Whose Land Is Palestine?

Whose Land Is Palestine?

The Middle East Problem in Historical Perspective

FRANK H. EPP

WILLIAM B. EERDMANS PUBLISHING COMPANY
Grand Rapids, Michigan

Dedicated to Fahed and David*

Fahed is a Palestinian, a refugee of the 1967 War. David is an Israeli soldier. The author met them in the summer of 1968. Fahed was a fellow passenger in a taxi from Amman to Jerusalem. He had received permission to return to his West Bank village for a few days to see his home and his relatives. He was hoping against hope that his return would be permanent. David was one of the guards at the newly established Israeli customs and check-point at the Allenby Bridge on the Jordan River. The customs process was a long one, and Fahed and I struck up a conversation with David. When it was time to go, I invited them to shake hands. They were reluctant at first, but finally they agreed. David put his gun aside, and they shook heartily, not once but twice, the second time being for a photograph. Both of them asked for prints which subsequently have been sent to them. Back on the dusty road, Fahed became uneasy about what he had done, feeling strongly that he had compromised the Arab position. Then he asked, "What does it mean?" "It means," I said, "that you are a gentleman, that's all!" He seemed relieved, and I added, "It also means that you are brothers." "I wish you were right," Fahed replied. This book is dedicated to Brothers Fahed and David and to the proposition that Arabs and Jews are not only cousins, but, under God, brothers, and that they should and can live together in the same land.

foreword

This is a book that needs to be read widely by the public, particularly by those persons in governments and on delegations to the United Nations who have responsibility for formulating policies that pertain to the Middle East. Its value is enhanced by the fact that it has been written by an articulate and well-informed young man — reared in a Mennonite home in Canada and son of refugee parents after World War I — whose personal background gives no reason for personal bias towards either the Arabs or Israelis.

The distinguishing feature of this book is that it is directed to Western Christians — particularly those in Canada and the United States. Dr. Epp is critical of past Western policies, contending that they are based on "a historical view that is too short and a theological stance that is too narrow." Accordingly, he has undertaken to place the problem of Arab-Israeli conflict in an appropriate historical perspective that encompasses all essential considerations as he sees them, including those which have a theological base.

In attempting this task, Dr. Epp has introduced few facts that have been heretofore unknown. However, he has placed greater emphasis than other writers on "the prominence of God or gods in the minds of men in the long history of the Middle East," believing that an understanding of this will facilitate insights relative to a solution. In that portion of the book that relates to background, Dr. Epp has presented the facts simply, interestingly, accurately and in a manner that likely will not be seriously challenged, even by readers who begin the book partial to one side or the other.

Dr. Epp's major contribution to better understanding of Arab-Israeli conflict is in the latter part of the book where he deals with the general subject of "Christian involvement" in Middle East conflict. It is his thesis that Christian theology has not only been a factor contributing to Jewish persecution

5

in the past but that more recently it has contributed towards
the persecution of certain Arab peoples — particularly the
Palestinian Arabs — as Christians have placed on these Arabs
the price of Christian atonement to the Jews. In Dr.
Epp's words, *"an old anti-Semitism directed against the Semitic Jews
now became a new anti-Semitism directed against the Semitic
Arabs. As the old anti-Semitism terribly wronged the Jews
so the new anti-Semitism terribly wronged the Arabs."*

Dr. Epp challenges Western Christians to take the lead
now to redress the wrongs they have helped to inflict on Arab
peoples and to do this in a manner that avoids new persecution of Jews. To this end he admonishes Christians to "accept their Messiah and become Christians," and that in so
doing "they will make their most important contribution to
peace." From this premise the author outlines a new approach
to peace that merits studied consideration by all persons concerned with peace in the Middle East. Dr. Epp's insight into
the problem of Arab-Israeli conflict and his sensitivity to underlying issues and the attitudes of both Arabs and Israelis are
reflected in such comments as:

> We must recognize . . . that the Palestinian struggle for lib-
> eration . . . of their homeland is at the root of the current
> problem.
>
> To the Palestine Arabs security for Jews and sovereignty
> for Israel were always two separate questions. They were al-
> ways prepared to guarantee the former but never to accept
> the latter.
>
> The Jews who have already made Palestine their homeland
> have a right to stay there, but it would be difficult to accept
> further immigration until the requirements of justice to the
> Arabs have been met.
>
> In the long run an Israeli state is as insecure in the Arab
> world as white regimes are insecure in Africa.

The world in general and Western Christians in particular
should feel indebted to Dr. Epp.

JOHN H. DAVIS
*International Consultant and
Former Commissioner-General of
the United Nations Relief and Works
Agency (UNRWA)*

Washington, D.C.

Preface

In the summer of 1969 I had the privilege of leading a seminar group of twenty-one persons in a unique study experience in Egypt, Jordan, Lebanon, Israel, and the occupied territories. In the forty-five major briefing, interview, and lecture sessions we attended, the most frequent questions concerned who was at fault in the Middle East: "Who bears the responsibility for the continuing hostilities?" "Who actually is the chief aggressor?" "Who is taking the land away from whom?"

The answers, we soon learned, were predictable. When we talked to the Arabs, the Israelis got all the blame; when we spoke to the Israelis, the Arabs were the undoubted disturbers of the peace. The farther we traveled and the more we listened, the more confused the seminar participants became.

One Middle Easterner we met, however, suggested a new approach to finding the answer. "There are two ways of looking at the conflict," he explained. "One way is that of the tourist, summer seminarian, or the journalist-in-a-hurry; the other way is that of the historian.

"In the first approach you look at contemporary events only. You isolate them and try to determine who fired the first shot. On that basis you identify the aggressor. But it's an inadequate approach, because it's like analyzing a newsreel on the basis of one or two frames or like judging a football game on the basis of one or two isolation replays. To get the whole story, you have to see the whole film. And the Middle East story is a very long newsreel. The more of it you see, the better you understand."

Our educated informer was correct, of course. Western conclusions on the Middle East conflict, as on the war in Vietnam, have been based too much on the daily snatches of news, which are rarely, if ever, placed in historical context. It is difficult, of

7

course, always to know how far to roll back the Middle East reel. Must one go back to the war of 1967, or to the United Nations Partition Resolution of 1947, or to the Balfour Declaration in 1917, or to the First Zionist Congress of 1897, or to the conquest of Palestine by the Turks in 1517?

In this present work we try to roll the reel back five thousand years or more, admittedly a difficult task because it really means dealing with the beginning of civilization and most of the history of man. However, we have accepted the risks and pitfalls of treating such a big subject in so little space on the assumption that what is needed, particularly among North American Christians (the primary audience of this study), is the kind of historical and theological understanding that comes from historical perspective in length and breadth. In other words, we hope to help overcome two weaknesses in the western approach to the world in general and the Middle East in particular, a historical view that is too short and a theological stance that is too narrow.

I am indebted to a large number of people who have assisted in the preparation of this volume, in particular a group of six manuscript readers. But my thanks must also go in a special way to more than one hundred Middle Easterners who, in my 1968 field research trip, first opened up to me the breadth and depth of the problem, and to the 1969 seminar resource people who helped to sharpen up the insights gained from field and library research, which was sponsored by the Mennonite Central Committee Peace Section. The responsibility for the contents of this book, of course, is mine alone.

—FRANK H. EPP

Ottawa, Canada

Contents

List of Tables

11

List of Maps

1. Claims for Good Reasons

> *...that most desirable area basking under the Mediterranean sun, washed by a lovely ocean, redolent of the most sacred history and religious associations of Muslims, Christians, and Jews, a land of spreading orchards, a Middle Eastern crossroads!* —John Nicholis Booth[1]

The Middle East is rapidly shaping up as one of the most critical areas of international conflict since World War II. The geographic region that encompasses the world's oldest centers of civilization now presents to the modern world one of its most complicated political situations.

The problem would not be so difficult nor the conflict so critical if throughout history there would not have been so many competitive claims to the area. These claims have not been ordinary expressions of interest in a given piece of land. The region has, for very good reasons which we will presently explore, always possessed an unusual attraction for peoples and empires both near and far.

The Land Called Palestine

At the heart of the current conflict, which is but another repetition of history, lies a dual claim for the same parcel of land, commonly called Palestine, the crossroads of the Middle East. Both the Palestinian Arabs and the Jews of Israel say that Palestine belongs to them. The former are supported by the surrounding Arab states and the latter by world Jewry, in particular by the Zionists. Additionally, both sides draw moral and material support from one or more of

[1] "The Moral Case for the Arabs," *The Middle East Newsletter,* III:5-6 (September 1969), p. 11 (10-13).

13

the big powers, thus turning the Middle East into an arena of East-West confrontation.

The name Palestine gives a general rather than a precise description of the contested area. The word Palestine is derived from the Philistines, a migrating twelfth-century people from the Aegean civilization (3000-1100 BC). The name appears to have been used first by Herodotus, the Greek "Father of History," and after him by early Christian historians. An earlier name for the area was Canaan, after *kinakhu,* a much-prized purple dye obtained from the shellfish for which the coasts were known.

While Canaan usually referred to the precise region between the Mediterranean Sea and the Jordan River, the term Palestine has had a much more flexible usage.[2] On the one hand, Palestine has described an area as small as the coastal regions occupied by the Philistines or as circumscribed as the Roman Judea in Jesus' time, and, on the other hand, as large an empire as the Kingdom of David and Solomon (1000-925 BC), extending, in general, from the Nile River to the Euphrates.

The maps most common and familiar in the West until recently identified Palestine with the Canaanite territory between the Jordan River and the Mediterranean Sea, extending about 150 miles from Dan in the north to Beersheba in the south. Actually, under the British Mandate for Palestine (1923-48), when the present territorial image was formed, a spur of land to the Gulf of Aqaba extended the length to 270 miles. In older times, Palestine sometimes included territories east of the Jordan, and in modern times these have occasionally been referred to as Eastern Palestine or more recently as the East Bank.

Uncertain Boundaries

As the Palestinian boundaries have shifted in the past, so the outside limits of the present quarrel are not easily determined. Long-term Israeli goals and ambitions, for instance, remain somewhat in doubt, as do the interests of some of the Arab states. When Prime Minister Levi Eshkol early in 1968 asked US President Lyndon B. Johnson to guarantee the borders of Israel, Johnson pointed to the crux of the matter

---

[2] John Grey, *The Canaanites,* p. 15.

when he replied, "You are asking me to guarantee your borders? What borders do you want me to guarantee?"[3]

Various spokesmen for the cause of Zionism and for Israel have, with their statements from time to time, illustrated the uncertainty concerning the extent of the claims and the location of the desired borders.[4] Theodore Herzl, the founder of Zionism, for instance, described the area of the Jewish state he envisioned as stretching "from the Brook of Egypt to the Euphrates."[5] The World Zionist Organization, in submitting its official plan to the 1919 Versailles Peace Conference for the creation of a Jewish homeland, specified the minimal territories necessary as follows: the headwaters of the Jordan River in Syria and Lebanon, the south of Lebanon up to the town of Sidon, the southern Bekaa Valley in Lebanon, the Hauran Plain in Syria, and the control of the Hijaz Railway running north-south considerably east of the Jordan from Derra in Syria to Amman and Aqaba in Jordan. Control of the Gulf of Aqaba itself was set as a requirement (*see Map 1*). The larger area identified by Herzl, however, was not quite forgotten. Nearly three decades later, shortly before the Jewish state came into being, Rabbi Fischmann, a member of the Jewish Agency for Palestine, recalled the founder's territorial vision. Fischmann declared in his testimony to the special United Nations Committee of Enquiry that "the promised land extends from the River of Egypt up to the Euphrates" including parts of Syria and Lebanon.

Fischmann's conception was never granted. On November 29, 1947, the United Nations recommended and authorized a Palestine partition plan that gave to the Jews a fraction of that dream, though the fraction represented 55 percent of the land west of the Jordan River. With the Palestine War of 1948, an additional 22 percent of this land was incorporated into the newly self-proclaimed State of Israel. In 1967, the territories under Israeli control were further extended to include all the land west of the Jordan, plus the Sinai Peninsula and the Golan Heights of Syria.

At the conclusion of the 1967 June War, Premier Levi Eshkol began to speak of a "Greater Israel," as did the new

---

[3] Quoted in *Newsweek*, January 22, 1968.

[4] See *The Arab Case: Documents and Testimonies,* II:11 (May 1969), pp. 82-96, for documented statements and illustrative maps.

[5] Herzl, *Complete Diaries,* Vol. II, p. 711.

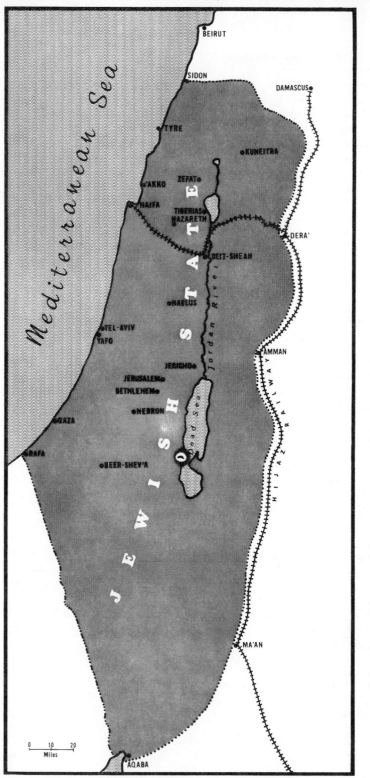

Map 1 — *The Jewish Area Proposed by World Zionist Organization in 1919*

maps. The Israeli army's chief, General Itzbak Rabin, identified, at least for the time being, the Suez Canal, the Jordan River, and the Golan Heights as the "natural frontiers" of Israel. Even so, the Arab states bordering Israel were not sure that the Israeli claims for territory had been satisfied.

As Israeli ambitions have remained in doubt, so there has been little certainty concerning the full claims of the Arabs. That the Palestinian Arabs themselves want to return with first-class citizenship rights to their homeland west of the Jordan is clear, and they want little else. The ambitions of Egypt under President Nasser are now said to be limited to regaining Gaza and the Sinai, but his dreams of a greater United Arab empire have not completely faded either. And King Hussein, whose father annexed the Palestinian UN Partition Plan, seems to be as much concerned with maintaining and restoring the Hashemite kingdom as with recognizing the rights of the Palestinian refugees. Similarly, other Arab governments, being normal nationalistic states, want to advance rather than retreat in their struggle for a share of Middle East power.

Generally speaking, the Israelis believe that the Arabs want to push them into the sea, and the Arabs, who are being pushed into the desert, are sure that the Israelis are after much more than any borders they have yet achieved. Speaking for themselves, both sides admit to no such ambitions. Thus the exact size of the area in dispute is impossible to determine. No doubt it varies from time to time between the extremes mentioned above.

Though the quarrel over land is basic, there are other important differences between the two parties. Some of these are cultural differences, as the Palestine Royal Commission of 1936 reported:

> There is no common ground between them. The Arab community is predominantly Asiatic in character, the Jewish community is predominantly European. They differ in religion and in language. Their cultural and social life, their ways of thought and conduct, are as incompatible as their national aspirations.[6]

Be that as it may, the present conflict in its regional and international dimensions is not a phenomenon new to the area. As "the middle of the earth," Palestine and the regions

---

[6] Julia E. Johnsen, *Palestine: Jewish Homeland?*, p. 9.

surrounding it have had their attractions and been competitively claimed from the beginning of time — or at least as long as the historical record reports — by a variety of claimants.

The Oasis in the Desert

A look at the geography gives the first indications why this should be so. Palestine, taken as a whole, can be considered an oasis on the edge of the vast southern and eastern deserts, the Sinai Peninsula and the great Syro-Arabian desert. To this oasis the nomadic peoples of the desert have gravitated and migrated quite naturally, seeking temporary resting places or permanent settlements in the river valleys, plains, or hill country of this desirable strip of real estate along the Mediterranean Sea.

The same was true, of course, of the fertile Nile and Tigris-Euphrates valleys, to the west and the east of Palestine, where the nomads brought their herds and were attracted by the prospect of establishing more sedentary settlements. Syro-Palestine, however, had the additional attraction of being located midway between these other two river valleys, forming together with them the so-called Fertile Crescent, along which and into which the ancient people moved.

Palestine and Syria may be considered as the single region of Syro-Palestine because together they form a continuous 500-mile strip, a series of successive valleys and plains between the desert and the sea. Both southern and northern parts of this strip have a large north-south cleft, which divides them into eastern and western parts. In Palestine, the cleft is the familiar Jordan Valley ending in the Dead Sea or even farther south in the Gulf of Aqaba.

The geography and climate of this Syro-Palestine region are widely divergent, serving a variety of needs, and this has contributed to its continuing, often universal, appeal. Within a very small geographic region variations of topography can be found to meet varying needs at different times of the year. The elevation, for instance, varies from the 9,232 feet of snow-capped Mount Hermon to the 1,286 feet below sea level of the surface of the Dead Sea.

In between these extremities are the fertile valleys and plains: the Jordan Valley running north-south the full length of the land; the east-west Jezreel Valley or Plain of Esdraelon between the hills of Samaria and Galilee; and the Sharon Plain on the coast connecting the north with the Judean hills and the Negev to the south.

As the elevation, so the climate has its variations and extremes, and this, no doubt, is one reason why Jewish immigrants from so many parts of the world have found in Palestine a little bit of home. The cold and wet winter winds from the north and west contrast with the hot and dry desert winds sweeping in occasionally from the east. While the snow still glistens at the head of the Jordan, temperatures soar to 100 degrees and more at its mouth. Moderation of both these extremes is provided by the influence of the Mediterranean Sea and the mountain breezes of the hills. Rainfall varies from forty inches in Galilee to a little more than one inch in the Negev, with the coastal plain striking a happy medium. C. C. McCowan has observed that the presence of all varieties of climate from sub-tropical to sub-arctic within a distance of 100 miles (Jericho to Mount Hermon) is one reason for the universal appeal and understanding of the land: "One reason the Bible is intelligible in nearly all parts of the earth is that it so nearly runs the gamut of the world's climates, land forms, and living conditions."[7]

Others have noted "a symbolic universality" of plant and animal life in Palestine. The flora and fauna found there are representative of almost every other region of the globe, from the Arctic circle to the tropics:

> The plants of northern Europe flourish in Lebanon, those of central Europe at the level of Jerusalem and Carmel, and those of the West Indies on the plain of Jericho near the Jordan. As for the animals, some are denizens of Alpine districts, and others the fauna of the plains of India and the rivers of Africa. . . .[8]

One of the favorite points of entrance from the desert into this beckoning region was near the junction of the Jordan River and the Dead Sea. There where the Judean hills and the Jordanian plain meet at a spring-fed oasis, nomads first began to settle down to develop more permanent agricultural communities and urban life. The place was called Jericho, and

---

[7] "Geography of Palestine," *Interpreter's Dictionary of the Bible,* Vol. 3, p. 636.

[8] Madeleine S. and J. Lane Miller, *Harper's Bible Dictionary,* pp. 514-518.

archaeological digs have provided evidence that here we have
the development of the earliest city, dating back to 5,000 BC
and perhaps much earlier.

The Middle of the Earth

However, not only the nomads of the desert found themselves moving into, and through, the Syro-Palestinian crescent.
With them, and partly because of them, came also the traders
and the conquerors, both of whom found "the middle of
the earth" to be a bridge, from the west to the east and from
the north to the south. Through Palestine and Syria lay the
caravan trails with direct connections to Egypt, Mesopotamia,
Asia Minor, South Arabia, and other regions of the ancient
world (*see Map 2*).

Known from earlier times also as the "Land of the Five
Seas," the "middle of the earth" accommodated not only
the traders, exploiters, and conquerors of the Fertile Crescent
but also those who traveled to and from distant regions.
Whether the men of commerce and conquest were based in
the territories beyond the Mediterranean, Black, Caspian, Red,
or Arabian seas, and whether they traveled by land or sea,
they found in the Fertile Crescent the all-important intersection of all their routes.

Since the greatest travelers, traders, and conquerors turned
out to be Europeans, it was they who eventually named the
area. To them the Land of the Five Seas was the gateway
to the Far East, and so they referred to it as the Near East.
In the nineteenth century, when European powers developed
a stronger interest in the middle itself, the gateway name of
Near East became less satisfactory. When, therefore, the
American naval historian, Alfred Thayer Mahan, in 1902 used
the term Middle East to designate the strategic naval area
between Arabia and India (the Persian Gulf), it was soon
picked up for official use by the British government.

Indeed, the term was found to be so useful that it was
soon applied to a much larger area, sometimes stretching from
the Black Sea to equatorial Africa and from India to the At-
lantic.[9] The US State Department has limited the Middle
East region to the eighteen countries listed in Table 1. The

---

[9] Bernard Lewis, *The Arabs in History,* p. 9.

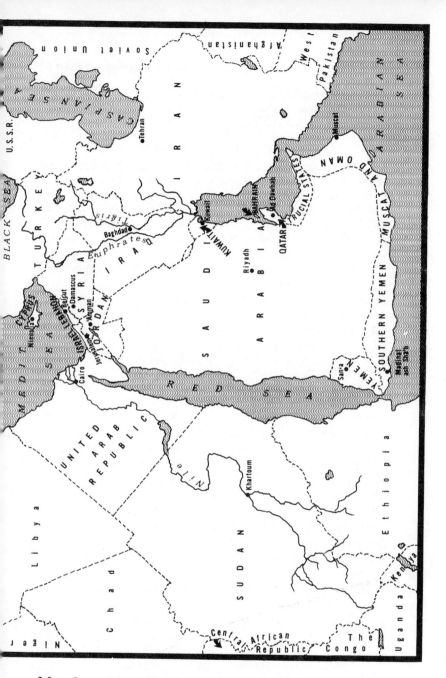

Map 2 — *The Middle East Lands of the Five Seas*

TABLE 1

SUMMARY DESCRIPTION OF MIDDLE EAST
COUNTRIES

(*As defined by US State Department*)

Name	Area in Sq. Mi.	Population in 1000s	Majority Group	Dominant Religion
Bahrain	256	216	Arabs	Islam
(British-protected sheikdom)				
Cyprus	3,572	622	Greeks	Christianity
(republic)			Turks	& Islam
Iran	636,293	28,166	Medes &	Islam
(constitutional monarchy)			Persians	
Iraq	169,284	8,766	Arabs	Islam
(republic)				
Israel	7,993	2,882	Jews	Judaism
(republic)				
Jordan	36,500	2,133	Arabs	Islam
(constitutional monarchy)				
Kuwait	7,450	532	Arabs	Islam
(sheikdom)				
Lebanon	4,015	2,580	Arabs	Christianity
(republic)				& Islam
Muscat &			Arabs	Islam
Oman	82,000	750		
(sultanate)				
Qatar	4,400	100	Arabs	Islam
(British-protected sheikdom)				
Saudi Arabia	873,972	7,100	Arabs	Islam
(kingdom)				
Southern				
Yemen	121,000	1,369	Arabs	Islam
(republic)				
Sudan	967,491	14,979	Arabs	Islam
(republic)				
Syria	71,498	5,738	Arabs	Islam
(republic)				

Name	Area in Sq. Mi.	Population in 1000s	Majority Group	Dominant Religion
Trucial States (7 British-protected sheikdoms)	32,278	133	Arabs	Islam
Turkey (republic)	301,380	34,375	Turks	Islam
United Arab Republic (republic)	385,237	32,501	Arabs	Islam
Yemen (republic)	75,290	5,000	Arabs	Islam

recent history of the countries suggests the extent to which the Middle East has been an attraction to, and dominated by, outside powers.

The importance of the Middle East as a crossroad was recognized, of course, long before Europeans built the modern Suez Canal in mid-nineteenth century (1859-69). Improvements and short cuts to international trade routes were attempted as early as the twentieth century BC, when a series of canals were built by Egyptian kings to extend the northern reaches of the Red Sea. Today the Suez Canal has, because of the conflict, fallen into disuse, but the utility of the Middle East as a crossroads has not been eliminated. On the contrary, the region is more significant than ever, because no all-weather global air route can be developed without it.[10] As Ilene Beatty has written:

> ... Palestine is today a crossroads to an even greater degree than ever before. The radius it draws from is enormously expanded, and the Middle East is now a four-way intersection for the criss-crossing airlanes of the world. Planes from the western nations fly in over the Mediterranean; Egypt and Africa come up from the south; Iraq and Iran, Pakistan and India from the East; and Turkey and Russia have a near approach from the north. All gravitate centripetally toward the crossroads vortex, and the avaricious among them scheme more subtly and psychologically than their ancient predecessors dreamed.[11]

[10] Johnsen, *op. cit.*, pp. 88-89.
[11] *Arab and Jew in the Land of Canaan*, p. 44.

Wine, Milk, Honey, and Oil

Not only were the waterways and land corridors of the Middle East lucrative commercial routes, but the area itself, parts of which were a veritable Garden of Eden, was rich in natural resources. These resources, however, were shamelessly devastated by invading armies and ruthlessly exploited by selfish rulers. This was particularly true of Palestine and Syria where the natural mineral wealth and forest resources vanished almost entirely already millennia ago. More recently, the Dead Sea has been discovered as an unparalleled source of potash and bromine.

Olive oil and the fruit of the vine were throughout history the region's most stable crops, because the olive trees and vines grew on almost every rocky hillside. In springtime, the otherwise barren hills blossomed with a colorful profusion of flowers, including the hyacinth, crocus, and narcissus followed by anemones, tulips, iris, and daisies, the resource base for bees and the honey industry. Thus Palestine "flowed" not only with olive oil and wine, but also with honey, and, of course, milk. Large herds of goats and cattle grazed near the springs and streams of the region, especially during the summer months when the deserts were hot and dry.

The fertile valley soils were conducive to raising grain, and both wheat and barley became staple crops. As time went on, figs, almonds, and bananas were introduced with profit along with citrus fruit, for which the coastal plain, when irrigated, offers the world's most favorable combination of soil and sunshine. The early growth of onions and garlic was later supplemented by such vegetables as tomatoes and potatoes. Cotton, groundnuts, and sugar-beets have also been successfully introduced on a comparatively large scale.

In the twentieth century, the area gained new economic significance. The search for oil, beginning in 1908, uncovered the fabulous petroleum reserves under the Middle East deserts in both Asia and Africa — perhaps as much as 62 percent of the world total.[12] The irrigation of dry land and the reclamation of waste hills brought new life to desert sands and stony slopes.

---

[12] Philip K. Hitti, *A Short History of the Near East*, p. 4.

Culture, Civilization, and Religion

Besides its strategic geographic location as an intercontinental crossroads and its resource potential, the Middle East has had historical significance and attraction also as the cradle of human civilization. There we discover not only the first domestication of plants and animals, but also the earliest development of urban life, with its political, social, and economic institutions. The employment of metallurgy, pottery, numbering, and writing, with their many scientific and cultural applications, all appeared first in the Middle East.

Common words like algebra, zero, mathematics, alchemy, mattress, orange, and atlas testify to the impact that one group of people, the Arabs, has had on western civilization. Later, a related group, the Jews, made staggering contributions in science, literature, music, finance, and philosophy, winning no less than twelve percent of all the Nobel prizes in physics, chemistry, and medicine.[13] Both of these peoples originated in the area in question.

The ancient people in the middle also excelled in religion. Indeed, it can probably be argued that it was religious as well as commercial impulses that provided much of the motivation for their cultural achievements. These impulses developed and matured as much in the desert as in the cities, not least of all because the nomadic experience came first. The wide horizons, the open sky, and the solitude of the shepherd together made possible and necessary the thought and reflections that gave to humanity the wisdom and insights later identified as the revelations of the gods.

As the tribes and settlements came in conflict with each other in intertribal warfare there were conflicting revelations, with the resulting plethora of deities to support the various claims. Such a state of affairs never proved satisfactory in the long run, and the tendency to return to the simpler, more unified, and universal notions of deity remained very strong. In the end, the monotheistic revelations had the widest and longest appeal, and so it happened that the people in the middle of the world gave to that middle and to the entire world an unparalleled spiritual heritage, complete with very precious shrines and powerful religious symbols. As Philip Hitti has written:

---

[13] Max I. Dimont, *Jews, God, and History,* p. 14.

Both Judaism and Christianity were nurtured therein. Their
daughter, Islam, the third great monotheistic religion was
cradled in an adjoining territory. All three religions are the
products of the spiritual experience and genius of the same
people, the Semites.[14]

Each of the three religions had at least one thing in common with the ancestral nature worship, which established very
close links between man and his land and his god. Jews,
Christians, and Muslims alike tended to see humanity, geography, and deity as a "holy trinity." To all of them Palestine
became a holy land. It was this notion of sacred ground being
indispensable to religious experience that gave all three religions an unholy character. The Jews became napalm-drop-
ping Zionists, Christians became bloody crusaders and free-
spending tourists, and Muslims turned into zealous conquerors
and determined guerrillas.

All of them made too sacred too small a piece of land,
thereby doing an injustice to that land and to religion, which
was never intended to promote so much unholy carnage in
the name of holy gods. But the higher intentions of religion
are another subject to be discussed a little later. Suffice it to
say here that religion became an important factor in the historic struggle of control over Palestine. All other good reasons
for wanting the land were reinforced by the most important
reason of all, religion.

If then we consider all the geographic, economic, political,
cultural, and religious factors that gave the Middle East and
its Palestinian hub so much appeal, it is not surprising that
so many people and empires have laid claim to the area. The
resulting claims have led to conflicts so serious that the Holy
Land has often had the character of an unholy place. Or, to
use the words of Gobineau,

The Middle East is a delicious meat, but it poisons those
who eat it.[15]

---

[14] *Op. cit.,* p. 3.
[15] Richard Meinertzhagen, *Middle East Diary, 1917-56,* p. 1.

2. The Claims of Many Gods

Nature' made Syria and Palestine the inevitable meeting-place and battleground of all the migratory, commercial, and military movements of the Near East. . . . Historically, we see the rise of the idea of universal kingship under the aegis of the god whose people prevails over the others.
—Sabatino Moscati[1]

In our historical survey of people and empires claiming the land of Palestine it will become obvious that there is nothing new under the sun. The people are claiming, as they always have, that they were there first. The empires are claiming, as they always have, that they are intervening for good reasons. And both people and empires relate their claims to the gods, as they always have, either explicitly or implicitly.

On Being There First

When Arabs and Jews today claim Palestine as their own, they do so in part on the grounds that they were there from the beginning, the first to occupy the area effectively and to establish a permanent society. Like the Indians of North America, they rest their case for first rights to the Palestinian real estate on their having been the earliest indigenous populations of the land. In doing so, they tend to forget that the human presence in Palestine goes back much further than most of us have ever believed, though this fact does not necessarily nullify either or both of the claims.

The Jews push their claim back to the patriarch Abraham, who early in the second millennium brought his family from Haran for permanent settlement in Canaan. Since the exact date of this "descent" down the Fertile Crescent is unknown,

---

[1] *Ancient Semitic Civilizations,* pp. 20, 235-236.

Jewish chronology tends to argue for the earliest possible date. The earlier to have been there the better, when it comes to claiming land. As far as Jerusalem itself is concerned, the Jewish identification may go as far back as the somewhat mythical Melchizedek, even though the city did not fall into Hebrew hands until early in the first millennium. Apparently, Melchizedek was priest and king of Salem when Abraham arrived, and the patriarch recognized the king as a priest of the highest God and offered to him the tenth of his possessions (Gen. 14:18-20).

The Arabs press three possibilities when it comes to determining who was there first. On one level, the Arabs argue that they have been there longer than any of the present-day Israelis, most of whom are recent immigrants without any prior connections to the land. Most frequently, the Arab claim at this level dates back to Islam's spread of Arabic culture in the seventh and eighth century. Individual Arab families, on the other hand, will recall the known history of their location in any one place. An example of such a claim is that of Rouhi Khatib, ex-mayor of Arab Jerusalem, whose family lived in that city for 700 years prior to his exile to the East Bank in 1968.[2]

At another level, the Arabs go back in their claims at least as far as the Jews. Arabs too claim possession through Abraham and his descendants, pointing out that Ishmael was born before Isaac and Esau before Jacob, and, they say, Ishmael and Esau belong to them. Indeed, they go as far as to indicate that Jacob may have succeeded in tricking Esau out of his birthright once, but that he surely won't get away with it the second time (Gen. 25:19-34). Finally, the Arabs identify with the Canaanites of earliest history to press their prior claim. Their ancestors were the indigenous population, they say. The Arabs cannot, of course, push the claims of birthright too far, because, as the years go by, the claims to land by right of birth undergo strange shifts.

The present situation illustrates this fact. Although most of the older Jews in Israel today are immigrants to that country, most of the younger ones were born there. Conversely, the older Palestinians who want to return were born in Palestine, but many of the children were born in camps away from their

---

[2] Conversation with the author in Amman, Jordan, June 14, 1969.

homes. In one generation, most Israelis will be indigenous to Palestine while most "Palestinians" will not be. Yet, from these "non-Palestinian" Arabs will come the strongest claim for the Palestinian homeland — in the form of a determined guerrilla movement!

Generally speaking, however, the argument is a powerful one, not least of all because it has been used again and again by a multitude of other peoples throughout history. The first people to occupy effectively a given piece of land that was or appeared to be unclaimed were the ones who "owned" it. They needed no stakes, no deeds, and no land title offices to have their claims recognized in their ancient generations. Instinctively, they felt that the land belonged to them, and that they belonged to the land.

At first such a feeling of belonging was true in a general way only, because the migrant life of the nomadic herdsman preceded the settled life of the agriculturist or urban dweller. The immigrants to a new area tended to remain migrants for a time, always literally looking for greener pastures. Too content with wandering really to settle down, they seemed to know in their hearts that they were called to move about, for why else would the world have been made so wide. Filling the earth and subduing it (Gen. 1:28) meant first of all to wander over it. And this is no doubt one of the reasons why the endless deserts of the Middle East were so well known by the ancient *arabs,* meaning desert dwellers.

A Complicated Situation

When it comes to identifying the first inhabitants of Palestine and linking these with any specific people of the present day, we are confronted by an enormous problem, partly because of the migrating character of early peoples, partly because the history of those peoples goes back much further than was at first believed, and partly because there has been a great deal of mixing through the years.

There has been a tendency, both among western Christians and Jews, at least until recently, to assume the beginnings of Palestinian settlement to be at the time of Abraham, or just prior to it. But now it is clear from archaeological research that the second millennium lies nowhere near the dawn of time and the earliest Middle East settlements. As John Bright has well expressed, Palestine knew settlement and culture many millennia before Abraham was born:

> Horizons have widened amazingly in the past generation. Whatever one says of Israel's origins must be said with full awareness that these lie nowhere near the dawn of history. The earliest decipherable inscriptions, both in Egypt and in Mesopotamia, reach back to the early centuries of the third millennium BC — thus approximately 1,000 years before Abraham, 1,500 before Moses. There history, properly speaking, begins. Moreover, in the course of the last few decades discoveries in Egypt, in Palestine, in Syria, and in Mesopotamia, have revealed a succession of yet earlier cultures which reach back through the fourth millennium and the fifth and, in some cases, as far as the seventh. The Hebrews were in fact latecomers on history's stage. All across the Bible lands, cultures had come to birth, assumed classical form, and run their course for hundreds and even thousands of years before Abraham was born. Difficult as it is for us to realize, it is quite as far if not farther from the beginnings of civilization in the Near East to the age of Israel's origins as it is from that latter time to our own![3]

The historic details concerning these earlier population facts are, of course, very vague, but skeletal remains point to the existence of men dwelling in the numerous Palestinian caves perhaps as long as one hundred thousand years ago. The caves of Stone Age men eventually gave way to permanent villages, which have appeared as early as the seventh millennium BC. The founding of Jericho, for instance, may go back to about that time if the date given by radio-carbonology is to be believed. Archaeological findings point to the use of brick or perhaps even stone construction, to the worship of a father-mother-son trinity, to the domestication of animals, and to a system of irrigation.

This high culture came to an end, as did other early "permanent" settlements, for reasons which have already been suggested. Earlier populations were replaced by later ones, who moved in from the desert, from the sea, or from the upper and lower ends of the Crescent. Little is known of them before the third millennium, because historical records of any such specific consequence do not go back much further.

---

[3] *A History of Israel,* pp. 17-18.

The Semites Leave Their Mark

From that time on, however, one people of a particular character appears to have left its linguistic and cultural influence in the regions of the Fertile Crescent more than any other. These people have been called Semites by scholars since the eighteenth century, after the biblical Shem, whose descendants, according to Genesis 10:21-31, spread through greater Syria and Persia, north to Armenia, and south to the Persian Gulf.

Some historians 'claim that these Semites first developed a distinctive social and cultural community in northern and/or southern Arabia, but their original home is really quite difficult to determine. At the dawn of history, traces of the Semitic languages can be found all over the Fertile Crescent. Even the earliest Canaanites of history, who have been linked to the Hamites of Egypt as descendants of the biblical Ham, show a very strong Semitic influence.

Those who hold to the Arabian origin of these Semites also conjecture that waves of nomads periodically engulfed the Crescent, both in historic and pre-historic times. The geography of the area and its commercial and military history suggest some credibility for this migratory theme, or at least a variation of it. The keepers of herds of cattle and goats did move back and forth with the seasons. The hot and dry summers brought them to the streams and valleys of the Crescent, while the cooler and wetter winter seasons allowed a return to the wider and more open spaces of the southern deserts. Similarly, extended periods of famine sometimes drove them from one area to another. The commercial and military competition, on the other hand, also guaranteed periodic convulsions, which "coughed" people into the desert from whence they were destined to return at a later time with an even greater resolve to stay.

Whatever their theory about distant origins, historians acknowledge a major movement of Semitic tribes into the Fertile Crescent in the third millennium before Christ. They mixed with already existing populations in Canaan and along with them became known as Canaanites. In the Nile Valley they intermarried with the Hamites to form the Egyptians of history.

At the other end of the Fertile Crescent, the Semites encountered and mingled with the Sumerian people of the Mesopotamian Valley even before city-states were established there. In Mesopotamia, as elsewhere, the Semites thus had a share in developing the first high civilization of man, as the linguistic evidence everywhere indicates.

Father-Sky and Mother-Earth

The cultural influence of the Semites also had a religious element, in that their concepts of deity were transmitted throughout the Crescent. With some local adaptations of these notions, the same fundamental concepts of deity were found everywhere, including both male and female deities, a sky-god and an earth-god, respectively. Father-sky ruled the affairs of humanity, while mother-earth was the source of all fertility. Various names were used to express these concepts. In Mesopotamia the divine couple was once known as Iztar and Tammuz; in Egypt as Isis and Osiris; and in Canaan, El and Asherah.[4]

From these male and female gods were derived a host of lesser divinities with many local and tribal variations. The sky-god, for instance, could be surrounded by other heavenly divinities named after the stars and after such heavenly phenomena as sky and lightning. Mother-earth, on the other hand, was associated with other fertility goddesses, such as Anat or Astarte, known as Ashtoreth or Ashtaroth in the Bible.

The Canaanite sky-god counterpart of Ashtoreth was Baal, a god of the storm, of lightning, of rain, and also of agricultural processes. The proper worship of Baal and Ashtoreth called for elaborate rituals and rites of fertility in which both priests and priestesses took part. Fertility could not really be celebrated without reference to human reproduction, and for that reason sacred sexual intercourse was introduced in the temples of the gods.

The fertility theme — father-sky and mother-earth (or their offspring) united in the process of life and nature — led, as might be expected, to a close identification of deity with nature, more particularly with the land. The land was the gift of the gods to man. Man recognized this gift by giving back to the

---

[4] Martin Noth, *The Old Testament World*, pp. 280-297; H. and H. A. Frankfort, John A. Wilson, and Thorkild Jacobsen, *Before Philosophy: The Intellectual Adventure of Ancient Man*, pp. 238-249; John Grey, *The Canaanites*, pp. 119-138.

gods the first fruits of the harvest. If a man sinned, he not only corrupted himself but he also offended the land. Thus man and his god and land were intimately linked together.[5]

This relationship had its universal as well as more parochial applications. In the general and universal sense, the god gave all of the land and made it fertile for all of the people. In a more local or tribal application, a tribal god gave a particular piece of land to a particular tribe. Since the Semites as a people manifested the characteristics of tribalism as well as universalism, we find among them both applications, although tribal expressions tended to be the most common.

The Tribes and Their Deities

The tribes were the normal social units among the Semites. They were expanded families or households, held together by kinship. At the head of the tribe stood the patriarch himself. Sometimes the tribes could not stay together because of personality clashes or leadership struggles. Occasionally a tribe would be driven asunder by outside forces. Economics also played a divisive role. Small oases or narrow river valleys could not always accommodate a growing tribe, and so, as in the later days of Abraham and Lot, the tribes would divide to the left and to the right.[6]

The tribes each had their chieftains, patriarchs, or judges, and where they established permanent settlements there arose small sovereign city-states, each with a king and a military force to protect and advance its interests. Often these kings were at war with each other, while sometimes they formed alliances against a common enemy. At the time of the conquest of Canaan by the Israelites there were scores of such kings to be dealt with and subdued either individually, if they stood alone, or collectively, if they had entered into coalitions.

Along with new tribes and their territories came new tribal deities, who were identified with these tribes and were believed to defend their territories. This identification intensified with the degree of tribal feeling, because both the lands and the gods served the interests of the tribe. The land claims of

---

[5] Martin Buber, *Israel and Palestine: The History of an Idea,* pp. 10-19.

[6] C. U. Wolf, "Tribe," *Interpreter's Dictionary of the Bible,* Vol. 4, p. 699.

a given tribe were supported by the gods and vice-versa, and territorial ambitions and acquisitions were, more often than not, co-equal with the desires of the god.

The gods fought for the kings and their people, and commanded the kings and the people to fight for them. The close links of land (whether pasture, settlement, or city-state), tribe, and god could only be broken through defeat in war. This is why the chieftains and kings so frequently sacrificed all they had to destroy all of the enemy in order to protect or make a claim.

Wherever a people laid claim to a parcel of land by effectively occupying it, they clung to it with all the zeal that tribal religion could muster and with all the means at their disposal. Not infrequently their deities would ask them — so they understood them — not only to defend what was already theirs, but to acquire other territories. Occupation by military force was added to indigenous ownership as a new unwritten title for landed property. The gods sanctioned both.

The Gods Demand Expansion

Indeed, if a god meant anything at all to a particular tribe it meant that he was superior, more authoritative, than the gods of other tribes. This fact in itself called for a concern on behalf of the less privileged tribes. That this religious zeal expressed itself in military terms more often than not should not surprise us, for this was how the superiority of a tribe was proved and the authority of a god established.

The zeal of the gods for more property and authority increased with the advance of civilization. Thus the Sumerian originators of city-states, sculpture, art, cuneiform writing, and other forms of culture had a greater passion than many others to spread the good word abroad. The gods wanted it that way, because after all they guarded the interests of the city-states that belonged to them.[7] This is borne out in the early (around 3000 BC) evidence of Mesopotamian culture found in the lower end of the Crescent in the Nile Valley.[8] Cultural expansion was, of course, a commercial enterprise, which in turn required military protection.

---

[7] Henri Frankfort, *The Birth of Civilization in the Near East,* p. 59.
[8] J. A. Wilson, "Egypt," *Interpreter's Dictionary of the Bible,* Vol. 2, p. 43.

At a somewhat later time, the gods in the Nile Valley seemed to have gained the superiority, and military as well as commercial influence flowed in the other direction. Indeed, the pharaohs of Egypt, who themselves were the embodiment of the Egyptian gods, controlled Canaan and the Canaanites in a general way for a very long period of time. Abraham went down into Egypt when famine came to Canaan because this was the most natural thing for him to do, both politically as well as geographically.

When the Egyptian of today claims that he was there first and longest, he has a real point, because after the earliest Canaanite city-states, Egypt was the effective occupier for the longest period of time, as ancient strata remains uncovered at such places as Biblos and Megiddo indicate. Egypt's interests in Canaan apart from the turquoise and the limited copper in Sinai were the trees of Lebanon.[9] As the kings of Egypt expanded, they claimed the subdued territory for their gods, or, more correctly, for themselves, because their ambitions and the desires of the god were identical. Thus the testament of one Rameses says that he guaranteed to the god nine Palestinian towns that he had conquered.

The pharaohs and gods of the larger Egyptian kingdom did not always triumph, because they were faced by other gods and kingdoms. As united as the Old Kingdom — established around 3000 BC — was, with its glorious pyramid building, it could not last due to internal opposition. Disintegration came in the latter part of the third millennium before Christ.

Competition from Other Gods

The threat to Egypt from without came chiefly from the other Semitic civilization in the Tigris-Euphrates Valley. Just as the Egyptian gods sent their kings up the Fertile Crescent, so the gods of Mesopotamia sent its kings to the southwest, with Canaan paying the price for being a buffer state. Egypt and Mesopotamia together controlled the Crescent for hundreds of years (see Map 3).

Sometimes, the threat from the northeast originated outside of Mesopotamia, as in the second millennium when the so-called Hyksos kings (1710-1480) came down the Fertile Crescent and subdued the Middle Kingdom of Egypt, which had

---

9 Grey, *The Canaanites,* p. 26.

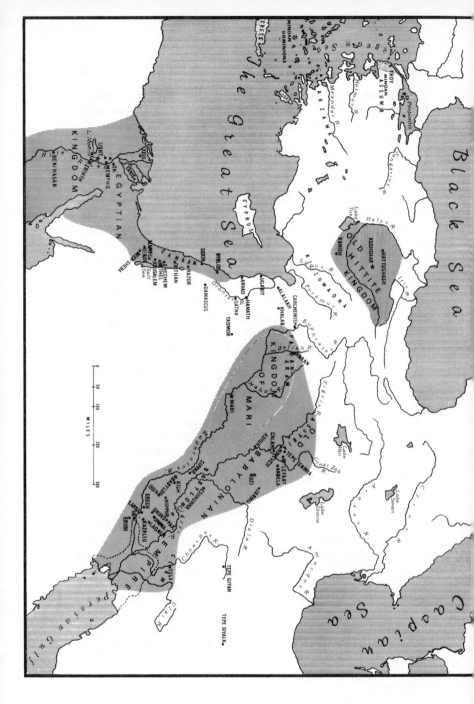

Map 3 — *Eastern and Western Power Centers in Ancient Times*

been united under the rulers of Thebes. Though the Hyksos too were Semitic in language and religion, they had links deep inside Asia and may have come from as far away as the Caucasus.

After the overthrow of the Hyksos, the reestablished New Kingdom extended the Egyptian empire farther than ever, and the mighty King Thutmose III (1490-1436) conducted seventeen campaigns into Asia and introduced military and civilian controls as far as the upper reaches of Syria. He too felt himself called by his god to smite the rulers of foreign countries, in particular the Hyksos and a coalition of 330 princes from Palestine and Syria that rebelled against him, each of them with a little army.

The big clash came at the Hill of Megiddo overlooking the Plain of Esdraelon in central Palestine, a site that had already become known as "the hill of the battles," and was forever to remain the symbol of the biggest battle to come in which the highest god would vanquish his enemies and establish his superiority. A fortress-city since about 3500 BC, Megiddo had dominated for many years the most important part of the Middle East crossroads, the intersection of two vitally important ancient trade and commercial routes. The fortress was set up high on a hill and had the additional advantage of abundant wells and springs and food resources, in the fertile plain below. Through this intersection had moved many of the hunters of the Stone Age, the caravans of endless traders traveling to Mesopotamia or Egypt, and the armies of many peoples. In days to come they would include not only Egyptians and Canaanites, but Assyrians, Israelites, Persians, Greeks, Romans, Saracens, Crusaders, Turks, and the British.

Whoever controlled Megiddo controlled the crossroads, and here Egypt had many confrontations with the kings and armies of foreign gods. Thutmose, for instance, confronted the mighty Canaanite coalition with a seven-month siege that yielded him four thousand horses and cattle, twenty thousand sheep, much gold and silver, and access to the Palestinian wheat harvest of 450,000 bushels. In subsequent Egyptian campaigns, the Pharaoh brought back ninety thousand Asiatic prisoners, including Nomadic Bedouins, many inhabitants of Palestine-Syria, and 3,600 Habiru peoples.[10]

---

[10] J. A. Wilson, *loc. cit.*

The Gods and the Empires

The expansion of the Egyptian empire also led to a review of the gods and a universalization of the deity. Amen-hotep IV (1370-1350), who renamed himself Akhenaton, after Aton the universal sun and supreme god, was a monotheist. Consequently, he was jealous of other gods and sent agents throughout the empire to remove their names and to eliminate them. The realignment of the deities was accompanied by sweeping political, religious, and social changes.

So it was throughout the ancient world. The religious and secular elements of life were completely interwoven with each other. Politics determined religion and religion politics. Every phenomenon and process of life was attributed to the agency of a god or gods. Art and literature, commerce and military expeditions — all were directly related to the deities.

Akhenaton's monotheism, however, could not save the empire, and after the Hittites from the north had seized control of Palestine, Egyptian influence in the Crescent was never restored to its former glory, although later rulers (including Nasser of the twentieth century) did manage to establish temporary alliances with the Syrian region.

After a period lasting about four centuries in the first millennium, when Canaanites, Philistines (a new people from the sea), and Hebrews (a new people from the desert) struggled for the control of Palestine, the initiative fell to new empires in the east, the Assyrians, the Babylonians, and then the Persians (*see Table 2*). More will be said about these peoples later. With the exception of some brief interludes, the imperial interests then shifted to Europe, with Greece opening the way for the mighty Roman empire, which as Byzantium remained in control into the seventh century of the Christian era.

Though the Europeans were more secularized than the Middle Eastern peoples, they too acted in the name of their gods, although they may have expressed it differently. Alexander the Great (365-323 BC), for instance, was anxious to establish some harmony between Europe and Asia, in the same way that the monotheistic pharaohs of Egypt felt called to impose a larger humanity on the many tribalisms.

Similarly, although the Roman Caesars made allowances

TABLE 2
LISTING OF PEOPLES OR POWERS IN EFFECTIVE CONTROL OF PALESTINE*

Peoples or Powers in Control	Time of Control	Length of Control-Years
Canaanites	From Earliest Times BC	?
Egypt (occasionally Mesopotamia)	3000(?) - 1710	1290 (?)
Hyksos	1710-1480	230
Egypt	1480-1350	130
Hittites	1350-1290	60
Egypt	1290-1154	136
Local (Canaanites, Philistines and Hebrews)	1154-1020	134
Hebrews (Saul, David, and Solomon)	1020- 925	95
Hebrews (two kingdoms)	1020- 587	433
Israel	925- 721	204
Judah	925- 587	338
Assyria and Babylonia (in Israel)	721- 587	134
Babylonia	587- 539	48
Persia	539- 330	209
Greece	330- 323	7
Egypt (Ptolemies)	323- 199	124
Syria (Seleucids)	199- 166	33
Hebrews (Maccabees, partial only)	166- 70	96
Seleucids (partial only)	166- 70	96
Armenia	70- 63	7

*The chronology of and division of power in history were rarely as precise and neat as suggested by the above listing. Moreover, the degrees and nature of control varied considerably throughout the 5,000 years of recorded history. The British, for instance, had a mandated control. The Ottoman empire, while it effectively came to an end in 1918, did not officially end until 1923. Control during the Crusades presents a fuzzy picture, as it does at other periods in history including the earliest named. The above Table should, therefore, be read for a general rather than a precise interpretation of Palestinian history.

Peoples or Powers in Control	Time of Control	Length of Control-Years
Rome (Western and Eastern Empires)	63 BC-AD 611	674
Persia	611- 628	17
Rome	628- 638	10
Arabs (Muslim)	638-1085	447
Turks (Seljuks: Muslim)	1085-1099	14
Crusaders (partial only)	1099-1291	192
Seljuks and Arabs (Muslim, partial only)	1099-1291	192
Egypt (Mamelukes: Muslim)	1291-1517	226
Turks (Ottoman: Muslim)	1517-1918	401
Great Britain	1918-1948	30
Jews (Israel, partial, west only)	1948-1970	22
Arabs (Jordan and Egypt, partial)	1948-1970	22

for many gods, they tried to establish a hierarchy of divinities with themselves assuming the deity of the highest level. Throughout the empire elaborate temples to the prevailing regional gods were built to help give the empire the legitimacy and sanctity it needed. The Islamic empire, which replaced the European influence, was similarly born out of a passion for unity and universality on behalf of a single god who was tired of all the tribal deities and tribal rivalries.

The claims of the various successive empires and their gods, of course, had important consequences for the "crossroads" of the region. As Ilene Beatty has said:

> Palestine is now and has been for thousands of years a trampled crossroads, a political pawn, traded, invaded, a subject people, sometimes a vassal, or a protectorate, or a satellite, or a mandate, annexed, dismembered, devastated, denuded, burned, partitioned. . . .[11]

Modern States, Peoples, Lands, and Gods

The ideological rationale for commercial and military expansion or intervention has, of course, never faded from the earth. As the Egyptians, Greeks, Romans, and Muslims

---

[11] *Arab and Jew in the Land of Canaan*, p. 85.

gave credit to the gods for their adventures, so also Britain and France had religious reasons for their Middle East intervention, as will be seen later. Today, the Soviet Union and the United States, both thoroughly secularized states, express their presence in the Middle East in religious terms, when they say, on the one hand, that they come as liberators (from imperialism) and, on the other hand, as protectors (of freedom). How divine sanction for imperial interests enters into the picture even today is well described by a recent Middle East editorial.

> Ever since the United States entered the Middle Eastern scene to fill the "vacuum" created by the departure of the former imperial powers, it has been persistently drummed into the Arabs that American interests in the area are as indivisible as the oneness of God, but as diversified as the concept of Trinity. . . . The elements of this Trinity of interests were explained to both Arabs and Americans as being in chronological order: *cultural* — American universities, missions, introduction of American values of democracy; *economic* — oil interests, investments; and finally *strategic* — sea and air routes, bases, etc.[12]

The universal theme of good land being promised to better people by superior gods has occurred frequently in history. Hundreds of peoples of all ages and regions have identified the promised land with the gods, who gave to them because they favored them. This is the basic and underlying theme of all history, not only of the Middle East but of the entire world.

America, for example, has become the promised land for uncounted migrating peoples. So strongly have they felt about the land where they settled and became prosperous that they wrote books and poems, made films, and preached sermons about it. And they heard their god commanding them to kill Indians, enslave Negroes, fight the Spaniards, incarcerate the Japanese, and even massacre the Vietnamese in order to make the promised land safe for the chosen people.

National environments like America, of course, cannot produce such pure and powerful religious symbolism as has been provided by Palestine, but this only serves to demonstrate that holy land notions can emerge from and be nurtured by "nonreligious" events like the breath of freedom, the experience of

---

[12] "American Eggs in One Basket," *The Arab World,* XV:10-11 (October-November 1969), p. 2.

raw nature, the conquest of native peoples, the emergence of a new group ego, and, not least of all, the discovery of rich corn fields, gold mines, and oil wells.

Yet symbols there are, and every chosen people soon establishes its substitute holy city upon which the gods bestow special favors and a special status. The attractive publicity brochure of Washington, D.C., for instance, says as much as it introduces the American capital to its many visitors, as follows:

> In every age, there has been one city which has seemed to be the center of the world, which the Fates have chosen to be the guardian for the hopes of all men, to hold and control their aspirations, to determine the probability of their glory, or their happiness or their misery, their bondage or their freedom. That world city in our time is Washington.[13]

We cannot be entirely sure, of course, that Washington is the holy city, because in the last decade two American presidents have identified Berlin as freedom's holy city. "We are all Berliners!" Kennedy and Nixon have said, and so one might suppose that the new city coming out of heaven could also be Berlin. The Russians feared that, of course, and so they built a wall through Berlin to confuse the gods. Russians have known since the fifteenth century that it was not Berlin but Moscow that was really the holy one, a Third Rome as it were, a successor to the first Rome (Jerusalem) and the Second Rome (Vatican City), which had failed their divine missions. In the meantime, millions of other people grew up believing in Rome as "the holy city" or the "eternal city."

Where there were holy cities there also were promised land and chosen people. Berlin was Berlin because it belonged to a *Herrenvolk,* a super-race. Moscow was Moscow because it was the home of the Great Russians, and London was London because from there the divinely favored Britains ruled not only the most land but also the waves. Little wonder that William Blake wrote:

> I will not cease from mental flight,
> Nor shall the sword sleep in my hand,

---

[13] Brochure "Welcome to the Nation's Capital." Distributed by the Washington Convention and Visitors' Bureau, 1616 K. Street, N.W., Washington, D.C. 20006.

       Till we have built Jerusalem
       In England's green and pleasant land.[14]

The claims of the gods and the identification of promised land, of holy cities, and of chosen people — that is what history and the Middle East conflict are all about. Let us now turn to some particular examinations of this theme with reference to Palestine.

---

[14] Quoted in Martin Buber, *To Hallow This Life,* p. 146.

3.   The Claims of Abraham, Isaac, and Jacob

> *...go in and take possession of the land which the Lord swore to your fathers, to Abraham, to Isaac, and to Jacob, to give to them and their descendants after them.*
> — Deuteronomy 1:8

After innumerable tribes or kingdoms and their gods had from time immemorial laid claim to the lands of the Canaanites, a new tribe, announcing a higher god and a prior claim, arrived from the desert around the year 1250 BC. Approximately the same time also a new people arrived from the sea. Both the Philistines of the sea and the Israelites of the desert now fought the inhabitants and each other for the coveted Canaanite real estate.

At the same time, these two determined peoples also had to come to terms with the major imperial powers from both ends of the Crescent — Egypt to the southeast and Assyria and Babylonia to the northwest — as well as with several minor ones. In the contest between the two peoples, however, the Israelites and their God established themselves most firmly, though the Philistines impressed posterity sufficiently to have the land named after them.

Migrations from the East

The Israelites or Hebrews, as they were also called, claimed the land on the basis of an oral tradition of some 600 years or more. That tradition, reported in Genesis 12-50, insisted that a man with the name of Abram or Abraham, the patriarch of the tribe, had received the promise of Canaan from his God. This promise had been passed on to his descendants, notably through Isaac and Jacob, though these were not the

44

only sons. Both Isaac and Jacob had older brothers, Ishmael and Esau, respectively.

The story, which was set down in its present Old Testament form centuries after the event, begins with the descent of Abraham and his family into Canaan from Haran. This latter settlement in the upper reaches of the Euphrates River had in turn become the home of the clan after a migration from Ur near the mouth of the Euphrates.

The exact chronology has not been determined (*see Table 3*),[1] but the migration probably came around the nineteenth century before Christ, when numerous other semi-nomadic Semites were descending into Canaan. It was a time of political instability in the east and a time of new opportunity in the middle, where a period of similar turbulence had just passed. Population movements in the Fertile Crescent were characteristic of such unstable times.

Thus, a drama that had been enacted in the Crescent countless times in preceding centuries now repeated itself in the family of Abraham. As another restless and wandering Semite, he nurtured the vision of an expanding clan, who would possess the entire world between the Euphrates and the Nile. As

TABLE 3
IMPORTANT DATES AND EVENTS IN HISTORY OF CHILDREN OF ISRAEL

Date	Event
c. 1900-1700	Age of the Patriarchs
c. 1700-1290	Sojourn in Egypt
c. 1290	Exodus from Egypt
c. 1250-1200	Conquest of Canaan
c. 1200-1020	Period of the Judges
c. 1020-1000	Reign of Saul
c. 1000-961	Reign of David
c. 961-922	Reign of Solomon
922-721 (Israel)	Divided Kingdom
925-587 (Judah)	Divided Kingdom
586-538	Babylonian Exile of Judah
538	Cyrus' Edict of Return
520-515	Rebuilding of Temple

[1] For a more detailed chronology of Israel in relation to the whole region see Bright, *A History of Israel*, pp. 460ff.

in the twentieth century (after Christ) Canadians thought of a promised "dominion from sea to sea" (Ps. 72:8) so the twentieth-century (before Christ) Canaanites thought of a promised dominion from river to river, more precisely "from the river of Egypt to the great river, the river Euphrates" (Gen. 15:18). In both instances, the seas and the rivers were the natural boundaries of lands of great promise.

Abraham's vision, in other words, appears to have had much in common with the ambitions of earlier and later tribal chieftains. He saw his tribe inhabiting and probably dominating the Fertile Crescent. Yet, his dream was also of a higher order. He anticipated a dominion that would not be yet another imperial imposition but rather a source of righteousness and justice and of blessing for other tribes and nations in the area. According to the Genesis story, Abraham's God was telling him: ". . . Abraham shall become a great and mighty nation and all the nations of the earth shall bless themselves by him. . . . I have chosen him to keep the way of the Lord by doing righteousness and justice . . ." (Gen. 18:19).

As many Semites before him, so Abraham too saw a close link between himself, his God, and the land which he was seeking and finding. But again, there was an important difference, because he was claiming land not in the name of a localized deity but rather at the command of El, the highest god in the Canaanite pantheon. It was the same, or almost the same, god worshipped by Melchizedek, the king-priest of Salem.

A higher god demanded a higher loyalty and a better religion. Thus Abraham disregarded the lesser deities and despised the idolatrous liturgies of other tribes. He also rejected the Canaanite religion of child sacrifice, and offered an animal instead. Altars were built to El, the highest god, and all the new ideas about the new society were credited to this god, whose wish was the patriarch's command. Abraham's grandson, Jacob (Israel), identified El as the God of Israel (Gen. 33:20).

Escape from Enslavement

Abraham did not see his dream fulfilled, nor did his immediate family, because there were discouraging delays. In the first place, he had no sons until he was old, and even then his first one was by an Egyptian maid. Although Abraham circumcised Ishmael and recognized that he would also be blessed by El, he expected the true fulfillment of his dream through Isaac, a son born of his wife and hence of purer birth and closer to his heart.

There were other problems. Isaac had only two sons. His family too was small, and his sons were jealous of each other. As the story goes, the elder son Esau broke with the clan when he was cheated out of his birthright by the younger Jacob. Thus Esau, like Ishmael and Lot before him, started tribal offshoots of the Hebrew family which, at least for the time being, followed an independent course in Canaan and surrounding territories.

A divisive tendency similar to that in the family of Abraham and Isaac appeared in the family of Jacob, whose sons sold one of their number to the Ishmaelites. But eventually all twelve sons and their families migrated to Egypt because of the famine in Canaan. Patriarch Abraham had gone that route before and for the same reason, while Jacob had returned at least once to the ancestral home in the east. Thus, we see how all the lands between the two rivers were not only a dream but an actual part of their experience. To traverse the whole region at least once in a lifetime was the normal Semitic thing to do.

In Egypt, the children of Israel, as they became known in that country, received a friendly reception. Indeed, Joseph was placed in charge of agricultural production and food distribution. This is not too surprising in view of the possibility that the Hebrews may have been related to the Hyksos who were now in control of Egypt. Both Semitic groups had come out of the Syrian east and beyond, and both had gradually moved through Canaan to Egypt, though not necessarily precisely at the same times.

In due course Hyksos control in Egypt came to an end, and a pharaoh "who knew not Joseph" used the tribe of Israel as slave labor, a practice not uncommon in those times. During their enslavement, the old vision of the promised land never left the Israelites, and indeed as a hope it was many times reinforced. At a time in the thirteenth century when the empire was crumbling and a series of natural disasters was complicating other domestic turmoil, the Hebrews made their dramatic — to them miraculous — escape under the leadership of Moses.

Moses appears to have combined within his total genius the gifts of law-making, administration, writing, and prophecy, though he was not as articulate as he might have wished. Enterprising and innovative, he had studied at Pharaoh's court, and monotheistic tendencies in Egyptian religion had given him much time for reflection on his own notions of deity, as he had learned them from his family. Somewhat a rebel, Moses fled from Pharaoh's court into the desert after he had killed an Egyptian in a fit of anger.

Moses' experience of some forty years with the Midianites in the Sinai also proved to be invaluable. He may have received further instruction in monotheism from Jethro, his Midianite father-in-law, and apparently he also gave a good deal of thought to law and order, inasmuch as he had found the Egyptian social situation far from satisfactory. On this latter matter he appears to have had at least some familiarity with the law codes of Hammurabi, a famous ruler of an eastern empire earlier in the millennium. In any event, the emerging Mosaic code bore some resemblance to the older Babylonian tradition, though the Mosaic code was superior and was presented in the nature of a covenant between God and his people.

Ten basic laws or commandments were central in the Mosaic code. Moses identified them as coming from God, whom he now knew as Yahweh. Although Moses named him, Yahweh really was a God whom no words or name could fully define. On the one hand, Moses identified him as the God of Abraham, Isaac, and Jacob, but, on the other hand, he knew him to be undefinable, and all he could say about him was "He is who He is" (Exod. 3:13). To Yahweh Moses attributed all of his new insights.

Hand in hand with these revelations from and about Yahweh, Moses received a call to be the liberator of his people, a possibility in his mind ever since he had turned his back on the royal court. Though reluctant at first to go all the way, he gave forceful leadership once he had made up his mind that the cause was worth it. Not only did he succeed in bringing his people out, but before their departure he demanded and obtained reparations for the slave labor of many years. The Israelites obtained much jewelry and precious metals, which later, in moments of idol worship, became a golden calf and, in days of Yahweh worship, the trimmings of a most extraordinary portable tabernacle.

The Covenant with Yahweh

The establishment of Yahweh worship, centered in the tabernacle, was Moses' first project in the first year of liberation. He took his people to Horeb where he shared with them the ten commandments. In the days and years thereafter he added many related instructions, dealing with slavery and concubinage, homicide and other crimes punishable by death, theft, seduction, witchcraft, and similar sins. The code enjoined justice and kindness to the stranger, the widows, and the fatherless, and it made certain demands regarding the use of the land and the disposition of the harvest.

Thus Moses spelled out the terms for his new society, the condition by which the descendants of Abraham were to become the universal blessing and receive the fulfillment of other promises. The most fundamental condition was the worship of Yahweh. He was one God and, as far as Israel was concerned, the only one. He was the one who had brought them out of the land of Egypt, the house of bondage. This God of Israel demanded absolute obedience, but he also promised many blessings. Indeed, according to the covenant relationship, which was now to be established, obedience meant blessing and disobedience meant cursing. Yahweh was not to be represented in any graven images. The tabernacle and the ark of the covenant should suffice as symbols of the holy.

In these terms Moses communicated Yahweh to his tribal society as the highest God he knew, and, indeed, a higher god the Middle East had not known. It was hard to know Yahweh because he was so different. The children of Israel had difficulty accepting him. It was easier for them to express their religion in calf worship, and in their minds Yahweh himself was reduced to other tribal deities, because in the competitive games of the gods (the tug-of-war of the tribes), he demanded what the gods had always demanded, complete annihilation of the enemy. The Amalekites were only the first of many to be hacked to pieces man, woman, and child. The annals of the Israelites later reported the meaning of that first of many slaughters:

And Joshua mowed down Amalek and his people with the

edge of the sword. . . . And the Lord said to Moses, "Write this as a memorial in a book and recite it in the ears of Joshua, for I will utterly blot out the remembrance of Amalek under heaven" (Exod. 17:13-14).

All of these experiences — the miraculous escape from Egypt, the rescue from other tribes, the provision of food and water in a dry desert, the receiving of the commandments, the building of the tabernacle, and the organization of the wandering society — had a profound effect on the people recently emerged from servitude. They were now a people, a nation, with a higher god. They had made their covenant with Yahweh, and they were now more certain than ever that they were destined to have their turn in the promised land, the crossroads of the earth.

The Conquest of Canaan

Moses had, in all probability, considered entry into Canaan at first by the Mediterranean coastal route, but Egyptian military installations discouraged such a short cut. An attempt to enter via the central route through the southern Canaanite hills likewise failed to materialize. Entry was finally made from the east after forty years of wandering in the wilderness and only after the unadaptive generation born in Egypt had died enroute.

Under Joshua, their new leader, the Israelites finally crossed the Jordan and captured the gateway city of Jericho. After that victorious entry there were numerous setbacks — the first attack on Ai, for instance, was a complete failure — but gradually General Joshua was able to assert himself against the Canaanite kings in the hills. Either these submitted themselves voluntarily to the Israelites or they were vanquished in battle.

In these conquests, the Israelites believed themselves to be doing the bidding of Yahweh, who was on their side in the same way that other gods assisted their enemies. The quarrel over land and the fighting between the tribes was a testing of the gods, as intertribal warfare among the Semites had always been. We may, therefore, not be too surprised to discover Yahweh, as the Lord God of Israel, smiting all their enemies. As it is written:

> When Israel had finished slaughtering all the inhabitants of Ai in the open wilderness where they pursued them . . . and

all who fell that day, both men and women, were 12,000, all
the people of Ai.... So Joshua burned Ai ... and he hanged
the king of Ai on a tree until evening ... (Josh. 8:24-25).

Before Joshua died and after some twenty-five years in the
land, it is reported that the land was sufficiently under control
that the tribes could be assigned to their respective territories,
several of them east of the Jordan. However, the conquest of
Canaan was not as quick or as complete as the somewhat
idealized presentation of military history in the Book of
Joshua might suggest. Later recollections, such as those in
the Book of Judges, indicate that many places were not subdued for a long time. The holdings of the children of Israel
constituted no well-rounded territorial units and the outside
borders of the tribes shifted constantly. The coastal plains and
Esdraelon were not easily conquered, and even in the mountains the Canaanites retained their enclaves. The mount of
Zion, for instance, remained a foreign city until the time of
David. During all this time Egypt, though greatly weakened,
remained an overlord for Canaan.

Joshua's advice to his people was later recorded as farewell
instructions and admonitions. As these were later remembered,
they forbade mixing with other tribes (though this happened
frequently), recognizing (naming and swearing by) other gods,
and marrying other women. Keeping the covenant with Yahweh
was of prime importance if the land was to be retained and
blessings were to flow. The people accepted Joshua's plea and
pledged themselves to obey only the God who had brought
them out of Egypt and into Canaan, with the following
covenant:

> Far be it from us that we should forsake the Lord, to serve
> other gods; for it is the Lord our God who brought us and
> our fathers up from the land of Egypt, out of the house of
> bondage, and who did these great signs in our sight, and pre-
> served us in all the way that we went, and among all the
> peoples through whom we passed; and the Lord drove out
> before us all the peoples ... therefore we also will serve the
> Lord, for he is our God (Josh. 24:16-18).

The Times of the Judges

After the death of Joshua the Israelites had no central
leadership. They were a loose confederacy of twelve independent tribes, whose unity lay in the worship of Yahweh,

in his commandments, rightly or wrongly understood, and in the ark of the covenant. With Yahweh as their leader, the Israelites needed no other government. In times of crisis they would look to leaders with special abilities to lead them against the enemies. When the emergency had passed, they would continue to seek the counsel of the successful leader, and he would be their judge. For at least two centuries the Israelites depended completely on these charismatic judges to save and guide them. They were their priests and their "kings."

The Israelites needed the judges frequently, because oppressions from outside tribes and chieftains were many. Thus Othniel saved Israel from the faraway Mesopotamians; Ehud from the Amalekites, as well as the Moabites and Ammonites, both descended from Lot; and Deborah and Barak from the Canaanites who after Joshua had become powerful again.

When the Israelites had once again been overcome and driven into the caves by the Amalekites, as well as the Midianites and Ishmaelites (all of them descendants of Abraham), they needed a mighty warrior like Gideon, who with his 300 courageous men gave them a victory long to be remembered. Another of the mighty judges was Samson, who on several occasions routed the Philistines.

The successes and failures of the Israelites and their judges were closely associated with the keeping and breaking of the covenant. The oppressions that came were seen as punishment for idolatry. This consequence of evildoing in turn prompted repentance, and when the people turned from their wicked ways Yahweh heard and gave them the needed saviors, the judges endowed with charisma and spirit. This is how later historians interpreted the experience of the people:

> And the people of Israel did what was evil in the sight of the Lord and served the Baals. . . . So the anger of the Lord was kindled against Israel, and he gave them over to plunderers . . . so that they could no longer withstand their enemies. Whenever they marched out, the hand of the Lord was against them for evil . . . and they were in sore straits. Then the Lord raised up judges, who saved them out of the power of those who plundered them. And yet they did not listen . . .
> (Judg. 2:11-23; *see also* 2 Kings 17:7-18).

In their new land, the Israelites had great difficulty in keeping the covenant they had made under Moses and renewed under Joshua. As they settled down to agricultural life, they learned many new customs from their neighbors. It was easy to accept also the Canaanite manner of harvest festivals, their liturgies, and their gods. However, whether or not they adopted other gods, their image of Yahweh was influenced by what they knew of Baal and the Asherah. Yahweh became a tribal deity, the Lord God of Israel. For this reason they heard Yahweh saying the kinds of things one might normally expect only from other tribal deities.

As interpreted by the tribalism of the day, Yahweh was as barbaric as any tribal god in the Crescent. He sanctioned the slaughter and extermination of the foes much in the same way that the twentieth-century Christian god, as interpreted by the nationalisms of the day, called for concentration camps, the use of nuclear weapons, and napalm drops. Israel's God allowed for every terror at the disposal of the Israelites, sometimes even against one of their own tribes. As it is written:

> And the Lord said, "Go up; for tomorrow I will give them into your hand." . . . And the Lord defeated Benjamin before Israel; and the men of Israel destroyed 25,100 men . . . the men in ambush moved out and smote all the city with the edge of the sword . . . and all the towns which they found they set on fire (Judg. 20:28-48).

The Demand for a King

The gods of other peoples, however, were equally jealous, and they pitted the tribes against each other. A contest on the battlefield usually demanded the extermination of one or the other of the tribes. Particularly troublesome to the Israelites were the Philistines, who had entered Canaan from the Sea. To them too Canaan was a promised land, and, since they could not be pushed out of their coastal strongholds, it was they rather than Israel that gave the name to the land. This too the Israelites could never forget, which is why the modern State of Israel, whose citizens, like the Philistines, also came by way of the Sea, determined once and for all to attach its "Land of Israel" label to the territory.

The continuing Philistine threat finally led the children of Israel to request, and their God to consent to, a king and a kingdom to replace the loose confederacy under the judges. Samuel, the last and perhaps the best of the judges, was upset about this development since he believed it to be a rejection

of himself. However, when there seemed to be no other alternative, he consented to the anointing and proclaiming of Saul,
a tall and brave Benjamite, as king (1020-1000 BC). Though
Saul was anointed king he was not a king in the later tradition. He made no administrative and structural changes. He
developed no bureaucracy, no splendid court, and no harem,
as was the kingly custom. Instead, he remained the charismatic
warrior-leader in the tradition of Joshua and the judges.

Even so, Saul's appearance represented an important transition in the development of the Israelite society. Until Samuel
the judges had represented more of a religious rather than
a political tradition. With them as leaders, the Israelites saw
themselves directly under Yahweh seeking to do his will. The
coming of the king Saul meant the emergence of the soldier
and patriot for whom religious considerations tended to be
secondary. Under a king the Israelites were becoming a society like other societies meeting them on their own, not
necessarily on Yahweh's terms.

Saul had weaknesses apart from his role. He seems to have
had a nervous disorder and was given to unreasoning fits of
terror and brooding. An evil spirit seemed to possess him,
and he needed the sound of music to bring temporary relief
to his unhappy soul. These personal weaknesses accentuated
the weaknesses of the monarchy itself and all of Samuel's
fears were confirmed then as well as in subsequent generations.
Samuel gave them the word of the Lord as follows:

> ... he will take your sons ... to be his horsemen ... and he
> will take your daughters ... he will take the best of your
> fields ... he will take the tenth of your grain ... your men-
> servants and your maidservants, and the best of your cattle
> and your asses ... and you shall be his slaves. And in that
> day you will cry out because of your king, whom you have
> chosen for yourselves; but the Lord will not answer you in
> that day ... (1 Sam. 8:10-18).

For the time being, however, the opposite appeared to be
true. Saul did not make many demands and both Saul and
his successors brought the Israelites the taste of glory they
had not known before. Saul was able to vanquish the Amorites
and thus secure the eastern front beyond the Jordan, but he
struggled all his life against the Philistines. Although he drove
them out of the central hills temporarily, they remained firmly

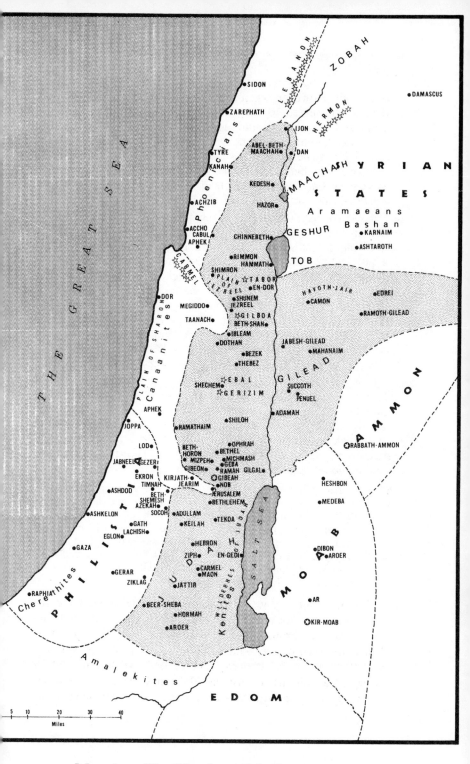

Map 4 — *The Kingdom of Saul at Its Peak*

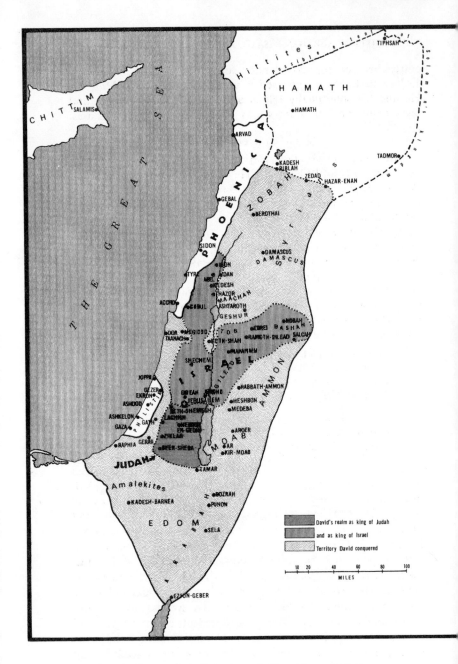

Map 5 — *The Empire of David and Solomon*

entrenched in the coastlands. Jerusalem and the Plain of Esdraelon likewise remained beyond his reach (*see Map 4*). He and his sons finally fell in a battle at Mount Gilboa, and once more the hill country was opened up to the Philistines.

David and David's City

After Saul, David the Bethlehemite took command as the new king (1004-961 BC). He had demonstrated military skill in Saul's army, established relations with the King of Gath, and perhaps also (through Ruth) with his relatives the Moabites. Like Saul before him, David was a charismatic leader chosen by the people for his gifts. Using both his military and diplomatic ingenuity, he rapidly advanced the kingdom. First he consolidated his position in the south with Hebron as his capital. Then he moved to conquer, control, and secure other territories, which he did so successfully that his reign was later seen as the golden age in Israel's history (*see Map 5*). David was a zealous prosecutor of war, as the historical chronicles reveal:

> After this David defeated the Philistines and subdued them ... and he defeated Moab ... and David also defeated Hadadezer ... king of Zobah, as he went to restore his power at the River Euphrates. And David took from him a thousand and 700 horsemen, and 20,000 foot soldiers ... slew 22,000 Syrians ... and David won a name for himself ... he slew 18,000 Edomites in the Valley of Salt. ... And the Lord gave victory to David wherever he went (2 Sam. 8:1-14).

Besides extending the borders of the kingdom to the Red Sea and the Euphrates River, David established a new capital, and this latter achievement brought him as much glory as the former. Hebron had served well when the country was not much larger than Judah, but for a growing nation it was too far south and too related to David's own tribe to serve as a rallying point for the entire nation. In one of his early campaigns against the Philistines, David's fancy was caught by the Jebusite stronghold of Jerusalem, which had withstood many onslaughts. David wanted to secure the fortress by peaceful negotiations, but since the Jebusites had never before had reason to surrender, they mockingly replied that if the walls were manned by the blind and the lame any assault would still be a vain undertaking. But one of David's warriors crawled

through one of the conduits with his bravest men and took
over. David was now the master of the stronghold, and he
named it the City of David (2 Sam. 5:5-9).

David wanted Jerusalem not only to be a royal fortress,
but also to carry religious symbolism and to have a sacred
character. Thus he linked the national center to the religious
traditions of Samuel and Moses as he transferred the ark of
the covenant to Zion. He also made plans to build a temple,
but its execution was left to the reign of his son. As Moses
before him, David was a man of many gifts, being a musician
and poet as well as warrior and king. In his literary works,
particularly his psalms, and in his political administration,
he sought to be a faithful worshipper of Yahweh.

David, however, also followed his own interests, in the
course of which he acquired many wives. He even committed
murder and adultery to win his favorite Bathsheba, the wife
of a Hittite mercenary. These acts in turn, however, also led
to deep remorse, and in his repentance he discovered person-
ally the same merciful, forgiving, and long-suffering God whom
the people collectively had experienced. Yahweh was jealous
and judgmental, but he also forgave all iniquity and acknowledged as favorites those who acknowledged him (Ps. 51).

David experienced forgiveness in his penitence but also
judgment for continuing cruelty, such as his blood revenge
against the house of Saul. The judgments caught up with him
in the disintegration of his family, the rebellion of his son,
and his inability to carry through his plans to build a magnificent temple. Yet so impressive had been his kingship in other
ways, that in later days of trouble he was always seen as the
prototype of an even greater messiah or deliverer for Israel.
The city that he had established was viewed thereafter as a
symbol of humanity's eternal and ideal city. Countless poems
were written and sung about Jerusalem or about Zion, as the
city was later also called (Ps. 122; Isa. 2). As for David, the
following words from modern Jewish historians seem to be
a fitting tribute:

> He left to his successor a rich heritage, and to his people the
> memory of glorious achievement. He had his faults; in the
> full record of his life, which is preserved in holy writ, there
> is no attempt to cover him up or condone them. He could
> be vindictive and then again magnanimous. He hated his
> enemies, but also loved his friends; he was an overindulgent

father; he was prone to sin, but was quick to repent. He rose
to his station by dint of an indomitable energy; a great
warrior, he also pursued the genteel arts of song and music;
he loved religious pomp and ceremony. Deeply pious by
nature, he divined his people's sacred vocation. The holy city
of Jerusalem was his foundation, the rocky hill for the rear-
ing of the temple was his choice. His dynasty continued down
to the Persian times; patriarchs and exilarchs reckoned themselves to his house. To the last days the hope of Israel is
bound up with this great figure, David the King, symbol of
the Jews' undying faith.[2]

Solomon and Solomon's Temple

Solomon (961-922), son and successor, brought additional
glory to the kingdom, chiefly with his extensive building programs, notably the magnificent temple in Jerusalem. The temple was built with architectural and construction help from
Phoenicia, and materials such as cedar and cypress timber
secured from Lebanon. Other building projects integrated with
the temple area included a king's palace, an armory, a treasury,
a hall of judgment, and a palace for Solomon's favorite wife,
the Egyptian princess.

The temple added very significantly to the attraction of
Jerusalem and to its religious and political significance, and
it is hard to overestimate the importance attached to the temple
by the Israelites in subsequent times. It gave rise to much
religious patriotism expressed in psalms and poetry, and this
literature in turn strengthened the image of the temple both
near and far. Beautiful in elevation, the city and temple were
"the joy of the whole earth" (Ps. 48:2; see also Pss. 84, 87,
122, 125, 126, 132, 135).

The temple was meant to bring glory not only to Jerusalem
and the kingdom, but to Yahweh himself, who with the growth
of the kingdom had also become more universal. Indeed, Solomon wanted foreigners to worship in his temple and he built
special chapels to accommodate them. While the temple was
meant to contain God, Solomon recognized that the temple
could no more contain him than could the heavens, as he
confessed in his prayer of dedication: "But will God indeed
dwell on the earth? Behold, heaven and the highest heaven

---

[2] Max I. Margolis and Alexander Marx, *A History of the Jewish
People,* p. 59.

cannot contain thee; how much less this house which I have
built!" (1 Kings 8:27).

Solomon's interest in building extended to military fortifica-
tions and commercial enterprises. Among the former we can
cite the establishment of Megiddo as one of his famous "char-
iot" cities, and among the latter the merchant fleet that operated from bases on the Red Sea. Megiddo helped him to protect his nation and the merchant fleet helped him to keep it
prosperous.

Solomon's programs involved considerable expense, and
soon the treasure accumulated by David was exhausted, in
spite of the more efficient taxation system that his son established. Like his father before him, Solomon used forced
labor extensively, and there is even a hint that he sold laborers
to Egypt to help balance his account. He lost some of the
territories acquired by David, and upon his death the kingdom divided into two parts and remained that way until they
were dissolved, each in its turn. Thus, while kingship brought
to Israel stability and splendor, it also exacted the toll that
Samuel had predicted.

The Divided Kingdom — Israel

When Solomon died, his son Rehoboam was accepted as
king by Jerusalem and the south, but the northerners, who
had resented Solomon's taxes the most, refused to accept
Rehoboam. Instead, they followed Jeroboam, who with the
assistance of Egypt staged a successful revolt and even forced
Rehoboam to empty the last of his father's treasures.

The political unity established by David and Solomon for
less than a century thus came to an end, as the two kingdoms fought against each other. In other ways, however,
they occasionally found a unity as their common faith and
tradition transcended their political disunity.

The kings of the northern state, which embraced ten tribes
and was called Israel, found themselves in almost continuous
confusion until Omri (876-869) in the early ninth century
did for the north what David had done for the entire kingdom. He established a new capital at Samaria, entered into
profitable alliances, and generally so impressed the Assyrians
to the east that they referred to Israel as "The Land of Omri."
Allied with Phoenicia, Israel was able to keep both the Ara-

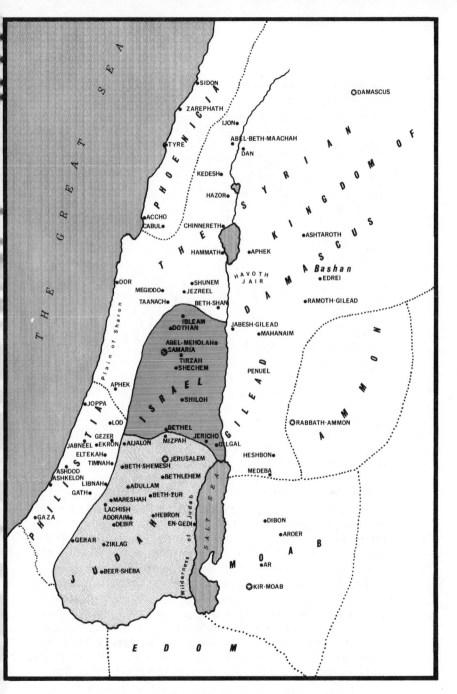

Map 6 — *Israel and Judah in the Ninth Century*

maeans of Syria and the Assyrians at bay, but only for a short while (*see Map 6*).

Ahab's continued alliance with Phoenicia brought Jezebel into Israel's ruling family and with her an autocracy and religious idolatry that brought much ill to the country. Prophets like Elijah were able to assert themselves against Ahab and the prophets of Baal, calling the people to repentance and promoting the righteousness of Yahweh while fighting for the maintenance of the covenant and individual rights against such autocratic oppression. However, their efforts to curb the growth of a wealthy class under the prosperous reign of Jeroboam II (786-746), which was likewise oppressive, were quite unsuccessful.

During this time the prophets took the place formerly held by the judges in calling people back to Yahweh. King David and King Solomon had not neglected religious functions, but the official priests of the kingdom did little more than sanction the policies of the kings. There were those in the kingdom, however, who felt that Yahweh could not always approve of the kings, and some with insight and courage rose up to prophesy against the evil. David, for instance, already heard the sharp rebukes of Nathan for his evils (2 Sam. 12).

In the north, where most of the nineteen kings and their priests served the Egyptian calf or the Canaanite Baal, the religious situation clearly demanded a new charisma. Elijah was one such prophet, and it was he who called the people back to the God of Abraham, Isaac, Jacob, and Moses: "How long will you go limping with two different opinions? If the Lord is God, follow him, but if Baal, then follow him" (1 Kings 18:21). Religious idolatry was accompanied by much economic inequality. Prophets like Amos and Hosea denounced the ill treatment of tenants and peasants and the injustice of the courts who favored the rich. Amos in particular saw Israel's breaking of the covenant in the oppression of the poor by the wealthy upper class, as we read in the book of his prophecy:

> For three transgressions of Israel, and for four, I will not revoke the punishment, because they sell the righteous for silver and the needy for a pair of shoes — they that trample the head of the poor into the dust of the earth. . . . Hear this word, you cows of Bashan, who are in the mountain of Samaria, who oppress the poor, who crush the needy . . . (Amos 2:6-7; 4:1).

Unable to reform society, the prophets predicted the judgments that inevitably followed. Internal disintegration was followed or accompanied by a repeated onslaught from Assyria, and in 721 Samaria was captured and destroyed after a three-year siege. Most of the kingdom was reorganized as the Assyrian province of Samaria, and large numbers of Israelites, perhaps as many as 30,000, were deported eastward (2 Kings 17).

The Israelites were replaced by Aramaeans from Syria and Bedouins from the desert. They intermarried with the remaining Israelites, and since the northern kingdom was now the Assyrian province of Samaria, they became known as Samaritans, a few of whom survive in the region around Nablus to the present day. The people's language also changed from Hebrew to Aramaic, the Semitic dialect of Syria, and this language was soon spoken throughout the land including Jerusalem. The ten tribes lost their identity both inside and outside of Canaan and became known as "the ten lost tribes of Israel," though some of the exiles did later return to the land.

The Southern Kingdom — Judah

The southern kingdom of Judah differed from the northern kingdom in several ways. It was much smaller and concentrated, and less exposed to the expanding eastern empires of Assyria and Babylon. Its kings — with one brief interruption — continued the Davidic dynasty, and officially they maintained the worship of God, though in Judah too there was much idolatry. The geographical, political, and religious factors, however, all contributed to a longer duration for the southern kingdom than the northern.

As Egyptian influence in the south declined, Assyrian and later Babylonian influence and control increased. After the fall of Israel, Judah was for all practical purposes also under the thumb of Assyria, but the eastern empire had no reason to press its claims any further, because Egypt was for the time being no threat to anybody.

Yet Judah was tempted to forge an alliance with Egypt to get out from under Assyria, and this was true especially after one of her greater kings, Uzziah (783-742), had died. It was in this situation that there arose in Jerusalem the first prophet to direct his message primarily to the southern kingdom, Isaiah. He was probably the greatest of the prophets of the children of Israel.

Isaiah, an articulate and sophisticated member of Jerusalem's privileged class, had a new vision of Yahweh in the year that Uzziah died. To him the Lord appeared once more with the majesty and intimacy that he had revealed to Moses. According to the prophet, Yahweh would remain true to his covenant. He would bless the people if they kept their promise, but all conceivable judgmental woes would befall them if they strayed away. Isaiah, however, did not limit his message to Judah. On the contrary, more than ever before Yahweh was presented as the universal God to whom all nations, including Egypt and Syria, were ultimately subject. Judah should, therefore, trust the Lord and not any one single nation:

> Woe to those who go down to Egypt for help and rely on horses, who trust in chariots because they are many and in horsemen because they are strong, but do not look to the Holy One of Israel or consult the Lord! . . . The Egyptians are men and not God; and their horses are flesh, and not spirit. When the Lord stretches out his hand, the helper will stumble, and he who is helped will fall, and they will all perish (Isa. 31:1-3).

Two prominent later kings, Hezekiah (c. 715-687) and Josiah (c. 640-609), sought to restore the worship of Yahweh in the temple; and Jerusalem was spared as Isaiah had promised. Josiah's reforms were aided by the discovery of a book of the law, probably the present Deuteronomy.

After Josiah Judah declined rapidly. Josiah's immediate successor became a vassal of Egypt, and this was a state of affairs which could not be tolerated by the east. Soon after the new Babylonian king Nebuchadnezzar had crushed Assyria, he extended Babylonian domains to the full extent of the Assyrian empire. Jerusalem was captured in 589, the king and the best of his subjects were sent into exile. Jerusalem and its temple were destroyed, and there were three additional major deportations in 589, 587, and 586.

Isaiah was not the only one to predict that idolatry, foolish alliances, and rebellion would bring the downfall of Judah. His message was later corroborated by the voices of Zephaniah, Habakkuk, Jeremiah, and Ezekiel. As the crisis deepened, Jeremiah called for a deeper knowledge of Yahweh and a more personal relationship to him. As his society was destroyed, the prophet went to Egypt, while his colleague, Ezekiel, joined the exiles in Babylon.

The Exile and the Return

The desolation of Jerusalem had been complete, and this fact added to the discouragement of the Babylonian exiles who now had to make their life in a new society. Under Nebuchadnezzar their existence was tolerable, but under his successors it became increasingly precarious. And even though they developed the synagogue to replace the function of the temple, they longed for a return.

They sang old and new songs of Zion, and prophets whose works were later incorporated into Isaiah saw the coming of a redeemer from out of the House of David who would be even greater than that great king. He would be a prince of peace, and his kingdom would have no end. Others like Daniel, who were favored in the highest courts, had visions and dreams regarding the inevitable downfall of various nations and the triumph of Yahweh. While Daniel had reference particularly to Babylon, Media, Persia, and Greece, his apocalyptic writings have had a variety of other applications in later times, and his "other horn" has been identified as the anti-Christ, the Roman pope, and such latter-day leaders as Stalin and Hitler.

Ezekiel, the earlier prophet of doom, now offered a message of hope. He announced a new day for Yahweh's faithful remnant and predicted that the dry bones of an exiled society would take on flesh with a new spirit. Yahweh's enemies would be defeated, and a new Jerusalem would appear among men. On behalf of Yahweh, Ezekiel promised:

> I will take you from the nations, and gather you from all the countries, and bring you into your own land.... A new spirit I will give you, and a new spirit I will put within you.... You shall dwell in the land of your fathers, and you shall be my people, and I will be your God (Ezek. 36:24-28).

Ezekiel read the signs of the times correctly. The Babylonian empire was declining rapidly, and under Cyrus the Persian empire was expanding. Cyrus reversed the policies of former emperors and returned exiled populations to their former houses. In 539 he issued an edict authorizing the return of the Jews. Only a few returned at first, but the first ones to return laid the foundations of a new temple. So difficult was their task that little progress was made for eighteen years.

A new impetus came under Cyrus' successor Darius, who

encouraged the Jewish governors of Jerusalem, descendants of Jehoiakim, the last king of Judah. With further impetus from a new group of prophets, including Haggai and Zechariah, work on the temple was resumed; but the restoration was not completed until Nehemiah became governor under the Persian overlord around 444.

With Nehemiah and Ezra the scribe, there came an emphasis that dominated Jewish thought until the time of Jesus. For Nehemiah the national Jewish identity, if not independence, and the purity of the Jewish congregation were all-important. For these reasons the returned Jews clashed frequently with the Samaritans to the north. Ezra directed the Jewish people to become a people of the book, which also remained a prominent characteristic.

The independent nationhood of the Jews, however, remained an elusive goal. The Persian empire ended with the conquests of Alexander the Great of Greece in 333. Though Alexander died ten years later, Greek influence prevailed for several centuries. The new conquest meant a new scattering of the Jews, and they became leading merchants and traders. So strong was Greek culture that the Jewish colony in the new Egyptian city of Alexandria proceeded to translate the Hebrew writings into Greek, and they became known as the Septuagint.

When Alexander died, the empire was divided by his generals, the Ptolemies based in Egypt and the Seleucids based in Syria. The latter controlled Palestine from 198. The introduction of Greek gods into the temple so offended some Jews that a minority, led by the Maccabeans, staged a revolt, and a period of independence began in 164. The temple was cleansed and rededicated, as the Maccabeans ruled as high priests and later as kings.

However, this time of independence came to an end a hundred years later as another empire appeared on the world stage, that of the Romans. Jerusalem was conquered in 63. While Roman administration of the region was not always direct, the Jews had lost political control of their destiny. The latest suppression renewed the hope of a king like David, but even though a messiah in the Davidic line did appear he was too unlike David to be recognized as the desired savior.

The Jews staged a series of revolts, and in the end the Romans like the Assyrians and Babylonians before them lost their patience and crushed the rebels completely. The temple, which had been built anew by Herod the Great, was destroyed in AD 70 and another wave of Jews was scattered.

The people lost their land, but not their sacred writings. Wherever these were read among the dispersed Jews, they became reminders of past promises and glories, and these in turn became the content of the future hope. For this reason the bygone realities of promised land, a glorious Davidic dynasty, a beautiful Zion, and a sacred temple remained future possibilities in a very literal sense. How could it be otherwise, if generation after generation kept singing the Israelite song composed and learned in Babylon: "If I forget thee, O Jerusalem, let my right hand forget her cunning" (Ps. 137:5)?

4. The Claims of Islam

The greatest achievement of Arabic civilization in Palestine is manifest in the Muslim religious buildings. Above all, the Mosque of Al-Aksa and the Dome of the Rock, both on the place of Hebrew Temple, stand out, and the latter is among the greatest monuments not only of its age, but of all times.
— Norman Bentwich[1]

As the Jews and their later religious relatives, the Christians, spread out from the Middle East, they carried with them the biblical literature, which repeatedly identified the children of Israel with the promised land of Palestine. In terms of historical and sociological reality, however, this association of one people with one land was only one part of the total human story. Another much-neglected dimension had to do with the other descendants of Abraham and of his Semitic relatives, who also became very much attached to Palestine for religious reasons.

The stories of Abraham, Isaac, Jacob (Israel), and their descendants were known and retold endlessly wherever the Judaic-Christian tradition established itself, while the stories of Isaac's brother Ishmael, Ishmael's cousin Lot, and Jacob's brother Esau were forgotten. Yet they and their offspring continued to exist as part of God's humanity. They too multiplied exceedingly, as did scores of closely or distantly related Semitic tribes around them. Like Jacob Ishmael gave birth to twelve tribes, which increased even more rapidly than the twelve tribes of Israel and became a great people who spread throughout the region, assimilating themselves to, and integrating with, other Semitic peoples.

[1] *Palestine,* p. 5.

68

Invasion from the Desert

Not infrequently Abraham's other descendants and relatives crossed paths with the Israelites in ways both friendly and hostile. The Ishmaelites, for instance, are known to have befriended Joseph and helped Moses, but they also joined other tribes in resisting the Hebrew conquest of Canaan, for they too had a claim on that land or a part of it. In other words, the Ishmaelites, like other Semitic tribes before, during, and after the times of the Hebrews, tended to move from desert areas toward the fertile areas and claim some part of them as their own.

The most desired section of the Crescent, as we have already seen, was the Canaanite territory halfway between the Nile and the Tigris-Euphrates valleys. Because this region was the most desired, it was the location of the most frequent invasions and expulsions of peoples. Like other tribes before and after them, the Hebrews were both the fortunate benefactors and the tragic victims of these patterns of population movement and conquest.

The most determined invasions came from the desert, and the most determined desert people were the inhabitants of the vast Arabian peninsula. Indeed, one theory has it that all the Semitic peoples eventually found in the Crescent (including the Syrians, Aramaeans, Canaanites, Phoenicians, and Hebrews) had their original home in Arabia. Ancient history is too vague to allow much confidence in this theory, but there is no uncertainty that the Arabian people did in later times spill out of the desert and into the Fertile Crescent in a magnitude unprecedented in both quantity and quality.

These migrating and conquering Arabians identified themselves as relatives of all other Semites. More specifically, they recognized themselves as sharing the religious and territorial inheritance of Abraham through Ishmael. For the patriarch's first son and his mother a sacred shrine was established in Mecca, the chief city of the Arabian peninsula.

The latest Arabian invasion became possible in the seventh century of the Christian era by the decline of other power centers, particularly the waning of the Persian and Byzantine empires, which until that time had vied for the control of the middle of the earth. The identification with Abraham and his people, on the other hand, came with the rise of a new

religious force, which also provided the motive power for expansion at the very time when power vacuums were begging
a new authority.

Muhammad — Prophet of Allah

This new religious and military dynamic appeared in the
commercial heartland of Arabia and was precipitated by Muhammad, who became known as a prophet of Allah and the
founder of Islam, a new religion that placed a premium on
man's submission to God.

Muhammad was born around AD 570 in the city of
Mecca, Arabia's most prominent population and business center. Brought up as a poor orphan, he acquired wealth and
position at the age of 25 by marrying the rich widow of a
merchant and becoming a merchant himself. In his later
teaching he spoke of God's providing guidance and en-
richment for an erring and impoverished orphan. His words
applied not only to himself but also to the impoverished slaves
of greedy masters and to destitute desert dwellers, all of whom
received his message with eagerness since it brought them so
much comfort:

> By the light of day, and the fall of night, the lord has not
> forsaken you, nor does he abhor you.
> The life to come holds a richer prize for you than this
> present life. You shall be gratified with what your lord will
> give you.
> Did he not find you an orphan and give you shelter?
> Did he not find you in error and guide you?
> Did he not find you poor and enrich you?
> Therefore do not wrong the orphan, nor drive the beggar
> away. But proclaim the goodness of your lord.[2]

Though Muhammad was in all likelihood not too well educated (some sources say he was illiterate), he was familiar
with the contents of the sacred writings and their ideas of
Jewish monotheism and Christian revelation. Jewish and Christian influences came to him not only from the writings but
also from the numerous traders and travelers coming through
Mecca and from actual communities of both traditions, which
had penetrated the peninsula. The Jews and Judaized Arabs
could be found everywhere, though mostly in Medina, a rival

[2] Translated by N. J. Dawood, *The Koran*, p. 24.

center to Mecca. The chief Christian center in central Arabia was in Najran, likewise a center of commercial and political power.

The "pagan" Arabians, like their Semitic ancestors, were open to new religious revelations, and a monotheistic God was usually only as far away as a leader and his tribe who would champion the monotheistic cause. During the latter part of the sixth century, the Hanifs in Mecca were most unhappy with the prevailing pagan idolatries, but they were not enthusiastic over either Judaism or Christianity. Among the dissatisfied was Muhammad, who felt the call to preach his new insights when he was about forty years old. His earliest and also his latest preaching had to do with the unity of God, the wickedness and idolatry of his age, and the imminence of divine judgment.

The only way to escape the wrath of God was to submit to his will. What this will was was spelled out more precisely as time went on. Like the Bible, the holy writings of Islam forbade lying, stealing, adultery, and murder. Warfare was justified if it served to unify the warring tribes and bring them into submission to the one God. Submission to God forged a brotherhood more binding than the ties of blood relationships. Indeed, those who died in the effort to bring about such intertribal brotherhood earned thereby a special reward in heaven. As it was spoken and written:

> Did you think that you could go to Paradise before Allah has proved the men who fought for Him and endured with fortitude? ... Many large armies have fought by the side of their prophet. They were never daunted by what befell them on the path of Allah: they neither weakened nor cringed abjectly. Allah loves the steadfast. ... Therefore Allah gave them the reward of this life, and the glorious recompense of the life to come; Allah loves the righteous.[3]

Reaction to Polytheism

Muhammad's emphasis on the unity of God grew out of his contempt for the polytheism he observed around him. At the Kaaba (a holy black stone where bloody sacrifices took place) in Mecca, for instance, the Meccans worshipped not only Allah, as the supreme Semitic god was known in those parts, but also a number of female deities. These derived their

[3] *Ibid.*, p. 408.

divine status from the fact that they were, as was believed,
daughters of Allah.

Similarly, Muhammad was not attracted by what he thought
was polytheism in Christianity as he knew it. He could not
reconcile the doctrine of the trinity as it was expressed (he
hardly knew the doctrine in the more classical formulation
of the Councils of Nicaea and Chalcedon), with his understanding of the unity of God. The trinity among the Christians
of Arabia included Mary and, in the prevailing culture of the
time, her divinity was seen as comparable with that of other
female deities, such as the daughters of Allah: Al-Lat (sun),
Al-Uzzah (Venus), and Al-Manat (Fortune).

For Muhammad such notions were scandalous, and he could
no more accept the idea that God had a wife than that he
had daughters. The Christian community believed Jesus to be
a member of the divine trinity as a physical offspring of Allah
and Mary. To Muhammad this was utterly unacceptable. The
unity and supremacy of God, therefore, became his primary
theme, which he proclaimed with all the vigor and energy
at his command. His message was later recorded in the holy
book Koran as follows:

> Never has Allah begotten a son, nor is there any other god
> besides him. Were this otherwise, each god would govern his
> own creation, each holding himself above the other. Exalted
> by Allah above their falsehoods ... he that invokes another
> god besides Allah — a god for whose divinity he has no proof
> — his lord will bring him to account. ...

> The Jews say Ezra is a son of Allah, while the Christians say
> the Messiah is a son of Allah. Such are their assertions by
> which they imitate the infidels of old. Allah confound them!
> How perverse they are!

> They worship their rabbis and their monks, and the Messiah,
> the son of Mary, as gods besides Allah; though they were
> ordered to serve one god only. There is no god but him,
> exhalted be he above those whom they deify besides him![4]

Muhammad's removal of Mary and Jesus from the deities
to be worshipped did not mean that he lost his regard for
them. On the contrary, he recognized that Jesus, as well as
Moses, had been sent by Allah to call the people to obedience.

---

4 *Ibid.*, pp. 220-221, 315-316.

But the people had refused to heed him. Indeed, they did not even believe the miracles Jesus did.

Allah, according to Muhammad, was a compassionate and merciful God, who desired the salvation of all mankind but who would judge all who refused to believe and obey, while they worshipped other gods. To such idolaters Allah was a God of terrible judgment. All men were, therefore, called to submit themselves to him, and this emphasis on submission gave to the new religion its name, Islam (meaning submission). Those who submitted themselves were Muslims, a name likewise derived from the act of submission.

From Mecca to Medina

Muhammad's message was not readily received by the lords and citizens of Mecca, but the people of the rival city of Medina responded to him with greater openness and eventually welcomed him as the chief magistrate of the community. The prophet's migration, or *Hijara* as it was called in Arabic, from Mecca to Medina came after a time of negotiations with the city fathers. The year of the Hijara, AD 622 by Christian reckoning, became the first certain and recognized date in Islamic history, and Islam's calendar begins with that event.

In Medina, Muhammad tried to win the Jews over to his side, inasmuch as he recognized them as the bearers of the same monotheistic tradition. He adopted Jewish practices and directed that prayers be spoken facing toward Jerusalem. When the Jews, however, rejected this "gentile prophet," he substituted Mecca, the traditional Arabian center of worship, as the direction of prayer. Jerusalem was, however, never forgotten and later it became a city as holy as Medina or Mecca.

While leading Jews, Christians, and Arab pagans alike rejected the prophet, he did not remain without some followers. Many of his kinfolk believed in him, and the slaves and poor people of his day also took to his message. This is not surprising, since his message was directed against the wealthy and powerful classes who had rejected him in Mecca.

Since the wealthy had also rejected Allah, Muhammad felt called to go out after them in his name and bring them to submission. The more they opposed him, the more he became determined to humiliate his enemies at Mecca and to cleanse the monotheistic religion of Abraham of its idolatrous Jewish and Christian accretions. In his zeal it was not always clear whether he was first a warrior or religious reformer. Most of the time he was both, seeking reform and demanding submission in the name of Allah. If this required war then so be it. Political and religious objectives were of one kind in the mind of the prophet, and methods appropriate to the one area applied also to the other. Since many citizens of Medina, most of all the poor, shared his feelings about Mecca, it was not too difficult for him to organize them for his campaigns against that city.

Meanwhile, brief returns to Mecca had won him new converts, among them Khalid ibn Al-Walid, who was to play a prominent role in the future. With his following reinforced by fresh converts, Muhammad was able to capture Mecca in January 630. Though he lived only two and a half years thereafter, Muhammad consolidated his victory and firmly established himself as a new religious and political authority to whom many Arabian tribes quickly submitted. When the prophet died, he had established a new community, a state well organized and armed, with power and prestige to unify the many Arabian tribes under Allah.

The New Unifying Force

A single God required a single people, and this new doctrine became the ideological foundation of the empire that emerged after Muhammad's death. The Middle East was ready and waiting for a new unifying force. The two contending empires of Persia and Byzantium had spent themselves in a series of wars from 602-628, both of them unaware of the new challenge that was to burst forth from the Arabian desert.

The military thrust of Islam was initiated by Muhammad's immediate successors, who had formerly been his deputies or caliphs. Their authority embraced the political, military, and religious spheres in which Muhammad had also been active, and this power became institutionalized in the office of the caliphate.

Abu Bakr, the first caliph, and Umar, his successor, did not automatically inherit all of Muhammad's authority and prestige. Both were confronted by rebellions, collectively known as the *Ridda* movement, which first had to be suppressed. This action to subjugate dissident tribes and their leaders turned into

a conquest, which ultimately led far beyond the borders of
Arabia. The key figure in this conquest was the prominent
Mecca convert, Khalid ibn Al-Walid, who established his military powers at a major successful battle as early as 633. From
that time on a series of expeditions radiated in all directions.

The Christianized Arabs to the north, no longer protected
by Byzantium, threw in their lot with the invaders, as did
many other tribes. The Islamic general kept advancing and,
supported by a few thousand Arabs, he routed a Byzantine army
of the Yarmuk River in 636, thus gaining access to all Syria
and Palestine. Jerusalem fell after a siege of four months and
so did Caesarea, Damascus, and Antioch in short order.

Following this early conquest of Palestine and Syria, Khalid
directed his armies against Egypt, North Africa, Tunis, Iraq,
and Persia. All were subdued by 661 (*see Map 7*). For Muhammad, the passion for a unified human race had arisen from
his belief in one God, but for his crusaders on the frontier
the rewards of booty also provided strong motivation. The
prophet justified the taking of the spoils of war if they were
taken from the rich and given to the poor, and most of his
followers happened to be poor. Very eagerly his generals rode
forth with hordes of untrained soldiers to spread the good
words of Allah, to enforce the new unity, and to gather in
the goods. One such general in 642 led 20,000 desert dwellers
as far as Alexandria, and sent back the kind of dispatch which
would easily generate enthusiasm for additional crusades. He
said: "Suffice it to say, I have seized therein 4,000 villas with
4,000 baths . . . and 400 royal places of entertainment."[5]

Special Attention to Jerusalem

The offer to surrender Jerusalem was made by Patriarch
Sophronius on condition that the Caliph himself appear to
negotiate the takeover. To this Umar agreed, for Jerusalem was
a city different from all the rest, since it was to Jerusalem that
Muhammad had made his miraculous nocturnal journey and
it was in Jerusalem that he had ascended on a celestial ladder
into heaven. The Caliph agreed with the Prelate to terms of
surrender expressed by the former as follows:

> In the name of Allah, the Merciful, the Compassionate. This
> is the covenant which Umar, the servant of Allah, the Com-

---

[5] Philip K. Hitti, *A Short History of the Near East*, p. 98.

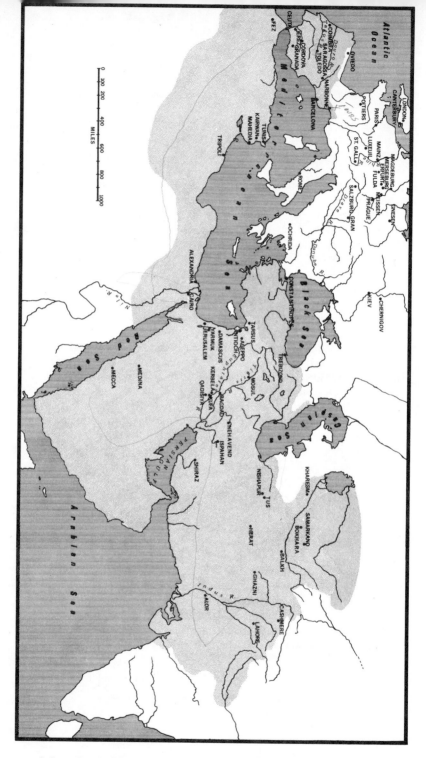

Map 7 — *The Expansion of the Muslim-Arab Empire*

> mander of the faithful granted to the people. . . . He granted
> them safety for their lives, their possessions, their churches,
> and their crosses . . . they shall not be constrained in the mat-
> ter of religion, nor shall any of them be molested. . . . And the
> people shall pay the poll-tax. . . . Whoever leaves the city shall
> be safe in his person until he reaches his destination. . . .[6]

Umar then proceeded to search out in the old Temple area the holy place, the Rock from where Muhammad had, so it was supposed, temporarily ascended into heaven, and in this he was assisted by the Patriarch. The Caliph directed that no prayers be spoken until the Rock, which had been concealed under a dunghill, had been washed by rain three times.

Furthermore, Umar directed that two of his deputies, former companions of the Prophet, take up residence in Jerusalem. One, a teacher, was made the first Muslim judge of Jerusalem, and the other was given special religious duties to perform. Both remained there until their deaths.

Before his departure from the city, Umar directed that a mosque, a place for prostration in prayer, be erected on the spot where he had led the Muslims in prayer. The first structure was very primitive, but it provided the beginnings for monumental Muslim structures later in the century.

Arabization and Islamization

While a new unity was being forged on the frontier of the advancing Arabic armies, dissension and factionalism appeared among the rulers at Medina. Of the first four caliphs (632-611), only the first died peacefully. The last three were murdered. In 661 the Umayyas, an aristocratic family from Mecca, seized the caliphate and in so doing edged out Hussein, a relative of Muhammad. The young contender was killed, but his descendants nonetheless worked their way up to an influential role, which culminated in the monarchy of Transjordan many years later.

The Umayyad dynasty ruled from Damascus. During its rule (661-750) Islam spread over Persia into central Asia and India, and over Syria and Egypt into Spain and finally France, where the Muslims were stopped in 732 near Poitiers by Charles Martel. The vast military conquest of the Arabs

---

[6] A. L. Tibawi, "Jerusalem: Its Place in Islam and Arab History," *The Arab World,* XIV:10-11, p. 10.

set in motion a two-dimensional cultural thrust: on the one hand, it resulted in the Arabization of the Middle East, and on the other hand it culminated in the Islamization of many peoples who because of distance did not become an integral part of the Arab culture, as in India and Indonesia.

The Arabization had both linguistic and racial dimensions. The latter was a consequence of the invasion and migration of the aggressive Arabic Semites from the Arabian peninsula. The resulting dominance of this breed of people led to the linguistic and cultural integration of the majority of the Middle Eastern Semitic tribes into an Arabic unity, although the separate dialects of the area remained in use a long time. This Arabization had begun in some areas before the Muslim conquest. In those instances, the armies speeded up and universalized the process:

> In less than three generations, the life of those countries was completely transformed. While a new religion preached by the invaders . . . allowed large communities in the conquered countries to retain their old faith . . . the Arabic language had unity and became uniformly dominant everywhere. Before the end of the seventh century, it had become the language of state. . . .[7]

Arabization in the Middle East, having begun earlier, proceeded more rapidly than Islamization. Indeed, the Muslim empire in its early generations contained many non-Muslim subjects, who for a long time constituted the majority of the population. These people were not all forcefully converted, as has sometimes been assumed, because Muhammad's words that there should be no compulsion in the matters of religion were taken seriously by most of the crusader armies. It was the tolerance rather than the sword of Islam that swelled the ranks of believers, especially in Syria and Palestine. Only deliberate unbelief and rebellion against Allah should be punished.

Autonomy in the Millets

Christian and Jewish communities were left largely undisturbed as long as they agreed to the payment of annual tribute and recognized the one God. Since Muslims were exempt from such taxation, the conversion of non-Muslims was actually

---

[7] George Antonius, *The Arab Awakening,* p. 17.

discouraged in order not to lessen the number of taxpayers. The taxes were raised through a system of self-administering religious communities or *millets*. Muslim law did not apply in these communities, inasmuch as in Islamic thought the religious and political orders were one. Thus the religious dignitaries of those communities were in charge of administering the civil code that had applied before the conquest.

Under the millet system some Christian and Jewish communities actually prospered. This was true particularly of the Jews, who felt that they had at long last been liberated from their oppressive Christian overlords. As Merlin Swartz has written: "For the Jews in the Near-East, North Africa, and Spain the Arab conquest marked the dawn of a new era. Those forces that had led to the progressive isolation and disruption of Jewish life were not only checked but dramatically reversed. . . ."[8]

In economics, in education, and in political life the Jews in the Arab world experienced a remarkable renascence, which was checked only when the Arab world itself entered a period of stagnation. Until then the Jews shared the prosperity of the Arab world and, under the Fatimid caliphs of Egypt, even political power. A Jewish governor ruled the province of Syria, and important positions in the caliph's court were also held by Jews. This Jewish influence caused one Arab poet to write a poem about the desirability of being a Jew:

Today the Jews have reached the summit of their hopes
    and have become aristocrats.
Power and riches have they,
    and from them councillors and princes are chosen.
Egyptians, I advise you, become Jews for the very sky has
    become Jewish![9]

Within the context of the millet system and religious freedom, Arabization was complete also in Palestine, where most of the inhabitants were Christians, though there were some Jews. The Arab tongue became the common cultural bond of the inhabitants, while religious liturgies continued the use of the Hebrew, Greek, and Latin tongues. The villages and

---

[8] "The Position of Jews in Arab Lands following the Rise of Islam," unpublished paper, January 1969.

[9] Mez, *The Renaissance of Islam,* p. 58.

towns, which had been Hellenized, resumed their former Semitic names.

Worship and Learning

The Umayyad caliphs took a special interest in Palestine. Umar's successor had himself proclaimed Caliph in Jerusalem rather than in his capital Damascus. Caliph Abdul-Malek, ruling from Damascus, strove to make Jerusalem a Muslim religious center to rival Mecca and Medina, which were not always under Umayyad control. Jerusalem should be El-Kuds, meaning the holy town, and Islamic Arabs forever after recognized it as such.

To turn Jerusalem into a holy place for Muslims, the caliphs built on the site of the Temple, which had become a heap of refuse in the Byzantine empire, two outstanding shrines of Islam, the Mosque of Al-Aksa and the Dome of the Rock. The rock on which the dome was built was believed to be the place where Abraham prepared to offer Isaac and to which Muhammad had made his nocturnal visit.

The mosque may originally have been a Christian basilica, but the Dome was an original creation completed in 691, and reflecting the genius of Byzantine, Persian, as well as Arabic craftsmen. Both the inner and outer walls were beautifully decorated with mosaics, the motifs being taken from nature with emphasis on floral designs. The two Islamic shrines endured for many centuries, longer than any of the Jewish temples. As it became necessary, the structures were restored, but any willful harm was looked upon as an offense against Allah and his holiest of holy places. This is why the fire in 1969, when the mosque was under Israeli control, was believed to be sufficient cause for a holy war by Islam against Israel.

The Umayyads had great achievements to their credit, but they lost control of the caliphate to the Abbasid dynasty in 750. The capital was moved from Damascus to Baghdad from where Islam ruled until 1258. While Palestine did not receive as much attention from the new, more distant capital, three Abbasid caliphs made pilgrimages to Jerusalem and one of them ordered major renovations and restorations of the Dome. From that time on many Muslim pilgrims went to Jerusalem, including state functionaries, commentators on the Koran, students of prophetic traditions, mystics, and pious men and

women in general. One Muslim author wrote concerning the
new majesty and significance of Jerusalem:

> As to her being the finest city, why, has any seen elsewhere
> buildings finer or cleaner, or a mosque that is more beautiful?
> ... And as to the excellence of the city, why, is this not the
> place of marshalling on the Day of Judgment? ... Verily,
> Mecca and Medinah have their superiority by reason of the
> Kaabah and the Prophet, but, in truth, on the Day of Judg-
> ment, both cities will come to Jerusalem, and the excellencies
> of them all will be united.[10]

The Abbasid period was one of general prosperity and cultural brilliance, and Jerusalem, along with Baghdad, Cairo, and
Damascus, became an important center of learning. The col-
leges of all four cities together formed a university that pre-
dated the oldest universities in Europe by hundreds of years.
These Arab centers of learning gave new life to the exhausted
culture of the Byzantine and Persian empires, while generat-
ing knowledge and insight distinctively Arabian in character.
Astronomy was revitalized, and mathematics, arithmetic, ge-
ometry, and algebra were developed anew. Many Arab scientific terms were destined for universal acceptance. And there
were other contributions:

> The astrolabe, which was a Greek invention of antiquity, was
> perfected by the Arabs to determine the hour of prayer and
> the position of Mecca. Geography became an important
> practical science because every good Muslim had once in his
> life to be a traveller and make the pilgrimage to Mecca,
> Medina, and Jerusalem. Road books consequently were multi-
> plied. Arithmetic was revolutionized by the arabic system of
> numbers which adopted the sign of zero (arabic ziphr) and
> so enabled an enormous development that was closed to the
> Greek and Roman scientists. Music flourished, and the Arab
> instruments, the lute and the guitar, were brought with their
> Arabic names to Europe.[11]

The cultural renaissance under the Abbasid caliphs was
equaled, and in part made possible, by the general economic
prosperity brought about by ambitious men of commerce. The
rapidly expanding trading empire of Islam extended to China,
Russia, Sweden, and Madagascar, bringing great material

---

[10] Tibawi, *op. cit.*, p. 11.
[11] Bentwich, *op. cit.*, p. 34.

wealth to Baghdad, which the *Arabian Nights* later turned into a legend. At first a blessing, the wealth became a double curse. On the one hand, it contributed to the corruption of the Islamic court, and, on the other hand, it became a temptation for outsiders.

Threats Within and Without

The empire was too huge and too young and the regional rivalries too great to allow for an easy holding together of its far-flung territories. As the Abbasids had in 750 overthrown the Umayyads, so the Fatimid dynasty wrested North Africa and Egypt from the control of the Abbasids in 1055, though the latter were to rule elsewhere for another two centuries.

Actually, the Turks first made their entry into Islam as slave troops, hired as mercenaries by the caliphs. In due course, they became masters in their own rights, and Turkish princes from North Syria joined Saladin of the Kurdish dynasty in Egypt in fighting off the Christian crusaders in 1171. From 1250, when the Abbasids were completely eclipsed, these mamelukes, as the Turkish mandarins were called, controlled Egypt, Palestine, and Syria, until in 1517 they too were dominated by another force. In the meantime they became strong enough for the sultan (or sovereign) himself to be elected from their midst.

In the eastern part of the Arab world the Mongols from deep inside Asia competed with the Turks for the riches of the decimated Abbasid caliphate. While the Mongols held the upper hand for several generations, the Turks won out in the end. The latter were rallied in the fourteenth century by a restless Turkish tribesman by the name of Othman, who by 1326 had extended his control through much of Asia Minor.

Othman's sons were no less ambitious than their father, and to his savagery they added an effective military organization at the heart of which was the famous corps of janissaries (from *yeni cheri* meaning new strength). Ironically, the new strength came not from Islamic Turks, but from Christian Greeks. The first janissaries were young lads taken from their Christian families and brought up as Muslims. Forbidden to marry, they had to submit themselves in every sense to military disciplines and training in order to become ideal fighting material for their leaders. In this practice the Turks were using the Greeks in the same way that the Arabs had used the Turks.

The Ottoman Turks took Jerusalem in 1516 and Cairo early in 1517. In the century immediately following, the Ottoman authorities took great interest in the Arab communities and did their best to promote positive development. Many of them enjoyed considerable autonomy, as long as the Turkish pashas, or viceroys, were able to collect taxes. Conscripts found their places and achieved stature and power in the Turkish armed forces.

As champions of Islam, the Ottoman leaders gave personal attention to the holy cities, particularly Jerusalem. Sultan Sulaiman of the sixteenth century carried out extensive restorations of the Dome of the Rock and gave Jerusalem a new water supply, including five fountains in the Haran area, the site of the Dome and the Al-Aksa Mosque.

Even after the decline of the empire, the sultans never gave up maintaining and further embellishing the mosques in Jerusalem, Medina, and Mecca. Eventually, in the nineteenth century, the floors of both mosques on the Haran were completely covered with priceless Persian rugs.

The End of Progress

As the quality of Ottoman leadership deteriorated and became a conservative force, the clock of human progress came to a halt in the empire. The discovery of new trade routes from western Europe to the East did not help matters, because the Middle East waned somewhat in importance as a trade route and a commercial center. The discovery of gold and silver deposits in the new world led to devaluation of the Ottoman currency, and external military threats demanded of the empire a large and expensive army. Agriculture also was seriously neglected, and, in the words of Anthony Nutting,

> . . . a system of absentee landlords and speculators grew up; a drift from the land followed immediately; and by the middle of the seventeenth century, the once prosperous rural areas of the empire lay derelict. Villages were abandoned, fertile plains were eroded and turned to deserts and, 200 years after the Ottoman occupation started, the population of all Syria had shrunk to little over a million and that of Palestine to a bare 200,000.[12]

[12] *The Arabs,* p. 215.

In a depopulated Palestine the taxes from pilgrim tourists became a most important source of revenue. The yearly rate of pilgrims rose from several thousand persons to some 12,000 in the eighteenth century. The taxes collected for visits to the Jordan River alone were three times the tax assessment in Gaza, the largest Palestinian town.

Egypt too suffered under the Ottoman maladministration. The irrigation system decayed, and the one-time granary of the Roman empire suffered from frequent famines and pestilence. The population of nearly ten million was reduced to an estimated one-fourth of that number.

The European Christian Concern

While the Sultan in Constantinople named himself as Caliph, head of the Muslim community as the successor of Muhammad and thus the commander of all the faithful Muslims, he allowed considerable religious freedom and independence to non-Muslim groups who remained organized as millets. The Greek Orthodox Church, with the later assistance of the Russian Tsar, became the main intermediary between the Sultan and many of his Christian subjects. In many ways the Christians in the Ottoman empire fared better than the Jews in Christendom. And for a long time Christians were better off in Turkey than were the Protestants in France or the Roman Catholics in the British Isles.

The Christianity of Europe, however, could not accept the Islamic empire of Ottoman any more than it had accepted the Islamic empire of the Arabs. While the latter had offended the holy places of Christendom in Palestine, the Ottomans in the early centuries were a constant threat to Christian kingdoms in southern Europe, a threat that neither the Orthodox of Russia, the Catholics of Rome, or the Protestants, somewhat farther away, could accept.

While Christianity was legally protected in the Ottoman empire, the social and economic pressures were such that its numbers declined as a result of intermarriage and the continuing process of Arabization and Islamization. European powers, therefore, felt themselves called to protect and, if possible, extend Christianity in the Middle East. When eventually the Ottoman empire weakened and became "the sick man of Europe," the protectors became rivals, all in the name of Christianity, and the crusader spirit of an earlier day manifested itself again, though this time in a more sophisticated form and with much less bloodshed.

5. The Claims of Christianity

The land where our Lord was born and died had a power-
ful attraction for the west from the time of the first Chris-
tian emperors. . . . —Philip Hughes[1]

The Christian religion was born six centuries before Islam, and, if historical sequence were to be followed consistently in this narrative, the earlier Christian claims on Palestine should have been presented before those of the Muslim faith. The totality of the Christian claim, however, has been so determined by the rise of Islam that some justification can also be made for following the present order. In any event, it was the Christian view of the Muslim threat as the anti-Christ that most determined the modern involvement of western Christianity in the Palestine question.

From the time of its beginnings in the first century, Christianity, like Judaism and Islam, could have given good reasons for claiming Palestine. Jerusalem and the country surrounding it had been important geography for Jesus. It was in the City of David that he had made his debut as a youth, where he had manifested his miraculous power, and where he had delivered some of his major speeches. Here he had given his famous Palm Sunday demonstration prior to his arrest, trial, and crucifixion. In Jerusalem was the nucleus of the first Christian congregation, and leading churchmen gathered there for their first major conference to settle important religious questions having international implications.

---

[1] *A History of the Church,* Volume II, *The Church and the World,* p. 463.

The Founder and the Holy Places

Yet, for good reasons the earliest Christians appear not to have made strong claims to the Holy City and the Holy Land. Their Master had discouraged that kind of religious concern. He himself had not attached much importance to real estate; indeed, at the time of his temptation and several times thereafter he had rejected the contention that property was essential to his cause and his kingdom. Most of the time he had no place he could really call his own where he could lay his head. Comfort, security, property, and the ordinary power of kings were not of prime importance in the order he had come to establish.

Jesus did not appear to have the usual human interest in the identification of holy places. While he respected and frequently visited the holy temple of his people, he seemed to find greater spiritual renewal in the deserts and mountains, where he went to pray in private more often than he did in Jerusalem. As precious as the hills were to him, however, he discouraged attaching any religious significance to particular mountains. On the contrary, he predicted a time when his followers would not be tied in their worship to specific hilltops and temples but would learn to worship God in spirit and in truth:

> Woman, believe me, the hour is coming when neither on this mountain nor in Jerusalem will you worship the Father. . . . But the hour is coming, and now is, when the true worshippers will worship the Father in spirit and in truth, for such the Father seeks to worship him. God is spirit, and those who worship him must worship in spirit and truth (John 4:21-24).

This they did and, as a consequence, Jerusalem was not as important to the early Christians as it was to the Jews and the Muslims. Christians believed that they had received a mandate to make the entire world a holy place and all of its people a holy race. The holiness or chosenness of a people was now based on faith in God, a relationship of obedience and servanthood, rather than on racial or related factors. Peter's identification and description of the new society was most precious to them, and they repeated these words with frequency especially when their persecutors sought to destroy them:

> But you are a chosen race, a royal priesthood, a holy nation, God's people, that you may declare the wonderful deeds of

him who called you out of darkness into his marvellous light.
Once you were no people but now you are God's people . . .
(1 Pet. 1:9).

Theology was one reason for the early detachment from holy
places; the other was the political and military realities of the
latter part of the first century. In many ways, the Christians
of the Roman empire shared the fate of Jews, for they too
were persecuted and scattered abroad so that they had little
time to form binding attachments. Their holy places, if they
had any, were the new outposts where they preached the gospel, the catacombs where they met in secrecy, and the stakes
where they were burned.

Bishops, Rites, and Basilicas

As the Christian church spread rapidly from Jerusalem
throughout the Roman empire, communities of Christians
headed by bishops were established in various districts and
cities. The bishop of the most important city in a district assumed responsibility over his fellow bishops. This development gave rise to the offices and districts of archbishops,
metropolitans, and patriarchs, which later had its significance
for the Holy Land.

Initially, Jerusalem was superseded in importance and rank
by such centers as Antioch, Alexandria, and Rome, which represented the only patriarchates until 451, when the Council
of Chalcedon raised the bishoprics of Constantinople and Jerusalem to patriarchal rank. Constantinople became second in
importance to Rome, due to its having been elevated and renamed by Constantine as his civilian capital.

The patriarch of Rome, who was assumed to be in the suc-
cession of the Apostle Peter, remained the acknowledged head
of the whole church, which developed varied liturgies and rites
in its several patriarchal parts. At first Greek was the dominant language of all the rites, but Latin was used in some
sectors of the Roman empire as early as 200, and also came
into prominent usage in Palestine. The various liturgies themselves became more sophisticated as time went on. In addition,
as soon as social and political conditions made the Christian
communities more secure than before, came the drive to build
better church buildings. In cities like Rome and Jerusalem, it
was believed that church buildings were most appropriately

constructed on sites hallowed by the heroes and martyrs of the faith, or by relics left behind or by events remembered.

The Emperors and Religion

The best religious sites of all were in Palestine, and when the emperors themselves became interested in buildings, some rather magnificent structures arose. The first thus to build was the emperor Constantine. Together with his pious mother St. Helena, he constructed stately basilicas, not only in Rome but also in Palestine and elsewhere in the empire.

In his policy of aiding the construction of religious buildings, Constantine was not initiating a new trend but simply following in the footsteps of his predecessors, who also had expanded and controlled their empires by recognizing existing religions and patronizing the influential deities. Emperors long before Constantine had discovered that the best way to get the gods to bless the empire was for the emperors to boost the gods. Once Constantine had decided that Christianity was the best religion for his empire, tradition dictated that he express his religious appreciations in massive building programs. In 324-325, Emperor Constantine gave specific instructions to Metropolitan Eusebius of Caesarea and Bishop St. Macarius of Jerusalem to preserve the holy places for Christian purposes. The pagan structures erected by Emperor Hadrian over the rock of Calvary and the empty tomb were demolished, and soon the Martyrium church appeared on Calvary and the Anastasis church over the Tomb. Additional basilicas were built over the Grotto at Bethlehem and on the Mount of Olives, where the Christian Lord and his disciples had often gathered for retreat and prayer. The completion of these churches was usually marked by an impressive ceremony, which officially was meant to advance the cause of the church, but which also improved the image and strengthened the hold of the empire. The Basilica of the Holy Sepulchre, for instance, was dedicated in the solemn presence of over 300 bishops from all over the empire in 335.[2]

This new association of, identification with, and cooperation between, the empire and the church and the emperor and the bishops was of itself to have profound significance for the

[2] *Government of Palestine. A Survey of Palestine. Memoranda Prepared for Anglo-American Committee of Inquiry,* p. 179.

future relation of Christianity to Palestine. Until that time, Christianity had more or less refused to be identified with the interests of the Roman empire. As Church Historian Lars P. Qualben has written:

> In the Graeco-Roman world the State was conceived of as the Highest Good. The State included all the possible good that could come to man, even religion, which was subordinated by the State. Hence supreme loyalty to the State was the great Roman ideal. Service to the State was the purpose of life. But the Christians were citizens of a Kingdom that was not of this world. They recognized an authority that was higher than the State, and if the law of the Empire came in conflict with the law of God, they would obey God rather than man. It was this supreme loyalty to a law outside the Roman law that irritated and worried the Roman authorities more than all the other accusations against Christianity combined. . . .[3]

As late as Emperor Diocletian (284-305) there were attempts to annihilate Christianity because of its refusal to bow down to the state. But when the great persecution of 304 and after, which offered the Christians either apostasy or death, failed, the emperors reconsidered their position. In 312 Constantine made the Christian cross his military insignia, and a year later he ended the persecution.

The Edict of Milan in 313 recognized Christianity as a lawful religion; and when Constantine became the sole ruler of the empire in 325, he began openly to favor and protect the church. Weary of many decades of persecution, the church soon welcomed his embrace and saw Constantine's conversion as a real victory over paganism.

The rise of Christianity to the status of state religion, however, had some by-products that changed Christianity's thinking on a number of points. Whereas God and his kingdom had previously reigned supreme above the empire, they were now more and more identified with — and often subordinated to — the empire. The process that became known as the Constantinization of the church allowed the church in subsequent history to ally itself so closely with the various empires and nations that it lost its earlier prophetic stance. More and more it tended to represent the claims of the national kingdoms, as

---

[3] *A History of the Christian Church,* p. 58.

more and more it endorsed the sword and the military crusade against the national enemies, a policy that continued centuries later through World War II in the twentieth century.

There were other important consequences. When Christianity became official in the Roman empire, the Persian archenemy of Rome closed its doors to the Christian gospel, and later the Muslim world became intolerant of Christianity to the extent that it represented the Byzantine empire in the Middle East. Similarly, the Communists suppressed Christianity because it had been the religion by which the Tsars had maintained their power.

In the light of the early persecutions, however, we can understand why the Christians in the fourth century enjoyed their newly won status, and the long-term implications of the change could not easily be foreseen at the time. In any event, joint pilgrimages of governors and bishops seemed infinitely better than persecutions.

The pilgrimages increased, especially as Constantine's immediate successors continued the building program he began. Before the end of the fourth century, the Church of the Ascension had been completed on the Mount of Olives as well as the Church of the Agony in Gethsemane, and a Spanish Abbess by name of Aetheria had written her famous "Pilgrimage to the Holy Places." This earliest antecedent of modern tourism brochures attached great importance to the holy places and the religious services conducted there. At the same time, according to Aetheria, various languages and rites (Greek, Syriac, Latin) were already being used to accommodate all Christians, though the church was as yet not divided.

The new basilicas in Palestine brought more pilgrims, and the pilgrims, it seems, brought more basilicas. The fifth century saw the construction of the Basilica of St. Stephen, the Church of St. Peter in Gallicantu (the site of Caiaphas' palace), and the Church of the Tomb of the Virgin at Gethsemane, among others. By the sixth century, Jerusalem had become, to quote one traveling father, "a treasure house of churches, monasteries, hostels, and hospitals."

Invasion and Insecurity

Where there are treasures there usually is insecurity, and so it was with the Byzantine investment in Palestine. The earli-

est threats from the Persian empire had been warded off in
the middle of the sixth century, but the Persians could not be
held back forever. Damascus fell in 613 and Jerusalem a year
later. As a result of that conquest, a considerable number of
churches were burned, including the Basilica of the Holy Sepulchre. Over 30,000 Christians were massacred and others were
sent into captivity. After fourteen years of great sadness for
Christianity, Byzantium was able once more to control Jerusalem, and the rebuilding of churches was immediately promoted.

Byzantium's imperial strength had, however, waned. When
the armies of Islam moved in from the south, Constantinople
could not come to the aid of Jerusalem, so the patriarch quickly made an agreement with the Muslim Caliph to guarantee
the Christians their security and their churches. When the
Caliph entered Jerusalem in 638, he was accompanied by Patriarch Sophronius. The church leader's cooperation with the
conquest had won him the concessions necessary for the Christian communities to live in relative peace, especially under
the Umayyad caliphs. And such a rapprochement was not too
difficult in view of Islam's theology, which tolerated Christians
as well as Jews.

There came a time, however, when Muslim tolerance and
good will towards the Christians diminished and the Christian
church felt itself severely threatened. Early in the eighth century, therefore, some Palestinian church leaders turned to the
Christian west for help, the Christian east having been at least
temporarily incapacitated by the political problems of Constantinople. Since the first King of France and his famous
son Charlemagne (742-814) had established diplomatic relations with some Muslim caliphs, France became the most
accessible and ready protector of Christian interests in Palestine. These agreements brought relative quiet for about a century, but renewed Byzantine offensives and victories near the
end of the tenth century embittered the Muslims, who burned
not only the Church of the Resurrection but also the patriarch
himself because of his relations and cooperation with the Byzantine emperor. The Christians, too, were harassed until an
agreement between the emperor and the caliph in 1027 once
more brought tranquility to the believers in the Holy Land.
The Byzantines had temporarily replaced western rulers as
protectors in Palestine and again large amounts of money were
spent to restore and build churches.

Massive Pilgrimages and Crusades

Pilgrimages, which were now organized on a massive scale, brought seven hundred Normans under the protection of the Duke to Palestine in 1027 alone, and no less than twelve thousand participated in a pilgrimage under the leadership of the Bishop of Romburg in 1065. It was a miniature invasion, inasmuch as it was a military expedition, which more than once fought for its life and which anticipated the crusades of the years immediately following.

The Byzantine protectorate, however, was effective only as long as the Byzantine empire was strong. In 1054, some 250 years of strained relations between the patriarchs in Rome and Constantinople came to a head. The patriarch of Rome — the pope — excommunicated the patriarch of Constantinople who, supported by the three other eastern patriarchs (in Alexandria, Antioch, and Jerusalem), now became the head of the Eastern Orthodox Church. Among the inevitable consequences was a continuing dispute between Orthodox and Catholic factions over the holy places in Palestine. (This quarrel has not come to an end to this very day, making it necessary for a Muslim family to hold the keys to the Church of the Holy Sepulchre.)

The two factions came together again a decade later, when the Seljuk Turks threatened the boundaries of the Byzantine empire and captured Jerusalem in 1070. By 1092 they had seized the whole of Asia Minor and pressed to regions beyond. With both Byzantium and the holy places threatened, the emperor appealed to the pope for help, suggesting the re-union of the church. Armed with the double cause of saving Palestine and reuniting the church, Pope Urban II in 1095 urged an assemblage of European clergy and barons to take up arms for the deliverance of the holy sepulchre. As a reward, he offered the remission of past sins to all participants, and they in turn replied with enthusiasm "God wills it." The papal appeal went as follows:

> These pagans have made a vigorous onslaught on the Christian empire; they have pillaged and laid waste the whole land with unheard of cruelties up to the very gates of Constantinople. They have occupied these countries with tyrannical violence and massacred thousands and thousands of Christians like beasts. If, therefore, we have any love for God, if we are truly Christian people, the unhappy fate of this great empire and the deaths of so many Christians must be

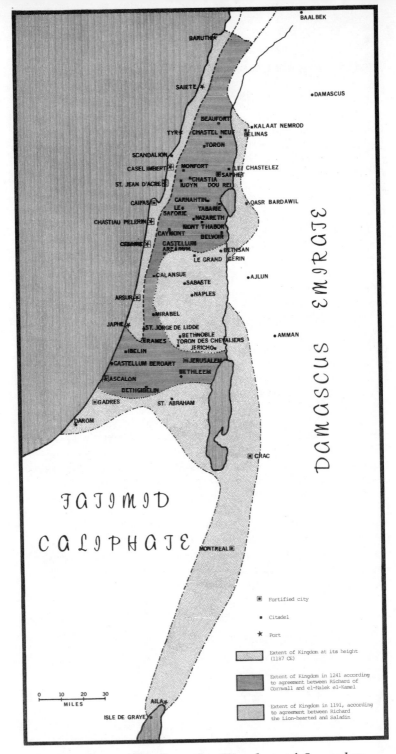

Map 8 — *The Crusader Kingdom of Jerusalem*

for us all a great anxiety. Our Lord's own example, who
redeemed us, and the duty of Christian charity, lead us not
only to lament these misfortunes, but also, if it be necessary,
to give ourselves in sacrifice for our brethren.[4]

Thus began the first of a series of three major and six minor
crusades, which did not come to an end until two centuries
later. The first crusading army, led by Godfrey of Bouillon,
captured Jerusalem on July 15, 1099 and established the Latin
Kingdom of Jerusalem, one of four such crusade states. Godfrey became the leader of the Jerusalem kingdom but he refused the title of King (*see Map 8*).

Bouillon's brother, who succeeded him, accepted the crown
and became Baldwin I of the Latin Kingdom. The fact that
the crowning took place on Christmas Day, 1100, in the Basilica of the Nativity at Bethlehem added to its sanctity, thus
helping to generate the religious energy needed for subsequent
crusades.

The Greek-oriented Christians did not very much appre-
ciate the Latin dominance which had now come to the Holy
Land — even the Jerusalem patriarch was now of the Latin
rite — and not a few fought with their Muslim neighbors
against the western crusaders.

If this eastern religious alliance appeared strange to the
western crusaders, the western coalition appeared equally
incongruous from the Christian point of view, if not more
so. Merchants of all sorts, released criminals, and a host of
adventurers made up the crusading groups, frequently numbering in the thousands. All were moving under the symbol of
the Christian cross, and, consequently, the crusades were called
the holy wars of the Middle Ages. As so often in history, so
also this holy war represented a strange mixture of religious,
political, and commercial motivations:

> The crusader period was not only one of warfare but also
> of intensive trade and cultural interchange, between western
> Europe and Islam, and "Frankish" knights who volunteered
> from all over western Christendom were invariably followed
> by traders from Venice, Pisa, Geneva, and Florence. These
> traders financed the crusades.[5]

In the Holy Land itself, the crusaders engaged in massive

---

[4] Quoted in Hughes, *op. cit.*, p. 252.
[5] Zoe Oldenbourg, *The Crusades,* p. 761.

construction and restoration programs. To the churches, hospitals, and hostels already there, they added monasteries and castles, of which some ruins can be seen to this day. The Basilica of the Holy Sepulchre was rebuilt to include both Anastasis and Martyrium. Dedicated in 1149 on the fiftieth anniversary of the capture of Jerusalem, the Basilica still stands, having been renewed in 1810. The Muslim Dome of the Rock was used as a Christian church as was the neighboring Mosque of Al-Aksa. The latter also served for a time as a palace for the king.

The building programs to boost Christianity were only one side of the story. On the other side was one of the darkest chapters of barbarity in human history. The victory of capturing the holy city of Jerusalem had been celebrated by wholesale and indiscriminate massacre of the Muslim population. Even the women and children were not spared, not even when they took refuge in the Haran and its mosques, which were desecrated and their treasures plundered. The anguish felt by the Muslims is illustrated by the following lines from a contemporary poet:

> Our blood we have mixed with over-
>   flow of tears
> When our line of defense was no more.
> A man's worst weapon is tears to shed
> When war is waged with cutting swords.
> Oh ye sons of Islam, behold
> Onslaughts on all sides!
> How can you close your eyes
> To a calamity that awakes the sound
>   asleep?
>
> How long will Arab heroes endure
>   such injury,
> And submit to disgrace from the
>   barbarian?[6]

The Loss of the Latin Kingdom

The Latin kingdom was not to endure forever. In 1187, before a century had passed, Caliph Saladin of Egypt and Syria took Jerusalem from the Christians. For him and his followers the campaign was as much a holy war as the crusades

---

[6] A. L. Tibawi, "Jerusalem: Its Place in Arab History," *The Arab World,* XIV:10-11, p. 12.

were for the Christians. When his victory was complete, all Christians had to pay a ransom to save their lives, but in spite of the payments many non-Palestinian Christians were not allowed to stay in the country. The mosques were restored to Muslim use, as were some Christian churches, but the Basilica of the Holy Sepulchre, soon to become a center of pilgrimage and an important revenue source, was spared.

In western Europe Saladin's conquests led to the dispatch of additional crusading forces, but Jerusalem could not immediately be recaptured. Pilgrimages to Jerusalem could be resumed freely under a truce agreed to in 1192. This agreement led to other concessions, including the reestablishment in Jerusalem of a western protectorate. Latin control ended suddenly once again in 1244, however, when a Tartar tribe from Central Asiatic Russia sacked Jerusalem. Soon thereafter the city fell into the hands of Egypt, which then controlled both Palestine and Syria until the coming of the Ottoman Turks in 1517.

The second and final loss of Jerusalem to the western crusaders did not, however, mean the end of their efforts. They managed to retain a foothold in the coastal towns of Palestine longer than anywhere else, but since their controls had been slipping and their energies had been dissipating for some time, they could not hold them beyond 1291. One cause for the weakening of the crusaders beginning early in the thirteenth century was the continuing church quarrel between east and west, which caused the crusader army to forget Jerusalem temporarily, and to concentrate on humiliating Constantinople instead.

While the crusaders lost their real power and their territory, they did leave behind some cultural evidence of having been in Palestine. The Latin rite remained strong until 1517, and certain religious orders like the Franciscans gained permanent bases in the country with their parishes, schools, convents, orphanages, and workhouses.

These "Franks," as they were called in the documents of the country, remained for many centuries the only representatives of western Christianity in Palestine. They were confirmed in their role as guardians "of the holy places on behalf of the whole of Catholic Christendom" by Pope Clement VI in 1342.

For a while thereafter it seemed that the Latin Western

and Greek Orthodox interests would be reunited, but the 1439 Council of Florence decree concerning the reunion of the See of Rome with the Orthodox East was effective only a short while. The reunion with Constantinople ended with the fall of that city to the Muslims in 1453, and Antioch, Alexandria, and Jerusalem likewise defected once more from Rome.

Under the Ottomans

From 1517, when the Ottoman Turks took control of Palestine, Orthodox churches were treated with greater favor than were the Latin ones. There was some Ottoman vacillation in granting favors, depending on diplomatic pressures and financial considerations, but two and a half centuries later the Orthodox had definitely superseded the Latins in Palestine.

After 1774 and the Russo-Turkish Treaty of Kuchuk Kainarji, the interests of the Orthodox in Palestine were championed by the Czar of Russia. For some time he and his predecessors had been waging war against the Ottoman Turks on the pretext of protecting the Eastern Orthodox everywhere and most of all in Palestine. The 1774 treaty established Russia's position officially. Thereafter funds for the building and restoration of churches flowed also from that part of the world, although pilgrimages had been made by Russian officials since the time of the crusades.

The extended influence and improved Russian position in the Middle East alarmed such western powers as France and Britain, who themselves were not always on friendly terms. For a while France had the greater international initiative, because the French ambassador to Turkey had established himself as the protector of Latin church interests in Palestine and the guarantor of Latin church cooperation with the Ottomans. The traditional Latin-Orthodox disputes over the holy places were intensified by French-Russian imperial rivalry, and the religious quarrel became one of the causes that led to the Crimean War.

Before that time the Protestant Christians of western Europe had likewise developed a very specific interest in Palestine, and their cause was championed by such political powers as Prussia and Britain. Indeed, Britain's national involvement in the Palestine question beginning in the nineteenth century became so interwoven with Protestant claims that the latter can best be treated in a later chapter. Suffice it to say here that the British (later the American) government and the Protestant churches served each other's interests in the nineteenth and twentieth centuries in the same way that the Catholics had found a convenient partnership with western European nations (particularly France) prior to that. The marriage between the Orthodox Church and eastern powers (Byzantium and Russia) was a similar arrangement.

In each instance, religious institutions were advanced under the protection of the national powers, while these powers, in turn, enjoyed the legitimization or sanctification that the religious cloak alone could give to their imperial ambitions. It is more than coincidence that Anglo-Saxon Protestants discovered Islam and the Ottoman Turks as the anti-Christ (as formerly the crusading Catholics had done) precisely at the time when Britain needed the Middle East as a shorter route to India and as a block to Russian expansion into areas of great interest to Britain.

Palestine and the Jews

Nor is it just coincidence that Britain and her Protestants were discovering "that Palestine belonged to the Jews," precisely at the time when their archenemy Napoleon of France was promising Palestine to the Jews. Arriving in Egypt and Jerusalem in 1799, he addressed himself to the Chief Rabbi of Jerusalem on April 20 with the following words:

> Israelites, unique nation, whom, in thousands of years, lust of conquest and tyranny have been able to deprive only of ancestral lands, but not of name and national existence. . . .
>
> The young army with which Providence has sent me hither, led by justice and accompanied by victory, has made Jerusalem my headquarters. . . .
>
> Rightful heirs of Palestine! The great nation which does not trade in men and countries as did those which sold your ancestors unto all peoples (Joel IV, 6) herewith calls on you not indeed to conquer your patrimony; nay, only to take over that which has been conquered and, with that nation's warranty and support, to remain master of it against all comers. . . .
>
> Hasten! Now is the moment, which may not return for thousands of years, to claim the restoration of civic rights among

the population of the universe which has been shamefully
withheld from you for thousands of years, your political existence as a natural right to worship Jehovah in accordance
with your faith, publicly and most probably for ever (Joel
IV, 20).[7]

The Rábbi of Jerusalem hailed Bonaparte as "the great and
highly enlightened Commander-in-Chief of the French armies
in Africa and Asia," and as "the man after God's own heart,"
and advised his brethren that the "glorious prophecies" were
being fulfilled by the victorious army of the great (French)
nation.[8]

The Rabbi's final salute and challenge — "Here the sword
of the Lord and of Bonaparte!" — was too much for Britain.
Like other western nations who had treated the Jews badly,
she was anxious to purge a guilty conscience. But more than
that, Britain like France needed the national and international
cooperation of the Jews in her imperial designs.

The notion that the prophecies should be fulfilled by Catholic armies was also too much for the Protestants. Thus it
happened that Britain's Christian community in the nineteenth
century developed an extraordinary interest in Palestine. This
involvement, with its several facets, could not reinforce British interests more handily. Islam, symbolized by the Ottoman
Turks, became the latest anti-Christ. The Jews, whose support
the British needed, were identified as the rightful heirs of
Palestine. But the British belonged there too, because, after all,
the world-wide mission of the church could not exclude Palestine. It was inconceivable that the Protestants should leave
Palestine alone to the Orthodox and Catholic Christians.

Prophecies and Predictions

The idea of the return of the Jews, of course, was not entirely new. There had been Jewish, Protestant, and British
expressions of it before Napoleon came to Cairo. It was new,
however, in the sense that neither the early church fathers nor
the leaders of the Protestant Reformation had been much concerned, if at all, with this dimension of the prophetic word.
While the early church knew several conflicting schools of

---

[7] *Three Historical Memoranda: Submitted to the United Nations Special Committee on Palestine,* p. 104.

[8] Royal Institute of International Affairs, *The Middle East: A Political
and Economic Survey,* p. 590.

thought on "the premillennial advent and personal reign of Christ," the territorial restoration of the Jews did not enter into the controversy, since none of the parties seemed to believe in it. Nor did the Reformers, so far as is known, hold to a literal restoration of the Jews to the land of Palestine.[9]

The French Revolution and the Napoleonic wars, however, had the effect of stimulating considerable interest in predictions concerning the future. The upheavals accompanying the revolution appeared to be the fulfillment of certain apocalyptic predictions, and some saw the mystical 1260 days referred to in the Old Testament Book of Daniel now coming to a close. In any event, the decisive conflict between the Kingdom of Christ and the anti-Christ appeared to be at hand. Some Christian teachers associated all of these events with the physical restoration of the Jews; others saw only the time of their general conversion approaching; still others believed that conversion would either precede or follow the return but that the return was as certain as the predicted conversion.

As a result of these speculations and projections, several works on "the restoration of Israel and the overthrow of the anti-Christ" appeared in Britain within a decade after Napoleon's dramatic entry into the Middle East. One of the most widely read publications appearing in both Britain and the United States in 1809 was George Stanley Faber's

A GENERAL AND CONNECTED
VIEW
of
THE PROPHECIES,
Relative To
The Conversion, Restoration, Union, and Future Glory
of the Houses of
JUDAH AND ISRAEL,
The Progress, and Final Overthrow,
of
THE ANTI-CHRISTIAN CONFEDERACY
In the Land of Palestine;
And the Ultimate General Diffusion of
CHRISTIANITY.

The common theme of the prophecy books fitted all of

---

[9] David Brown, *The Restoration of the Jews: The History, Principles, and Bearings of the Question,* p. 237.

the enemies of Protestantism and Britain into the prophetic scheme extracted from the Book of Daniel, much as the popes had done nearly a millennium before. France, Russia, the Ottoman Turks, and the Latin empire were now identified with the anti-Christ, whose downfall would be accompanied by the restoration of the Jews; and Britain was seen as Daniel's "great prince which standeth for the children of thy people" in the "time of trouble" (Dan. 12:1).

This restoration, however, was not seen in a narrow sense giving advantages only to the Jews. As it was interpreted, it meant giving both Protestants and British the long-coveted foothold in the Holy Land. Faber explained the future of the nations thus:

> At the period when these matters are transacting, the Ottoman empire will have been overthrown, and the great confederacy of anti-Christ will have been completed. It will consist of the Roman beast . . . and the subordinate vassal kings of the Latin empire. To these, Daniel adds a state . . . (with a king) that magnified himself above every God . . . the state in question I have shown elsewhere to be the anti-Christian France . . . this great northern power I have already conjectured to be Russia. . . .[10]

Post World War I American Christians may be surprised that Russia was identified as the northern power long before atheistic and Communistic rulers replaced the czars, but the national enemy of Britain, even if he was a Christian czar, was the anti-Christ long before the Communist revolution.

Faber visualized that the "times of the Gentiles" would run out in about 1866 (although one of his contemporaries had decided that the date was 1836) and that it would only be the faithful maritime power (meaning Britain) which, together with converted Jews, would stand up to the great anti-Christian confederacy, at the heart of which stood the Muslim "land of Satan."

These theological views applied to the politics of the time did not become, at least not officially, the stated views of the church. However, like the leaven that leavens the whole lump, the idea that "Palestine belongs to the Jews" gradually but surely became a basic religious and political assumption of British society. As Leonard Stein has written, "It is possible

---

[10] *Op. cit.*, pp. 1-4.

to compile a fairly lengthy list of English writers who between 1850 and 1880 pleaded the cause of the restoration of the Jews to Palestine."[11]

Thus, religious thought and writing in Britain was influenced by the national political ambitions of the day. And these aspirations in turn, in the balance of the century and into the twentieth, were affected by the religious-political thought, as Protestant missions and prophecy, British imperialism, and finally organized Zionism all reinforced each other in their respective goals.

---

[11] *The Balfour Declaration,* pp. 12-15.

6. The Claims of Zionism

The Jews have always hoped — it was an article of faith for religious and even non-religious Jews — that a day might come when they would be allowed to return to the land of their ancestors. They have never given up this claim.[1]
— Chaim Weizmann[1]

The idea that the Jews of Europe should and would find a new home in Palestine came to the fore, as already indicated, in the nineteenth century, and the vision was at first championed as much by non-Jews as by Jews. By the end of the century, however, the Jews themselves were the strongest advocates of the "return" to Zion. These zealous promoters of Jewish resettlement were called Zionists, and the movement itself became known as Zionism.

While the end of the nineteenth century saw the establishment of the Zionist movement, it must be remembered that the idea of a return to Palestine by the descendants of Abraham was not really a new one. After Abraham, the idea to go to Canaan was reborn nearly as often as there was a voluntary or involuntary departure from that country. Famine drove Abraham out to Egypt but he had to return. His grandson Jacob left for Mesopotamia to get himself a wife, but he too went back. The entire tribe was driven westward to Egypt in search of food, but under Moses and after 400 years of enslavement, the Israelites returned. The same was true of the exiles to the east some 600 years later. In due course, some of them too came back.

---

[1] Quoted in *Great Britain and Palestine 1915-1945,* pp. 17-18.

The Songs of Zion

Inasmuch as history repeated itself once more in a later expulsion of the Jews, so the longing to return repeated itself. Indeed, all the prayers, promises, poetry, and folklore arising from earlier exiles very appropriately spoke the language of the later exiles. Thus, the songs of the Jews deported to Babylonia remained on the lips of generation after generation of European Jews much in the same way that German emigrants kept singing about the *Heimatland* and Russian emigrants never stopped singing about the Volga River and its boatmen.

The Babylonian song in its origin was a Jewish response to their tormentors who taunted them to "sing the songs of Zion." The exiles took this teasing seriously and proceeded to express themselves in the sad songs of a homeless people. Their favorite one was the following one about remembering Jerusalem:

> If I forget you, O Jerusalem,
> let my right hand wither!
> Let my tongue cleave
> to the roof of my mouth,
> if I do not remember you,
> if I do not set Jerusalem
> above my highest joy! (Ps. 137:5-6).

As the song was sung by succeeding generations, it strengthened the memory of Jerusalem in the hearts of those who had been expelled and of their descendants. The Jews may have been far away from Jerusalem in body, but Zion continued as an experience in their hearts and minds, most of all when it was difficult to find a friendly environment in Europe. Persecution always intensified their longing for a homeland.

Dispersions and Conversions

The Jews had originally migrated to Europe voluntarily and involuntarily in several waves, beginning in the days of the Greek empire centuries before Christ. They arrived at the Mediterranean peninsulas of Greece, Italy, and Spain, some as traders and some of them as slaves and prisoners. In the early days of the Roman empire in Palestine (beginning 63 BC) an estimated three million Jews could be found from Asia Minor to Spain. They constituted about seven percent of the empire's total population. Most of the estimated one million Jews inhabiting Palestine proper later in the first century of the Christian era also went into this diaspora.[2] From southern Europe they eventually spread inland.

As Greek colonies were established in southern Russia, Jews moved along and founded their trading outposts on the Black Sea as well as farther inland. Whole tribes, such as the Khazars, were converted to the Jewish faith through these Jewish outposts, and these conversions account in part for the large Jewish population later found in Russia.

The most religiously active Jewish communities, however, appeared in Italy, particularly in Rome, from where the missionaries of Judaism went out to central Europe. They were accompanied and also followed by other Jewish migrants, most of whom specialized in trade and commerce and who assisted in establishing permanent settlements. So effective was Judaism in converting the Gentiles that the Roman writer Seneca complained: "The customs of this criminal people are gaining so much ground that they find followers in all countries, and thus the defeated have imposed their law upon the victors."[3]

In some ways, it might be said that the Jews prepared the way for Christianity not only in the Middle East but also in Europe; for wherever the Christian missionary Paul went, he began his work in established Jewish settlements and their synagogues. His desire to go to Spain appears to have been linked to firmly established and well-known Jewish communities there. Eventually, the Christian evangelists overtook the Jewish missionaries and the Jews were thus confronted not only by rivalry from the Romans but also with competition from the Christians, though the latter was not serious as long as the Christians themselves were despised.

Elevation and Segregation

In the Mediterranean basin and the regions beyond, the Jews attained key positions in the economy of the Roman empire. After operating as trading intermediaries, they became great merchants and shipowners, while also excelling as farmers, lawyers, physicians, manufacturers, and goldsmiths.

In some places, the Jews were also found in high govern-

---

[2] Leon Poliakov, *The History of Anti-Semitism,* p. 5.
[3] Quoted in Kahler, *The Jews Among the Nations,* p. 35.

mental positions, but generally they were held back inasmuch as they never reconciled themselves to Roman rule. They remained, generally speaking, a people apart, independent in spirit, persistent in the observance of their laws and customs, strictly observing the Sabbath, and stubborn in their insistence that Palestine belonged to them and not to the Romans.

Generally speaking, however, the pagan emperors treated the Jews better than they did Christians, at least in the first three centuries. The situation was reversed in 325 when Constantine gave official approval and legal status to the Christian religion and to the doctrine of the deity of Christ. From that time on Judaism and Jews were subordinated. Constantine ordered that the wealthier members be drafted into unwanted jobs in the civil service, and Christian leaders like Augustine assigned to the Jews the full guilt of Christ's crucifixion.

Such views and actions by the great Christian emperors and bishops, as well as the financial genius and stubborn separateness of the Jewish community, were largely responsible for the strife between the two groups. This early animosity in turn laid the foundations for the persecution meted out to the Jews by the Christian natives of Europe in subsequent generations. In the words of Kahler, the Christian majority now passed on to the Jewish minority their own experience of an earlier day when they were few in number:

> In its early period, Christianity had undergone the same ordeal that was to be Judaism's throughout its history. The Christians were accused of having no god and hating men, of setting themselves apart from the non-Christian community, of being unpatriotic, indifferent toward the state, arrogantly intolerant of all the pleasures of life, and of mocking all that was sacred to millions of people.[4]

Rules restricting the activities and rights of Jews were promulgated by Christian councils and emperors, but divisions in Christendom and the pervasiveness of paganism at first prevented their effective implementation. The pagan tribes were not as hostile to the Jews, and some Christian communities, particularly the Arians (the followers of Arius, who questioned Christ's deity), were friendly.

Arian Christianity, however, was defeated by the Nicene Creed, first promulgated in 325 and revised in 381, which

---

[4] *Ibid.,* p. 39.

insisted on the essential divinity of Christ. Those who opposed the Nicene Creed to any degree were called Judaizers; and Judaizers, like the Jews, were enemies of Christ. Since Nicene Christianity eventually conquered Europe, the Jews were in that conquest destined to be either converted or suppressed.

Friendship and Animosity

This influence of Nicene Christianity did not mean, however, that the Jews were entirely disadvantaged, because kings, princes, landowners, and even church dignitaries liked them as financial agents, personal physicians, and even diplomatic negotiators. One such king was Charlemagne (742-814), who, while promoting Christianity, resisted restrictions on Jews as landowners and international tradesmen.

Such royal concessions to the Jews were frowned upon by Christians, however, whenever and wherever the competition between Jews and Christians was extended from the areas of doctrine and missions to land-owning and commerce. While the Christians eventually won out in the former area, the Jews excelled in the latter and unquestionably became the financial leaders in Europe. Each group remained jealous of the other's successes.

More difficult days lay ahead for the Jews in both the economic and religious spheres. With the rise of feudalism Christian barons dispossessed Jewish landowners, as few and as small as they were. This displacement turned the Jews more than before to bartering and banking, which brought them much ill repute as time went on. The successful rise of Islam, on the other hand, had the effect of arousing among Christians a religious hostility that often treated Judaism and Islam as a single target.

Thus it happened that the Jews and Muslims embraced each other in certain places and at certain times as the common victims of Christianity. When the Muslims invaded Spain in 711 the Jews welcomed them. As a consequence, the Jews under Muslim rule experienced in Spain in the eight centuries following the golden age of European Jewry. Henceforth, the European Jews knew that under Islam there was greater tolerance than among Christians, and not a few sons of Abraham found their way to peace and security in Arab countries in subsequent generations. In the favorable climate of these

Middle East regions, as in Spain, they rose to positions of diplomatic, academic, and commercial prominence.

The Curse of the Crusades

Christian persecution of the Jews in Europe became very real early in the second millennium. The Christian crusades meant attacks not only on the Muslims in the Middle East but also on the Jews in Europe. They were plundered and massacred by undisciplined mobs, who could not be restrained by horrified princes and humanitarian Christians like Bernard of Clairvaux. From that time on the Jews were harassed and blamed for every evil that befell Europe.

The unorganized Jew-baiting so characteristic of the tenth, eleventh, and twelfth centuries turned into a system of repression and banishment in the thirteenth. Pope Innocent III's internal crusade against Waldensians and other heretics included the Jews. Their holy places were desecrated, and the Talmud was publicly burned in Paris in 1242. Jewish apartness resulting from this religious persecution was further reinforced by official industrial restrictions. More than ever they were pushed into ghettos or forced to scatter to the far-flung regions of Europe, including the British Isles.

In England, Jews were tolerated as long as they were indispensable to economic mobilization. Once the balance of power was favorable to the lords and clerics, they sought in every way to limit the Jews and drain away their wealth. Massacres in 1189 were followed by expulsion in 1290. Not until after 1656, when the Puritans brought them back, were Jews found in England again in significant numbers. The stricken English conscience thus tried to redress some wrongs, but complete reconciliation was not achieved. Eventually, the English concluded that the Jews belonged more to Palestine than they did to England — a conclusion that made both groups much happier.

Jewish communities in eastern Europe too had relative peace until the crusades brought ravaging gangs into their territories. In Hungary where Jews, Christians, Muslims, and pagans had lived together in peace, the Hungarian king treated the crusading hordes as robbers. He had many of them killed, thereby earning Hungarians the title of "pagan" or "Jew" in western Europe.

Needless to say, the financial and administrative power position achieved by the Jews in the east was one of the reasons for the hostility from the European west. But there were also indigenous rivalries. One of the worst persecutions in the east came in the mid-seventeenth century in Poland, when Ukrainian Cossacks and peasants rose up against the oppressions of Polish nobles, most of them Jews, and virtually destroyed 90 percent of the Jews in 700 communities.

In Orthodox Russia, the struggle between Christian and Jew was similar to that in early Catholic Europe. The ideological reason for keeping the Jews at bay was the protection of the realm against Judaizing challenges to the doctrine concerning the divine Christ. The more practical, and perhaps the more real, reason again was the financial and administrative power that Jews seemed to achieve so quickly. The results of the clash were repeated pogroms against the Jews as late as the twentieth century.

Enlightenment and Emancipation

In western and central Europe, the Protestant Reformation brought only temporary relief. Luther at first censured the church for persecuting the Jews, but when he could not win them to his side he too turned his fury against those "stubborn people." Only the humanists, pioneers of the later enlightenment, came to the defense of the Jews. In Holland, the first great seat of the enlightenment, the Jews first experienced the benefits of free thought, and in Amsterdam they founded their largest shipping and banking firms. Enlightenment influence also led to the loosening of intolerable restrictions elsewhere in Europe. Christian scholars and writers, influenced by humanism, now joined in the struggle for Jewish emancipation. Equality of rights for Jews was proclaimed first in 1776 by the American Declaration of Independence, followed in 1790-1791 by the granting of full rights by the Constituent Assembly of the French Revolution. Emancipation was advanced in neighboring countries by the armies of the revolution, but some of the new freedoms thus won were repealed by the Congress of Vienna in 1815. The equality of the Jews was not finally recognized in most countries until well into the nineteenth century, as can be seen from Table 4.[5]

---

[5] *Ibid.*, p. 83.

TABLE 4
CHRONOLOGY OF JEWISH EMANCIPATION IN EUROPE

Date	Country
1796	Holland
1830	France
1849	Denmark
1858	England
1867	Austria-Hungary
1870	Italy
1871	Germany
1874	Switzerland
1876	Spain
1878	Balkan States
1917	Russia

Theories of equality were more easily preached than practiced, and prejudice continued strong, not least of all because the Jews remained a power factor. As new freedoms were gained, the Jews rushed to take advantage of the situation, and their zeal and genius led them onward and upward in many fields. Before long, they had entered and excelled in the professions much in the same way that they had monopolized banking and trade.

As the twentieth century dawned in Germany, the minority Jewish population had produced forty-five times more lawyers, eight times more writers and scholars, and six times more physicians per capita than had emerged among non-Jewish people. The result was a moving out of the ghettos, and following the nationalistic spirit of the times the Jews also participated in patriotic identification. "There were no prouder Germans than the German Jews; there were no more enthusiastic Frenchmen than the French Jews. This was true of the Jews of every nation."[6]

Nationalism and Zionism

Such proud identification with the nation-states of Europe may have been somewhat exaggerated, because another kind

---

[6] Solomon Grayzel, *A History of the Jews,* p. 571.

of nationalism was now maturing in the Jewish mind. This
nationalism was in conflict with the larger society much like
the former social separateness had been. It was a nationalism
that envisaged the Jews in their own homeland and in full
control of it. Thus, even while a brighter day was dawning for
European Jewry, the nationalistic stirrings were strengthening
the memories of Palestine that had been kept alive by the
darker days.

Perhaps the new day was appearing only faintly because
the new legal position of the Jews had by no means eliminated
anti-Semitism in the European heart, as the twentieth century
was to reveal only too clearly. But even before that, anti-Jewish
feelings erupted in both Germany and Russia, and it was in
these countries that the Jewish nationalism, known as Zionism,
found its earliest and most articulate expression.

The Zionists pointed to recent historical precedents for the
desired return. When Palestine had come under the control
of the Turks in 1517 the country had been opened to Jewish
immigration, and in 1563 Don Josef Massic led his Spanish
followers to found an agricultural colony on the shores of
Lake Tiberias. Other "messiahs" of the sixteenth and seven-
teenth century, notably David Reubini and Sabbatai Sebi,
advanced plans for the settlement of Jews in Palestine.

Mordecai Manuel Noah, on the other hand, was ready to
found the Jewish State of Ararat on Grand Island in the
Niagara River. When that plan failed, he switched his efforts
to Palestine. The coming of the nineteenth century, however,
gave new strength to these older minority ideas, not only because more Jews accepted them, but because there were more
Jews to accept them. Jewish population in the world enjoyed
a fourfold increase in the nineteenth century, from 2,500,000 to
over ten million (*see Table 5*).[7]

At the same time, Christian millenarians were suggesting
the movement of the Jews to the Holy Land as a step toward
the realization of a world-wide messianic dream. Since such
proposals were being advanced at the very time that European
powers, particularly Britain and France, were scrambling to
pick up the pieces of the crumbling Turkish empire, it seemed
to be a propitious time for the cause of Zionism.

---

[7] *Encyclopedia Americana,* Vol. XVI, p. 128.

TABLE 5
WORLD JEWISH POPULATION FROM 1800 TO 1949

Year	Population
1800	2,500,000
1825	3,280,000
1850	4,750,000
1880	7,650,000
1900	10,600,000
1914	14,000,000
1939	16,725,000
1946	10,750,000
1949	11,000,000

Early Ideas and Writings

The first problem to be overcome by the Zionists was the prevailing Jewish notion that the return would be associated with the coming of the Messiah and hence be supernatural in nature. It was the Polish Rabbi Hirsch Kalischer who tried to convince the Jews with biblical and talmudic citations that the redemption of Israel was to be accomplished in a natural way. The Messiah, he said, would come only after a number of Jews had already gone to Palestine. While trying to convince the masses, he also sought to persuade such wealthy Jews as Asher Meyer Rothschild of Frankfort to offer financial and organizational assistance. Neither the masses nor the millionaires were yet ready to respond, but Kalischer nonetheless succeeded in establishing an agricultural school called Mikveh Israel ("ingathering of Israel") near Jaffa in 1870.

The theory of Zionism was more significantly advanced by the German Socialist, Moses Hess, who in 1862 published a small book entitled, *Rome and Jerusalem: The Latest National Question*. Hess objected to the effort of reform Jewish leaders to achieve national and social integration as Germans while following the Mosaic religious tradition. These Jews were eliminating references to a return to Zion in the prayer books, and Hess felt that this was a big mistake. In his opinion Jews could make their contribution to the world only through a renascence of their national consciousness, and such regeneration could be achieved fully only in the ancient homeland:

The acquisition of common ancestral soil, the organization of

the work on a legal basis, the founding of Jewish societies of
agriculture, industry, and commerce on the Mosaic, i.e. social
principles, these are the foundations on which Jewry will rise
again and in its rise will kindle the glowing fire of the old
Jewish patriotism and light the way to a new life for the
Jewry of the entire world.[8]

After Moses Hess, the most important figure in the development of the Zionist movement was the Russian physician, Leo
Pinsker, of Odessa. Pinsker at first felt that the emancipation
for the Jews would come with assimilation, but pogroms and
restrictive settlement measures in 1881 and 1882 led him to
review his position, and he concluded that deliverance for the
Jews could only come if they reestablished themselves as a
nation in a territory of their own.

Reestablishment meant the acquisition of the normal attributes of a nation — a common language, common customs,
and a common land. Pinsker recognized that this would take
time, but suggested that a first step should be taken by calling
a congress of Jewish notables. His pamphlet, *Auto-Emanci-
pation: An Admonition to His Brethren by a Russian Jew,*
was well received by Jewish intellectuals in his country, and
soon he found himself heading up the Lovers of Zion movement.

At first favorable to the idea of a homeland for Jews in
America, Pinsker soon accepted the view that *Eretz* (land of)
Israel was the only territory where the Jews could reestablish
themselves as a nation. To help raise funds for the immigration to Palestine, he founded the Odessa Committee (the Society for the Support of Jewish Agriculture in Syria and Palestine), which anticipated the founding of, and later merged
with, the World Zionist Organization. Actual colonization in
Palestine, sponsored by this movement, began in 1882 by
Bilu (a word formed from the first Hebrew letters of Isaiah
2:5 — "House of Jacob, come, let us go"), a society of 500
young people dedicated to the idea of pioneering in Palestine.
It was their initial effort that inspired Baron Edmond de Rothschild of the French section of the famous banking family to
support Palestinian colonization.

---

[8] Esco Foundation for Palestine, Inc., *Palestine: A Study of Jewish,
Arab and British Policies,* p. 12.

Herzl and the Big Push

With all these efforts, political Zionism was slowly but surely establishing itself in both theory and practice in a limited way, thus preparing the way for others to give it a major push. The leader to give the big promotion at the turn of the century was Theodore Herzl, a Viennese writer and journalist, who published his *Der Judenstaat* (The Jewish State) in 1896. This book became the foundation-stone of world Zionism.

Herzl came from a well-to-do, conventional, liberal-reform type Jewish family in which German classical literature was almost as much appreciated as the Jewish tradition. Liberal Jews called for the assimilation of Jews to the larger society as a way of escaping the ghetto, and this also became Herzl's earliest proposal for solving the problem of the Jewish middle class.

Herzl advocated mixing the oriental and western races in the context of a common state religion or nationalism, but he changed his mind after he was faced by the realities of anti-Semitism. This confrontation came in two ways. He read Eugene Duehring's 1881 book, *The Jewish Problem as a Problem of Race, Morals, and Culture,* which presented the Jewish people as racially inferior. Then as a journalist in Paris he witnessed the trial of Alfred Dreyfus, a Jewish French patriot with a military career who had chosen the path of assimilation, apparently without success. The Dreyfus Affair revealed the depths of anti-Semitism. A loyal Jewish Frenchman was denounced by other Frenchmen as a lowly Jew. A Jesuit journal asked for the withdrawal of all civil rights from the Jews, saying that they were nothing but spies.

As he observed this anti-Semitic outburst occurring one hundred years after the Declaration of the Rights of Man, Herzl resolved that the only way out of the ghetto was to get out, physically and environmentally. His first new goal now was to persuade Jewish philanthropists to aid in resettlement. Meeting with considerable opposition he directed his energies to a more careful formulation of his ideas instead. *Der Judenstaat* was the result. In it, he gave up assimilation as an answer to the Jewish problem. Theoretically, it might be possible through intermarriage, and practically this would happen to some Jews, but it could and should never happen to the whole

Jewish people. So he advanced what to him was a "perfectly simple plan," the Zionist idea, as follows:

> Let the sovereignty be granted us over a portion of the globe large enough to satisfy the rightful requirements of a nation; the rest we shall manage ourselves.[9]

The Organizing of Zionism

Herzl's heart was not definitely set on Palestine, because some of his negotiations were with a Jewish philanthropist who was then resettling Jews to Argentina. He thought that the Society of Jews, an organization to be formed and an authority to be recognized as a "state-building power," should finally determine the location of the Jewish sovereignty. The Jewish Company, a second organization to be founded, would be the financial instrument for resettling the migrating Jews.

In his essay Herzl envisioned a mass emigration from Europe taking place over several generations. The exodus would be in accordance with a prearranged plan of building up the new land. The upbuilding itself would employ the latest instruments of science and technology, and the result would be a model also along social lines. He concluded his pamphlet with a challenge and a promise:

> Let the word be repeated here which was given at the beginning: the Jews who will it shall have their state. We shall at last live as free men on our own soil and die peacefully in our own homeland. The world will be liberated by our liberation, enriched with our wealth, made greater by our greatness. And that which we seek, therefore, for our own use will stream out mightily and beneficently upon mankind.[10]

Herzl's call was received both favorably and unfavorably among his own people. Some identified him as a crackpot, others as a modern Moses. Christians as well as Jews, leaders as well as the masses, hailed his suggestions. Chaplain Heckler, of the English embassy in Vienna, wrote a tract prophesying that Palestine would be restored to the Jews by about 1897-1898.

In 1897 Herzl did succeed in calling the First Zionist Congress in Basel, attended by 197 elected delegates from Europe, Palestine, and the United States. The representatives, who quick-

---

[9] Kahler, *op. cit.,* p. 34.
[10] Quoted in Bein, *Theodore Herzl: A Biography,* p. 170.

ly agreed that the homeland should be Palestine, adopted a four-point plan for colonization and development. Subsequently called the Basel Program for World Jewry, the plan read as follows:

> The aim of Zionism is to create for the Jewish people a home in Palestine secured by public law.
>
> The Congress contemplates the following means to the attainment of this end:
>
> 1. The promotion, on suitable lines, of the colonization of Palestine by Jewish agricultural and industrial workers.
>
> 2. The organization and binding together of the whole of Jewry by means of appropriate institutions, local and international, in accordance with the laws of each country.
>
> 3. The strengthening and fostering of Jewish national sentiment and consciousness.
>
> 4. Preparatory steps towards obtaining government consent, where necessary, to the attainment of the aim of Zionism.[11]

External and Internal Opposition

After Herzl was elected president of the new World Zionist Organization, he wrote in his diary that on that day he had "created the Jewish state." Much work, however, still needed to be done before his creation was actual. First of all, he needed recognition for the proposed state from the Turkish Sultan, and he also sought approval for his plans from European powers.

Herzl's appointment with Kaiser Wilhelm was achieved through his millennial friend, the Christian Zionist, Reverend Hecklin. Herzl was cautious, however, and suggested to the Kaiser only the establishment of a Land Development Company that would operate in Palestine and Syria under a German protectorate. The Kaiser was enthusiastic, motivated in part by the anti-Semitic view that wanted the removal of some "usurious" Jews from Germany.

Soon thereafter, the Kaiser cooled toward the proposal, when he realized that the Sultan as well as France, England, and Russia would look with disfavor upon such a German protectorate. He was in no mood to jeopardize other German interests affected by international power plays at the time.

---

[11] Esco Foundation, *op. cit.*, p. 41.

Herzl was disappointed; but he had believed all along that England would be a better natural ally for the Jews than Germany.

The Sultan likewise was not interested in Jewish colonization in Palestine, though he welcomed a few Jewish families in Turkey to help him with his finances. Herzl concluded that if the Jews could fund the public debt of Turkey — more than a million pounds — the Sultan would be more cooperative. But the Rothschilds and other Jewish bankers could not be interested, and the fund-raising efforts of the Jewish Colonial Trust, later succeeded by the Jewish National Fund, had not been too successful either.

Since little progress was achieved on Palestine settlement, Herzl presented to the Sixth Zionist Congress in 1903 a British proposal for a Jewish settlement in Uganda in east Africa. Herzl advocated settlement in Uganda only as temporary haven enroute to Palestine. Even so he won little encouragement. His suggestion that an investigating commission be sent there was approved only by a narrow margin and only on condition that no Zionist funds be expended for the purpose. The Congress heard the Commission's report two years later and rejected the Uganda idea overwhelmingly. Herzl was not present to experience this discouragement. He had died in the summer of 1904.

The opposition for territorial reasons was not the only obstacle that Herzl had experienced before his death. Even though enthusiastic federations of Zionists were established in every land, including England and the United States, prominent Jews did not really accept the Zionist idea. There was the influential Ahad Ha'am (pen name of Asher Ginzberg), who insisted that the revival of Jewish values was much more important than a strong economy, thriving race, or sovereign territory. A cultural identity, he said, was more important than a national homeland. Close to Ginzberg were those Reform and Orthodox Jews who felt that Jewish claims to universal religion would be compromised by the revival of a Jewish nationalism. One American rabbi insisted that his Zion was Washington. Some Orthodox Jews, on the other hand, objected to Zionism because, in their opinion, natural means should not be used to attain its goals.

Opposition to Zionism on the basis of nationalism was particularly strong among liberal European Jews who believed that assimilation was the answer. Others, like the influential historian, Simon Dubnow, did not believe that Jewish survival depended on either kind of nationalism. In his opinion, the Jews had demonstrated that the core of unity and existence was not territory or statehood but a simple communal organization that provided for and allowed the functioning of spiritual power.

Significant opposition to, as well as support for, Zionism came from the Jewish American community, which had increased its population dramatically from 250,000 in 1815 to three million by 1914. Over one million of these were immigrants who had found their promised land in America and who could see no reason for promoting another elsewhere. But Zionism did have its strong supporters, and not many years later American Jewry became an all-important factor in the establishment of the national homeland for the Jews in Palestine.

Limited Immigration and Colonization

Meanwhile, a limited amount of colonization was taking place in Palestine. Before 1900, seven new colonies of settlers were added to the 34,000 Jewish inhabitants in the land in 1882. These old settlements were concentrated mainly in Jerusalem, Hebron, Safed, and Tiberias. The new agricultural colonies were supported largely by the Rothschild administration.

More settlements were established in the twentieth century. Between 1901 and 1907 a number of colonies founded in the wheat country of Lower Galilee were also funded by Rothschild. The Zionist Organization itself began colonization in 1908 and by 1914 had helped to increase the agricultural settlements to forty with a population of 12,000. Hebrew was established as the language of Jewish school instruction in Palestine. Communal life manifested its earliest organization and labor groups were formed, anticipating the later establishment of a national state.

Such a state, however, was not really in sight until either the Turks or some of the leading European powers would lend support and sponsorship. That the hundreds of thousands of native Arabs, the very unwilling and restless subjects of the tottering Ottoman empire, should also have a say in the question was hardly considered. The Jews, like other Europeans, had no difficulty in assuming that the Arabs were of little consequence.

The European power most anxious to be consulted by the Zionists was England. Precisely at the time that the Zionists needed an imperial sponsor, the empire itself needed Jewish support for its own international schemes. Thus dreams and schemes flowed into each other as the Zionist ambition found itself in partnership with the British expansion.

7. The Claims of the British

While the direct responsibility for the calamity that over-
took the Palestinian Arabs was on the heads of the Zionist
Jews who seized a Lebensraum *for themselves...a heavy*
load of indirect, yet irrepudiable, responsibility was on the
heads of the people of the United Kingdom....
—Arnold Toynbee[1]

In spite of the enthusiastic and aggressive efforts of Zionist nationalism to establish a national homeland for the Jews, it is doubtful that its program would have progressed as it did if it would not have been for the help of British imperialism at the most opportune time. The British help in turn, it must not be forgotten, was supported by a Protestant millenarianism, which helped to make imperial expansion and Zionism a holy cause, in much the same way that Catholicism in an earlier day had strengthened Roman and French imperialism, and Orthodoxy had provided the ideological base for the empires of both Byzantium and Russia.

Serious British interest in Palestine began in 1798, when Napoleon entered Cairo with 15,000 troops and prepared to march across the Middle East bridge to Asia in order to threaten British power in India, while offering to return Asian and African Jews to Palestine. The British quickly entered into an alliance with the Turkish Sultan, and a year later forced the French troops to surrender at the border of Egypt and Palestine. The British victory did not yet mean easy access to Palestine — a consulate was not established until 1842 — but a European return to Palestine after centuries of absence now appeared quite certain.

---

[1] In *A Study of History* (Vol. VIII), quoted in *Tension and Peace in the Middle East,* p. 7.

The Religious Developments

The British victory over the French had significant national and international consequences. British prestige increased within the Ottoman empire, and on the British domestic scene internationalist (i.e., imperialist) interests — commercial, religious, political, and military — were definitely escalated. The religious developments are particularly important because the British overseas missionary interest went hand in hand with the expansion of the British empire.

In much the same way that certain later American Christians viewed troop movements to Japan and Vietnam as "a highway for the gospel" to Asia, so the British Christians could not help seeing the victory over Napoleon as another open door for their missionary enterprise. This time the gates were opening to the Middle East, where Islam the anti-Christ reigned and where Orthodox Christians under Russian protection didn't appear to be capable of fulfilling the Christian task. This moment of opportunity for Protestant Christians in Britain was a clear responsibility, and their leaders could not allow it to slip by.

Two missionary societies were formed in London in 1799 and 1804, respectively, and both were destined to play an important role in the injection into Palestine of both the British and the Protestants. They were the Church Missionary Society and the London Society for Promoting Christianity Amongst the Jews (which in abbreviated form became known as the London Jews Society). As the two major English-language religious and educational agencies in the Holy Land, they formed the cultural dimension of the general British thrust.

Sometimes the cultural-religious presence preceded and prepared the way for commercial, political, and territorial expansion; at other times the missions simply accompanied or even followed the general British involvement. In any event, the imperial leaders welcomed and even promoted the religious missions, not least of all because they provided concrete evidence of high moral purpose on the part of the British.

The activities of the missions led to the introduction of a chain of teaching, preaching, and relief stations. A school system covering Jerusalem and a large number of Arab towns and villages was established, as were churches, hospitals, clinics, and centers for distributing religious literature. A learned society for the exploration and elucidation of the background of the Bible came into being and with it the beginnings of western-sponsored archaeological excavation.

The approach to the peoples of the Middle East was not always circumspect. An American Committee, which followed the London Committee, and which was likewise interdenominational, looked upon its missionary assignment as including Jews, Muslims, and Christians almost equally. All of them needed the enlightenment which the Protestants could bring. No contact was sought with the legally constituted Christian ecclesiastical authorities in the Ottoman empire.

The missionary-minded Protestants were not yet in a mood to recognize, certainly not to learn from, the Christianity of either the Catholics or the Orthodox. Latin and Eastern Christians were believed to be superstitious and idolatrous, the clergy ignorant and hypocritical. Muslims, of course, needed Christian missions most of all:

> If the Protestant missionaries' approach to the eastern Christians was one of superiority, the approach to Islam was manifestly one of hostility. The Christians were merely ignorant brethren and all that was needed was to rekindle the light of faith in their hearts and minds. With Islam and Muslims it was quite different. Beyond the shores of the Mediterranean the false prophet exercised his tyrannical sway. Therein lay the mission's opportunity, if they could only distribute enough tracts, deliver enough sermons, teach enough boys and girls, light was bound to prevail upon the darkness.[2]

Christianity and the Consulate

Closely connected with the new Protestant community was the British presence in general — business interests, such as banking and shipping, and the tourist and retail trades. One of the first tasks of the first resident missionary in Jerusalem upon his arrival there December 26, 1825, was to secure the appointment of a British consul. Jerusalem was to be a special case, for consuls were usually placed in seaports and commercial centers, and Jerusalem was neither. Besides, no other European power had a consulate in Jerusalem. Still, the British felt that they needed an official presence in Jerusa-

---

[2] A. L. Tibawi, *British Interests in Palestine (1800-1901): A Study in Religious and Educational Enterprise,* p. 21.

lem, and the Protestants fully agreed and helped to achieve this goal.

The Turkish Sultan was not too responsive to the request for an official British post in Jerusalem, but the occupation in 1831 of Syria and Palestine by Muhammad Ali, an Egypt-based rebel against Ottoman authority, changed the situation. Muhammad Ali's temporary Palestinian regime was more favorable to the British, and he quickly issued a proclamation to the civil and religious authorities in Jerusalem and elsewhere to relax restrictions on foreigners, particularly Christians and Jews.

In this new atmosphere, the Anglican bishop, who in the interests of Protestant unity was also financially supported by the King of Prussia, was successful in bringing a consul to Jerusalem on January 21, 1842. Both Bishop Alexander and Consul-General Hugh Rose rode into Jerusalem at the head of a very impressive cavalcade.

With the arrival of the Consul-General, the British became the official protectors of the Protestant Christians and Jews in the Holy Land under the millet system of the Ottomans, the autonomous religious communities of non-Muslims in the Ottoman empire, whose patriarchs or rabbis were responsible to the Turks for the payment of taxes and other conduct of their members.

Competition in Protection

The Latin and Orthodox Christians stood under the protection of France and Russia, respectively. This did not improve their relations with the Protestants, especially when the protectors of all three — the British, French, and Russians — were in international competition with each other. All wanted a strong lease in the Middle East generally, and to strengthen their hold on Palestine in particular.

Thus, even before the end of Muhammad Ali's occupation, Russian pilgrims in Jerusalem were predicting that Palestine would soon fall under Russian control. The prediction was not fulfilled, but the Russian consul in Beirut did arrive in Jerusalem with an Ottoman decree in his hand extending his jurisdiction also to Jerusalem and its dependencies. Immediately, the consul had buildings erected in Jerusalem for occupation by Russian subjects.

The British and French watched this development very closely. Since the Ottoman empire was obviously on the decline the European powers were considering various schemes for the advancement of their interests. In so doing they anticipated developments that became reality in the twentieth century under the so-called Mandate government. Norman Bentwich has reported the scheming as follows:

> The French proposed to establish an ecclesiastical enclave for Jerusalem and an area around it, to be governed by a Christian municipality under the direction of the Christian states. Prussia proposed a European protectorate over the holy cities, Jerusalem, Bethlehem, and Nazareth. Certain sections in England advocated a policy of restoring to Palestine the Jewish people. . . . The Frenchman Laharanne advocated an independent Jewish State. Russia ridiculed all of these proposals.[3]

One of the most vigorous British promoters of Jewish settlement in Palestine was Lord Shaftesbury, who felt that the development of the immense fertility of the country between the Euphrates and the Mediterranean Sea would be served thereby. A Christian millennialist, Shaftesbury believed that Palestine belonged to the Jews and should be returned to them, hopefully as converts to Christianity. Since the first Anglican bishop in Jerusalem was Jewish by race, the restoration, so it appeared to Shaftesbury and others, had already begun.

The Holy Places and War

For the time being, however, the Turks remained in control. The British were not particularly bothered by this, because they recognized Turkey as a convenient roadblock in the way of Russian expansionism. The British-Turkish alliance reached a peak of cooperation during the Crimean War (1853-56). British Christians, who had identified Turkish (Islamic) domains as the land of Satan, had their problems with this relationship. In the end, however, they adjusted to the alliance much in the same way that American Christians a century later adjusted to the American-Soviet alliance against the common enemy of Germany in World War II.

The Crimean War, which had its origin — at least by pretext — in the question of control over the holy places, did

---

[3] *Palestine*, p. 44.

not resolve that problem, and the treaties of Paris in 1856 and of Berlin in 1878 among the leading European powers (Russia, Britain, France) merely confirmed the status quo. The continuing quarrel over the holy places between the Latins and the Orthodox was left to plague the British Mandate government a half century later. The Protestants eventually developed their own happy solution to the problem of the holy places. They identified a new sepulchre (the Garden Tomb) and a new (Gordon's) Calvary as the most likely scenes of the crucifixion, burial, and resurrection of Jesus.

The Crimean War had generated new interest in the Holy Land and European pilgrims by the thousands went to Palestine to view the holy places. Jews, too, became interested and several permanent settlements and institutions were established in the 1860s and 1870s. At the same time, a German Christian community, known as Templars, settled near Jaffa and Haifa in order to be near Jerusalem at the time of Christ's second coming.

The British pilgrimage interest led to the establishment in 1865 of the Palestine Exploration Fund, which brought scores of explorers and archaeologists to Palestine in the decades following. The first main survey of western Palestine was prepared in the 1870s. Among the participating engineers was Horatio Herbert (Lord) Kitchener, whose resulting lifelong devotion to Palestine and the Near East was to have a dramatic effect on its subsequent history.

Territorial and Commercial Expansion

British engineers and financiers gave some thought to building a canal, as a rival to the predominantly French-controlled Suez, from Haifa to the Gulf of Aqaba, but later gave it up as too expensive. When the British occupied Egypt in 1883 and gradually supplanted French dominance, a second canal was no longer necessary.

Thereafter, the British expanded east of the Suez to control as much of the Sinai as the Turks would allow. In Palestine itself, the British competed with the Russians, French, and Germans in building hospices, churches, cathedrals, and schools and in sponsoring pilgrims.

The visit of the German emperor to Jerusalem in 1899 was so impressive that Theodore Herzl believed that Wilhelm II would be the man to help the Jews to establish their national homeland. The Kaiser proved to be a disappointment to the World Zionist Organization, but the British were definitely interested in Zionist goals. The new Jewish settlements had already been establishing economic ties with England, the latter buying oranges and barley from Palestine and shipping in cotton and iron goods in return. More Jewish immigration was seen as the key to further economic development of the area and to further political control for the British.

Then came the discovery by British engineers of some of the huge oil reserves in the Middle East and the formation of the Anglo-Persian and other oil companies. The Middle East was soon estimated to contain half of the world's oil resources, and since Britain was almost completely dependent on outside petroleum resources, her interest in the area became more intense than ever.

By 1913 First Lord of the Admiralty Winston Churchill had replaced coal with oil as fuel for the British navy. To guarantee the necessary supply of oil he arranged for the British control of the Anglo-Persian Oil Company. That was the beginning: other oil companies were formed with British assistance and protection, including those in which Americans were eventually to have a dominant economic interest. These investments in Middle East oil gave first to Britain and then the United States a strong and undeniable vested interest in the area, as can be concluded from Table 6.[4]

---

[4] Royal Institute of International Affairs, *The Middle East: A Political and Economical Survey,* pp. 568-569.

TABLE 6

PRINCIPAL OIL-PRODUCING COMPANIES AND CONCESSIONS IN THE MIDDLE EAST

Country and Operating Company	Parent Companies	Interest in Operating Co. (per cent)	Period of Concession
Persia			
Anglo-Iranian Co. Ltd.	British Government	56	(1901)
	Burmah Oil Co.	22	1933-1993
	Public Holdings	22	
Iraq			
Iraq Petroleum Co. Ltd. (IPC)	Royal Dutch/Shell	23.75	
	Anglo-Iranian Oil Co. Ltd.	23.75	1925-2000
	Compagne Francaise des Petroles	23.75	
	Socony-Vacuum Oil Co. Inc.	11.875	
	Standard Oil Co. (New Jersey)	11.875	
	Participations & Explorations Corp.	5.0	
Basra Petroleum Co. Ltd.	Same as for IPC		1938-2013
Mosul Petroleum Co. Ltd.	Same as for IPC		1932-2027
Qatar			
Qatar Petroleum Co. Ltd.	Same as for IPC		1935-2010
Shell Overseas Exploration Co. Ltd.	Royal Dutch/Shell	100	1952-2027

Kuwait			
Kuwait Oil Co. Ltd.	Anglo-Iranian Oil Co. Ltd.	50	1934-2026
	Gulf Oil Corp.	50	
Saudi Arabia			
Arabian American Oil Co.	Standard Oil Co. of California	30	1933-2005
	The Texas Co.	30	
	Standard Oil Co. (New Jersey)	30	
	Socony-Vacuum Oil Co. Inc.	10	
Bahrain			
Bahrain Petroleum Co. Ltd.	Standard Oil Co. of California	50	(1925)
	The Texas Co.	50	1940-1995
Egypt			
Anglo-Egyptian Oilfields Ltd.	Anglo-Iranian Oil Co. Ltd.	100	Individual leases expire between 1957 and 1978 (some are renewable for 15 years)
	Royal Dutch/Shell		
	Egyptian Government Public Holdings		
Kuwait-Nejd Neutral Zone			
American Independent Oil Co.	U.S. independent companies, including Phillips Petroleum Co., Signal Oil & Gas Co. Ltd., Ashland Oil & Refining Co., and Hancock Oil Co.	100	
Pacific Western Oil Corp.			

Country and Operating Company	Parent Companies	Interest in Operating Co. (per cent)	Period of Concession
Trucial Coast			
Petroleum Development (Trucial Coast) Ltd.	Same as for IPC	Various concessions granted for 75 years from various dates during and since 1937.	
Oman			
Petroleum Development (Oman) Ltd.	Same as for IPC		1937-2012
Jordan			
Transjordan Petroleum Co. Ltd.	Same as for IPC		1947-2022

* At the end of the First World War ownership of the Turkish Petroleum Co., now IPC, was divided between Royal Dutch/Shell, Anglo-Iranian, Deutsche Bank, and Mr. C. S. Gulbenkian. By the San Remo Agreement in 1920 the German share was transferred to France and in 1928 a group of American companies acquired a share.

The War and Arab Nationalism

The coming of World War I in 1914, which saw Turkey allied with Germany, made Britain's goals and priorities very clear. Turkey had to be defeated and British interests in the Middle East made secure. In this undertaking, Britain needed the cooperation of the Arab world, in which a strong nationalism and desire for self-determination was stirring. Arab leaders were not sure, however, whether the goal to independence lay in cooperation with, or opposition to, the Turks.

The British helped the Arabs to decide against the Turks by explaining to them that nationalist aspirations could best be obtained in cooperation with themselves, who were renounced as champions of freedom everywhere in the world. The explanations were followed by promises as soon as the British sensed that Arab cooperation was indispensable to victory over the Turks in the Middle East. Until then neither the British nor the other European powers had expressed much concern for the Arabs. British writers had distorted the Arab image by concentrating on one meaning of Arab at the expense of another. Thus the Arab was identified almost exclusively as a desert dweller, a Bedouin living in a tent and riding on a camel. Forgotten was the Arab who had nurtured a brilliant civilization with outstanding achievements in mathematics, astronomy, and science, and the more modern urban Arab, well educated in classical English or French, sophisticated, in close contact with European thought, and well able to take care of himself.

It was true, of course, that the Arab peoples had, so to speak, fallen into a great sleep during Ottoman rule. But the Arab awakening was well on its way at the end of the nineteenth and the beginning of the twentieth centuries, when the British felt that the Arabs could not possibly manage the Middle East without Europeans. American and European teachers in Syrian and Lebanese schools since the middle of the nineteenth century had contributed substantially to the Arab awakening. Many of the educators were Protestants; and, if western Christianity failed the Middle East in other ways, it did stir in the Arabs the desire for dignity. The impact of American and European thought was felt most of all in the growth of nationalism, which for Arabs meant two things: independence from Turkey and any other outside interference, and the restoration of the united Arab world that had been part of their past and whose glory now exhilarated them.

The Arab national consciousness at the turn of the century was strongest in Syria-Palestine and in Egypt. In the former area, it was stimulated by a new Turkish despotism, which, while it was prepared to recognize equality of rights for Arabs, foresaw emancipation only in the context of a reborn and democratic Turkish empire. The Arabs, however, felt that the so-called "sick man of Europe" was nearing the end of his days and they saw no reason for assisting in his resurrection. Arab nationalistic eagerness, therefore, turned into widespread agitation and revolt after the death of Sultan Abdul Hamid in 1908.

Egypt, on the other hand, as a huge millet in the empire, had been domestically independent and developing as a self-contained nation-state since the days of Muhammad Ali. The government and army, however, retained a strong Turkish complexion. This remaining Turkish influence led to the Egyptian revolt, which in turn gave the British their excuse for occupying a coveted area in 1883, thus once more usurping the French.

The British presence stimulated Egyptian political ideas and administrative know-how. On the other hand, the occupation aggravated those Egyptians who wanted to be rid of all foreign control, British as well as Turkish and French. The Egyptians were unhappy particularly because Britain was using their land as a base for the extension of its influence throughout the Middle East. From the two sides then, Syria and Egypt, Britain was confronted by a strong and determined Arab nationalism.

British Promises to the Arabs

By 1915-16, Britain's position in the Middle East war theatre was a precarious one. The Turkish-German forces were threatening not only the Suez Canal but also the overland route to India. The Arab role in the struggle was crucial. The Sultan of Turkey as the Muslim Caliph had issued a call to all the Muslim subjects of the British empire to rise up in a holy war against England. The Caliph was most anxious to have this call supported by the Sharif of Mecca, Hussein Ibn Ali, a man of prestige in Muslim eyes because he was a descendant of Muhammad and the custodian of the holy places of Islam.

The British, for obvious reasons, now also sought discussions with Hussein. The negotiations were begun by the aforementioned Lord Kitchener, who since his role as engineer in Palestine had been British high commissioner in Egypt and who was now the British war secretary. Kitchener promised personal security to Hussein and support for the Arabs in their struggle for independence.

Hussein was most receptive, and the detailed negotiations were left to him and Sir Henry McMahon, Kitchener's successor in Egypt, to complete. Hussein was joined in the consultations by his two sons, Abdullah and Feisal, and the three entered into an agreement on January 1, 1916, to join the allied side on conditions outlined by McMahon as follows:

> Subject to the above modifications [he had reference to parts of Syria in which France was vitally interested] Great Britain is prepared to recognize and support the independence of the Arabs in all the regions within the limits demanded by the Sharif of Mecca. Great Britain will guarantee the holy places against all external aggression and will recognize their inviolability. When the situation admits, Great Britain will give to the Arabs her advice and will assist them to establish what may appear to be the most suitable forms of government in those various territories. . . .[5]

With these guarantees, the Arabs revolted against Turkey and, under Feisal's leadership, fought side by side with the troops of British General Allenby until the strategic center of Damascus fell. In this struggle the Arabs rendered invaluable service to the allied cause, and when victory came they were certain that they had won their independence.

Agreements with the French

However, the British had been negotiating not only with the Arabs. Indeed, even while the discussions with Hussein were in progress the British foreign minister was also contacting the French ambassador in London to discuss the interests of their respective governments in Ottoman Asia. The details of the Anglo-French negotiations were entrusted to the two men after whom the ensuing Sykes-Picot agreement was named.

The provisional formula for the division of the Arab prov-

---

[5] Quoted in Hurewitz, *Diplomacy in Near and Middle East: A Documentary Record*, p. 15.

inces between Britain and France was shared with the other ally, Russia, who agreed to the division on condition that she, in turn, receive certain other areas controlled by Turkey. The final agreement reached on October 23, 1916 recognized that independent Arab states or a confederation of states was to be established, but it also specified that in given areas France or Britain should have "priority rights of enterprise" and supply the advisors or functionaries deemed necessary for this enterprise. Generally, this meant that the Syrian-Lebanon area would fall to France and the Palestine-Jordan-Iraq area to Great Britain.

To the dismay of the allies and even more of the Arabs, the Turkish government obtained the text of the Sykes-Picot agreement and drew it to the attention of the Arabs, who were furious about the plan to divide and control their territories. To pacify the Arabs, the British government assured Hussein that there were no designs on the Arab country and that the liberation of the Arab peoples remained a firm pledge. The Arabs were not easily pacified, however, and seven leading Arabs meeting in Cairo demanded an explanation. Again, the British gave assurances of complete independence and that no regime would be set up anywhere that would not be acceptable to the native peoples.

British Promises to the Jews

The assurances left many doubts in the minds of Arabs, not least of all because yet another negotiation with yet another party had been in progress. The British were seeking help in winning the war not only from the Arabs and all possible allies, but also from the Jews and, through the latter, also from the Americans. In 1917 the British themselves announced a policy regarding Palestine and the Jews, which policy became known as the Balfour Declaration.

The Jews had been very much alert to possible changes in the status of Palestine resulting from the war, and so they had petitioned the emerging victor for their share in the territorial pie to be divided. The Zionist movement, now led by the British chemist, Dr. Chaim Weizmann, presented its case anew; and, since Britain wanted international Jewry to support its cause and, more importantly, to get the United States to join the war on the British side, Britain was open.

Assisting Dr. Weizmann in the Zionist petition to the British were Baron Lionel Walter Rothschild, president of the English Zionist Federation, and the Honorable Louis D. Brandeis, Associate Justice of the Supreme Court of the United States and the leader of the American Zionist Movement. Brandeis was entirely clear on what he wanted for the Jews. In an address delivered in New York two years before the Balfour Declaration was issued, Brandeis stated that the aims of Zionism were as follows:

> Zionism seeks to establish in Palestine for such Jews as choose to go and remain there, and for their descendants, a legally secured home, where they may live together and lead a Jewish life, where they may expect ultimately to constitute a majority of the population, and may look forward to what we should call home rule. The Zionists seek to establish this home in Palestine because they are convinced that the undying longing of Jews for Palestine is a fact of deepest significance; that it is a manifestation in the struggle for existence by an ancient people which has established its right to live, a people whose three thousand years of civilization has produced a faith, culture, and individuality which enable it to contribute largely in the future, is not a right merely but a duty of the Jewish Nationality to survive and develop. They believe that only in Palestine can Jewish life be fully protected from the forces of disintegration; that there alone can the Jewish spirit reach its full and natural development; and that by securing for those Jews who wish to settle there the opportunity to do so, and that the long perplexing Jewish problem will, at last, find solution.[6]

Brandeis apparently succeeded in persuading President Wilson that a pledge of support to the Zionist organizations would be a good thing not only for them but for him. The words of the Balfour Declaration were checked out with Wilson by Brandeis, and the Declaration apparently became Britain's part of the deal that brought America into the war. Winston Churchill, more than twenty years later, stated that "in consequence of and on the basis of this pledge . . . we received important help in the war, and after the war we received from the allied and associated powers the Mandate for Palestine."[7]

---

[6] *Book of Documents, General Assembly of the United Nations Relating to the Establishment of the National Home for Jewish People,* p. 2.

[7] *Ibid.,* p. 3.

Thus, with American (and apparently also French) help and considerable domestic pressure, the British foreign secretary, Arthur James Balfour, issued the famous "British Declaration of Sympathy of Zionist Aspirations" of which the first draft had been drawn up by the Zionist leaders Weizmann, Rothschild, and Brandeis.

Brandeis' contribution to the agreement was no secret, and on the centennial of his birth in 1956 he was hailed as one of Israel's founding fathers. The Zionist Organizations of America recognized that: "Brandeis played a major part in assuring the approval of the United States Government for the issuance of the Balfour Declaration."[8] It was also Brandeis who gave to American Zionists their slogan "To be good Americans we must be better Jews ... and to be better Jews, we must become Zionists. ..."[9]

The November 2, 1919 Balfour Declaration was addressed as a letter to Baron Rothschild with the request that it be communicated to Zionist organizations throughout the world. The text of the letter reads:

> I have much pleasure in conveying to you, on behalf of his Majesty's Government, the following declaration of sympathy with Jewish Zionist aspirations which has been submitted to, and approved by, the Cabinet: —
>
> His Majesty's Government views with favour the establishment in Palestine of a national home for the Jewish people, and will use their best endeavours to facilitate the achievement of this object, it being clearly understood that nothing shall be done which may prejudice the civil and religious rights of existing non-Jewish communities in Palestine, or the rights and political status enjoyed by Jews in any other country. I should be grateful if you would bring this declaration to the knowledge of the Zionist Federation.[10]

The Arabs were entirely dismayed when the Balfour Declaration, not meant to be a secret document, became public knowledge and when post-war immigration policies were announced. But the British continued to reassure the Arabs, who took new courage also from the famous Fourteen Points Speech of President Wilson. On July 4, 1918, the American leader

---

[8] *Program and Source Book; Brandeis Centennial.*
[9] *Ibid.*
[10] Hurewitz, *op. cit.,* p. 26.

declared that post-war settlements would be based on free acceptance of those settlements by the people immediately concerned. The Arabs believed that this meant them, but they were soon to learn that they as a people would not be much consulted.

The Eager Zionist Lobby

Following the issuance of the Balfour Declaration, the Zionist Organization lost no time in establishing its new position and gaining further ground. It influenced the substance of the "Tentative American Proposals at Paris," presented its own memorandum regarding the "historic title of the Jewish people to Palestine," and subsequently addressed itself also to the San Remo conference of victorious World War I powers in 1920 and the newly founded League of Nations. Zionist leaders were instrumental in drafting the proposals and plans that led to the establishment of the British Mandatory Government for Palestine.

The Mandate for Palestine, which was finally approved by the Council of the League of Nations on July 24, 1922, and which officially came into force on September 29, 1923, established effective British control over Palestine. The Mandate referred in specific terms to the Balfour Declaration and gave the Mandatory the responsibility of "placing the country under such political, administrative conditions as will secure the establishment of the Jewish national home."[11]

The Mandate also specified that "the civil and religious rights of all the inhabitants of Palestine irrespective of race and religion" should be safeguarded. Arabs already knew, as the British were to learn from bitter experience, that these two parts of the Mandate were incompatible, not least of all because the Arabs were the dominant group and the British were at this stage more inclined to satisfy the aspirations of the Jews.

The Mandate provided for the establishment of an appropriate Jewish agency that would advise and cooperate with the administration of Palestine in matters related to the establishment of the national home and the interests of the Jewish population in Palestine. Actually, all of this had already happened before the Mandate had spoken. The British administration, cooperating closely with the Jewish National

[11] Martin Wight, *British Colonial Constitution 1947*, pp. 99-137.

Agency, had already in 1919 provided for a quota of 16,000 Jewish immigrants for the year 1920.

The Arabs, quite understandably, were furious. Before their very eyes they saw eroding the self-determination for which they had hoped so long, which they had been promised, and for which they thought they had fought. Their claims to the land were, so it seemed, being minimized, but the British and Zionists were soon to learn that the Arabs could not be ignored forever.

8. The Claims of the Arabs

The Arabs also have rights in Palestine; the Zionist program threatens those rights. Arabs will fight and die in their own cause.
　　　　　　　　　　　　　　　　　　　　—Kermit Roosevelt[1]

Precisely at the time when British imperialism, Protestant millenarianism, and Zionist ambition were reaching a new peak of fervor, Arab nationalism was also appearing as a determined and irreversible trend, destined to make itself felt throughout the Middle East. Neither the British nor the Zionists anticipated that they would feel this nationalism so soon or as strong as it turned out to be.

It cannot be denied, of course, that the Arab world had been relatively docile for three centuries. Leading Arab thinkers referred to the era of Ottoman dominance as "the sleep of the ages," in which their world was culturally dormant, politically stagnant, and economically sterile. This sleep, no doubt, was one of the reasons why the West thought that the Arab could be ignored. But at that crucial point the West too was asleep, for it failed to recognize the extent to which the Arab world was already wide awake.

The Arabs had been influenced and affected by both nineteenth-century European nationalism and the twentieth-century awakening of colonized peoples. When World War I came, they knew that they wanted their independence and their own nationhood. This meant freedom from the old domination, which was Turkish, and from the new intervention, which was European. They were expecting that the war would fulfill their wish, and in that hope and for that reason alone they had fought on the allied side.

---

[1] "The Arabs Live There Too," in *Papers on Palestine,* II, p. 18.

Restlessness and Reassurances

Thus it was a cause for considerable concern, if not alarm, when the Arabs saw decisions being made in London, Washington, and Paris that seemed to contradict the British promise of independence, especially since these decisions were being made without consultation with them. The Husseins and the Group of Seven did raise their voice in protest in Cairo, but then too quickly accepted at face value the assurances that were being given.

Even General Allenby's entry into Jerusalem on December 11, 1917 (Beersheba in the south and Jaffa on the coast had already been captured from the Turks) was reassuring for the Arabs. While proclaiming the establishment of an administration under martial law, the British general guaranteed the protection of religious rights and properties for all, as follows:

> Since your city is regarded with affection by the adherents of three of the great religions of mankind, and since its soil has been consecrated by the prayers and pilgrimages of multitudes of devoted people of these three religions for many centuries, therefore do I make known to you that every sacred building, monument, holy spot, shrine, traditional right, endowment and bequest, or customary place of prayer, of whatsoever form of the three religions, will be maintained and protected, according to the existing customs and beliefs of those to whose faith they are sacred.[2]

The new Occupied Enemy Territory Administration consisted of a chief, 13 district military governors (10 after 1919), 59 British assistants, and 17 appointed Arab officers. The chief quickly granted the traditional authority to existing religious institutions, including the Muslim (Shaira) courts, to administer their own affairs. A local Muslim council for the administration of endowment funds was appointed to replace the one in Constantinople. Arab Muslims thus had nothing to fear, and Arab Christians were not unhappy either.

This early confidence in the British administration was soon to be undermined, however. Early in 1918 the administration authorized a Zionist commission to travel, investigate, and report on the prospects in Palestine of a national home for the Jews. Upon the completion of its work, the commission

[2] *Survey of Palestine, Prepared in December 1945 and January 1946 for the Information of the Anglo-American Committee of Inquiry,* p. 15.

asked for Jewish representation in the occupying administration, and this request was granted.

The Zionist group also proposed the appointment of a land commission, consisting of experts to be nominated by themselves, to ascertain the resources of Palestine, and claimed the right to select Jewish members for the police force. More than that, the commission insisted that Jews be granted freedom to train their own defense forces, which training was already in progress.

The King-Crane Commission

The Zionists were active not only in Palestine but also in Paris, where the Arabs too were determined to assert their rights. But when their representatives arrived in the French capital, they learned that the Zionists had arrived before them. Both parties tried to persuade the great powers of their point of view, although there also appears to have been at least a temporary rapprochement between Arabs and Zionists.

In March of 1919 Chaim Weizmann and Emir, later Prince, Feisal of Iraq reached an agreement that Arabs and Zionists should cooperate in the development of Palestine. Feisal assured the Jews "a most hearty welcome home," while Weizmann promised that "the Arab peasant and tenant farmers shall be protected in their rights."[3] The agreements between the two leaders, however, turned out to be of no consequence, since both sides found them unacceptable, and when Feisal tried to assert himself as king of an independent Greater Syria he was soon thrown out of Damascus by the French.

Meanwhile the French and British could not agree on the full meaning of the Sykes-Picot accord. Consequently, Dr. Howard Bliss, president of the Syrian Protestant College and spokesman with the Arabs, proposed that an inter-allied commission be sent to the Lebanon-Syria-Palestine area to determine the governmental wishes of the local population.

Both the French and British were reluctant to ask the Arabs, and so the United States alone sent Henry C. King and Charles R. Crane — they became known as the King-Crane Commission — to conduct the public opinion poll. The Arab nationalists took advantage of the presence of the Americans and convened a general congress in Damascus in July, 1919 with

---

[3] Maurice Samuel, *Light on Israel,* pp. 46-48.

delegates from the Ottoman province areas of Syria and Palestine. The congress unanimously demanded "full and absolute independence for Syria" (including Lebanon, Palestine, Trans-Jordan, and Cilicia). The congress also rejected Zionist claims to Palestine, and requested that, if a Mandate government was absolutely essential, the trusteeship be granted to either the United States or Great Britain, in that order. France was completely ruled out as a possibility. The King-Crane Commission noted the Arab position, but talked also to Jewish representatives. After hearing both sides, King and Crane came to the conclusion that the establishment by the Zionists of a homeland for the Jews really meant or would lead to the expulsion of the Arabs. They said:

> The fact came out repeatedly in the commission's conference with Jewish representatives, that the Zionist looked forward to a practically complete dispossession of the present non-Jewish inhabitants of Palestine by various forms of purchase.[4]

This chilling report on Zionism, however, was not taken seriously in the United States, mainly because the Zionists had an effective lobby against it. Thus it happened that in April 1920, France and Britain had their way concerning the mandates at the conference in San Remo. Lebanon and Syria were assigned to France, and Britain got Palestine, the boundaries of which still needed to be clarified. At this point the limits of Palestine were only vaguely defined.

British and American Interests

The Zionists wanted a large Palestine. They were bidding for a national home that included territories beyond the Jordan River, at least up to the Hijaz Railway. The first draft of the Mandate, therefore, included both sides of the Jordan River, including the area later known as Transjordan. Though this bid was not granted, the Zionists never forgot it, and maps of *Eretz Israel,* published after the 1967 war, included this area along with the occupied territories as part of Israel.

Britain did not bow to full Zionist demands but rather made a concession to the Husseins. In 1921 Abdullah Hussein was

---

[4] *The Political History of Palestine Under British Administration: Memorandum by His Britannic Majesty's Government Presented in 1947 to the United Nations Special Committee on Palestine,* p. 3.

recognized the emir of Transjordan, and the Mandate draft was withdrawn to exclude this new emirate from the territory in which the Jewish national home was to come into being. Though the national home had, literally, been narrowed down, the Mandate for Palestine as it was finally ratified by the Council of the League of Nations on September 29, 1923, was generally in favor of the Zionists.

Quoting the Balfour Declaration in its preamble, the Mandate acknowledged the historical connection of the Jewish people with Palestine, as well as the grounds for "reconstituting" the national home in that country. While the Arabs were not once mentioned by name in the entire Mandate, Article 4 provided for the establishment of a Jewish Agency, working hand in hand with the Palestine government in matters affecting the establishment of the Jewish national home, an agency that was already operative before the Mandate officially sanctioned it.

American Zionists, led by Louis Brandeis, had contributed their share to the wording of the Mandate but the United States government's position still remained somewhat ambivalent. In 1922, Congress passed a resolution, again as a result of Zionist pressures, favoring the establishment of a national home for the Jews in Palestine, but America's official policy of neutrality was emphasized in the Anglo-American convention of December 1924, when the United States insisted that all international agreements affecting Middle East mandated territories provide for equal American economic opportunity. From that time on American-owned oil companies obtained many concessions in the region, and that is why the United States eventually took on much of the British political burden in the area.

Arab Politics and Protests

The Arabs appeared to submit to all these decisions being made in foreign capitals about them and their territories without their being asked, but in their hearts they were not accepting what was going on. Arab nationalists, who had attended the Syrian Congress, now formed Muslim-Christian Associations in the Arab towns of Palestine to protest the establishment of the Jewish national home. The Associations met in a country-wide conference at Haifa in December of 1920 and called for the founding of an independent Arab state, in which all the residents of Palestine would be citizens.

In 1919 the population included about 65,000 Jews, many of them Arabized Jews of long standing, and ten times that many Arabs, about 650,000, of whom some 70,000 were Christians, the balance being Muslims. The first official non-Ottoman census taken by the British administration in 1922, as well as later similar counts, revealed substantial increases, as can be seen in Table 7.[5] The increases were due to the high Arab birth rate on the one hand, and the high Jewish immigration on the other hand.

TABLE 7
STATISTICAL SUMMARY OF POPULATION IN PALESTINE (1922-37)

Year	Muslims	Jews	Christians	Others	Total
1922	598,177	83,790	71,464	7,617	761,048
1924	627,660	94,945	74,094	8,263	804,962
1926	663,613	149,500	76,764	8,782	898,659
1928	695,280	151,656	79,812	9,203	935,951
1930	733,149	164,796	84,986	9,628	992,559
1932	771,174	180,793	90,624	10,281	1,052,872
1934	807,180	253,700	99,532	10,746	1,171,158
1935	826,457	320,358	103,371	10,896	1,261,082
1936	848,342	370,483	106,474	11,219	1,336,518
1937	875,947	386,074	109,764	11,520	1,383,305

The Haifa Conference, which proposed the establishment of an Arab state, also elected the first permanent Muslim-Christian Executive, which, though it lasted only until 1923, represented a good beginning for Palestinian political action. It came too late and was too weak to effectively challenge the developments resulting from decisions being made outside the country, but it came as soon as it could come after the Ottoman subordination.

In the meantime, Arab protests against Zionist policies had become violent. On Easter Sunday, 1920, five Jews were killed and 200 injured in Haifa. A military committee of inquiry determined that the outbreak was caused by Arab nationalism, which was now being threatened by Zionism. A year later Arab

---

[5] *Palestine: Blue Book, 1937,* p. iii.

attacks on Jaffa resulted in the death of 47 Jews and the wounding of 146 others. These protests and attacks were spontaneous actions of citizens and not coordinated by any central political or military force.

Again, Zionism was found to be the cause of the outbreak, but, since the irritation was not removed, these violent clashes were only the beginning. The Arabs were well aware that not only Jewish extremists but also the responsible representatives of Zionism were deliberately and carefully planning for a future Palestine in which Jews would be the majority.

Attempts at Democratization

Zionist progress in this direction did not suffer when the military administration was replaced by a civil government on July 1, 1920. Sir Herbert Samuel assumed the office of high commissioner. He was supported by an executive council and an advisory council consisting of ten nominated non-officials, of whom four were Muslim Arabs, three were Christian Arabs, and three were Jews. The small influence of a Jewish minority in the administration was offset by the influence that the Jewish Agency had with the British themselves. In less than a month, the first immigration ordinance was passed authorizing a quota of 16,500 immigrant Jews for the first year.

The next governmental development was an order to strengthen the Muslim organization. The Supreme Muslim Council was then created for the purpose of administering the Awqaf, the religious endowments of the Muslims and the Sharia religious courts, which had formerly been administered from Constantinople. The *mufti* (Muslim judicial official) of Jerusalem became the head of the Supreme Council. This development, however, did not satisfy the Arabs nor did it deter them from voicing their main grievance — that their independence was being denied them by the mandatory powers and being taken away by the Zionists.

On February 21, 1922, a delegation of Arab leaders appeared in London to inform Secretary of State Winston Churchill that they could not accept the Balfour Declaration or the proposed Mandate and that they wanted their independence immediately. They insisted that the Palestinian government should be responsible only to the Palestinian people. It would provide for the creation of a national independent government in accordance with the spirit of the covenant of the League of Nations. This government would safeguard and guarantee the legal rights of foreigners, the religious equality of all peoples, the rights of minorities, and the rights of the assisting power.

In the face of Arab pressure the British government issued a White Paper to interpret the Balfour Declaration to both the Arab delegation and the Zionist organization. This explanation, while it reaffirmed the Declaration, denied that it meant making Palestine "as Jewish as England is English" or that Britain had had in mind "the disappearance or the subordination of the Arabic population, language, or culture in Palestine."[6] The terms of the Declaration, it was further explained, did not mean "that Palestine as a whole should be converted into a Jewish National Home," but only that such a home should be *"founded in Palestine."* The home did not mean "the imposition of a Jewish nationality upon the inhabitants of Palestine," but rather the development of a center in which Jews could take an interest and a pride. For the fulfillment of this policy, it was believed necessary, so said the White Paper, to increase by immigration the size of the Jewish community in Palestine.

Soon thereafter, an order-in-council was issued by the British providing for the creation of a legislative council, consisting of the high commissioner and 22 members, 10 official and 12 elected (eight Muslim, two Christian, and two Jews). The Arab delegation, still in London, insisted again that only a constitution, which would give "the people of Palestine full control of their own affairs," could be acceptable to them. Mr. Churchill replied that the creation of a national government at that point would prevent the British from fulfilling their pledge to the Jewish people. Hearing this reply, the delegation concluded that the undertaking to provide a Jewish national home was the reason why Arabs were being denied their rights in Palestine and why Palestine could not have an independent government the same as Iraq and Transjordan. They also concluded that self-government would not be granted until there were Jewish people sufficient in number to satisfy the Zionists. Later events supported the delegation's conclusion.

Jewish immigration proceeded as planned. The 5,000 and

---

[6] Quoted in *The Political History of Palestine Under British Administration,* p. 4.

more who arrived in the last four months of 1920, nearly doubled to just under 10,000 in 1921. In the three years of 1924-26 nearly 60,000 arrived, largely as a consequence of economic difficulties in Poland. Even higher immigration peaks were reached in the 1930s after Hitler came to power in Germany (*see Table 8*).[7]

TABLE 8
NUMBER OF JEWISH AND NON-JEWISH IMMIGRANTS TO PALESTINE (1920-1944)

Year	Jews	Non-Jews	Total
1920	5,514	202	5,716
1921	9,149	190	9,339
1922	7,844	284	8,128
1923	7,421	570	7,991
1924	12,856	697	13,553
1925	33,801	840	34,641
1926	13,081	829	13,910
1927	2,713	882	3,595
1928	2,178	908	3,086
1929	5,249	1,317	6,566
1930	4,944	1,489	6,433
1931	4,075	1,458	5,533
1932	9,553	1,736	11,289
1933	30,327	1,650	31,977
1934	42,359	1,784	44,143
1935	61,854	2,293	64,147
1936	29,727	1,944	31,671
1937	10,536	1,939	12,475
1938	12,868	2,395	15,263
1939	16,405	2,028	18,433
1940	4,547	1,064	5,611
1941	3,647	623	4,270
1942	2,194	858	3,052
1943	8,507	1,360	9,867
1944	20,848	3,245	24,093

[7] Sophie A. Udin (ed.), *The Palestine Year Book*, Vol. I, pp. 172-173; and *Memorandum Prepared by the Government of Palestine for the Use of The Palestine Royal Commission*, p. 8.

The 1922 British White Paper had stipulated that immigration limits were to be determined by "the economic absorptive capacity of the country," but absorptive capacity meant
one thing to the Jews and quite another thing to the Arabs.
The Jewish Agency, rather well financed by international Zionism, saw to it that the land absorbed the Jewish immigrants,
but in the process many Arabs lost the lands for which they
and their ancestors had been working for many years..

The Conflict Over Land

Whose the lands actually were became a matter of considerable debate as the years went on. Both Jews and Arabs
were telling the world that all they wanted was to live in their
country, in their own homes, and on their own lands. Both
claimed historic rights to these lands. The resolution of all
the conflicting claims was made difficult in part by the poor
records of surveys and ownership that had been kept during
Ottoman days.

According to the best records available, however, Jewish
ownership of Palestine land was only about two percent in
1922. This was increased to about 5.67 percent in 1945 (*see
Table 9*).[8] This represented registrations in old and defective

TABLE 9
LAND OWNERSHIP IN PALESTINE IN 1945

Category	Acres	Percent
Individually owned by Arabs	3,143,693	47.79
Individually owned by Jews	372,925	5.67
Others	35,512	.54
Registered and recorded State Domain	3,028,625	46.00
Total	6,580,755	100.

land registers, but these acres of land could not easily be
found on the ground without overlapping with other property
that had been identified and claimed. Similarly, the Arab
figure could have been increased by 52,925 acres of good land
for which the Sultan held the title, but which the tenants
really assumed to be theirs by right of freehold tenure.

The so-called state domains were not all purely state domains. Land thus identified included government buildings,

---

[8] Sami Hadawi, *Land Ownership in Palestine*, p. 12.

forest preserves, road and railway allowances, as well as marshes and waste lands. In addition, there were cultivable lands held only nominally by the state. Arab farmers living on them possessed hereditary cultivation rights, and paid annual rental or tax. The state domains also included lands uncultivable by ordinary means but used by village people for grazing their livestock or for fuel gathering. Some cultivators could make a living, though a very meager one, by terracing small pockets of soil among the rocks and planting olive shoots. The Arab farmers had managed through the years to cover vast hillsides, rich in rocks but poor in soil, with olive orchards, and they owned 99 percent of the olive trees in the country, not an insignificant fact considering that most of these were in the stony hills.

Another block of uncultivable land in the state domain included the Negev with its 2,643,844 acres. On this land lived some 90,000 nomads whose tribes had grazed their flocks there from time immemorial. The rights of the nomads had never been challenged, and so government ownership was only "presumed."[9]

The Jewish Agency obtained land mainly from two sources: purchases from absentee landowners and grants from state domains. The Arab tenants did not always suffer when land changed hands, but more often than not they did. Tenants who had been on particular lands for generations were often evicted by the new owners to make room for Jewish immigrants. For the Jews the "economic absorption capacity" was always more than adequate; for the Arabs it had already passed the limit.

While some of the private lands were sold by Arab landlords voluntarily for pure economic reasons and without humanitarian considerations for the tenants, other owners were pressured to sell, since the new land and tax rules made continuous absentee ownership a burden. When the owners became willing to sell, the Jewish Agency stepped in and purchased the land at bargain prices. Sometimes the prices paid were very high. Tenants were often evicted soon thereafter. As Sami Hadawi reports:

> In one instance, over 40,000 acres, comprising 18 villages were sold, resulting in the eviction of 688 Arab agricultural

---

[9] *Survey of Palestine,* Vol. I, p. 256.

families. Of these, 309 families joined the landless classes, while the remainder drifted either into towns and cities or became hired ploughmen and laborers in other villages. Although eviction took place in 1922, the problem remained with the Palestine government to find land for some of these displaced persons until the termination of the mandate in 1948.[10]

Political and Economic Developments

The creation of large numbers of landless Arabs made the meaning of the Balfour Declaration very clear. The establishment of a national home for the Jews could only result in the destruction of the national home of the Palestinian Arabs. For this reason, the Arabs could not see themselves cooperating with British plans for the Jews to any degree, and they rejected election in the legislative council. They also refused to accept nomination to an advisory council that was subsequently proposed.

The British Mandatory government could not give up its attempt to "democratize" the administration, and so it tried next to establish an Arab agency to operate on a par with the Jewish Agency. The Arab agency would be consulted on such matters as immigration, since on this matter "the views of the Arab community were entitled to a special consideration." The Arabs declined this offer as well, on the grounds that the agency would not satisfy the aspirations of the Arab people. As far as they were concerned, the Jewish Agency had no status either, since the Arabs of Palestine had never recognized it. Having made the proposal, the high commissioner felt that he had no alternative but to continue governing exclusively with the aid of British officials.

As the 1920s came to a close the restlessness and agitation on the part of the Arabs decreased slightly. Their passivity at this point was mainly due to the drop in Jewish immigration due to the economic depression. While the population was not increasing as expected, the Jewish agricultural communities in Palestine were developing remarkably. The same was true of the cities. Modern suburbs were appearing in Jerusalem and Haifa. Tel Aviv showed the most growth of all. A village of 2,000 in 1914, the coastal city a decade later had a population of 30,000. Small industries were springing up everywhere.

---

[10] *Bitter Harvest: Palestine 1914-67,* p. 59.

The school system was flourishing, including the Hebrew university, which was founded in Jerusalem in 1925 to promote Hebrew as one of the three official languages of Palestine along with Arabic and English. Balfour himself had come from England to participate in the ceremonies opening this new school.

In the development of the Jewish community, the Jewish Agency did not forget its Hagana (defense) arm. The activities of these police units dated back to the 1870s, when the first of the new Jewish colonies had been founded in Palestine. After World War I the original Hagana Hashamen (defense watchmen) were organized into a paramilitary organization to recruit, train, and equip all able-bodied men and women to assist the long-term purposes of the Jewish Agency and the Zionist Organization, the establishment of a Jewish state.

The Arab community too developed and progressed as new roads were built, education was promoted, new agricultural techniques were introduced, and new markets established. In one decade the export of citrus fruits alone increased threefold to 2,610,000 cases in 1930. Most of the citrus plantations were owned by Arabs.

Disappointment and Disillusionment

The growing prosperity, however, did not decrease dissatisfaction with developments generally. On the contrary, by 1930 Arabs felt more keenly than ever that independence and control of their own destiny was further away than it had been at the time of the 1915 revolt against the Ottoman empire. A dozen years had now passed since the end of the war. The feelings concerning the lost cause were so sensitive that the slightest incident could touch off major disorders.

Such an incident had occurred in 1929, at the Wailing Wall, believed to be a fragment of Herod's temple, which in turn had been built on the site of the temple of Solomon. On the Day of Atonement, the Jews had introduced a screen to divide men and women during prayers. The Muslims, who had not been consulted, objected to this regulation on the grounds that the Jews were preparing to take gradual possession of the Mosque of Al Aksa by starting with control of this wall.

The National Council of the Jews denied this, but Arab nationalist agitators had once more been aroused. A Jewish demonstration, in the course of which the Zionist flag was raised and the Zionist anthem sung, was followed by an Arab counter-demonstration. These acts in turn led to murderous attacks on Jews in various parts of the country. The Jews suffered 133 dead and 339 wounded. The British police, on the other hand, killed about 116 Arabs and wounded 232 others.

A British commission of inquiry visited Palestine and reported that Arab fears for their economic and political future were the cause of the violent outbreak. The fears were not unfounded. A Zionist Congress in Zurich had just announced that a strong body of wealthy non-Zionists would join the Zionist endeavors and provide funds for further Zionist activities in Palestine. The commission recommended that the British define clearly what the Balfour Declaration and Mandate meant when they talked about safeguarding the rights of the non-Jewish communities, and that it clarify the policies of immigration and land tenure in relation to these rights. Immigration, said the commission, should be controlled to prevent the excesses of 1925-26, and the eviction of peasant cultivators from the land should be checked. Finally the 1922 statement specifying that the Zionist Organization would not share to any degree in the government of Palestine, should be implemented.

Soon thereafter the newly formed Arab Executive asked the British government to cease immigration, to declare Arab lands inalienable, and to establish a democratic government with representation on a population basis. The British were unwilling and declared that such demands required changes incompatible with the demands of the Mandate, but it had to do more than just say no.

On August 6, 1930 His Majesty's government issued another White Paper trying to satisfy both sides, but after conferring with Zionist leaders it assigned a larger role for an enlarged Jewish Agency. For the Arabs this was a clear sign that the Zionist lobby in London carried more weight than the wishes of the Arab population in Palestine.

Strikes and Rebellion

It was clear that there was more trouble ahead, and it came in spite of remarkable prosperity and development in Palestine in the early 1930s, while the rest of the world was sunk in depression and stagnation. Arab disturbances in 1933 were directed not so much against the Zionists as against the British who, the Arabs were sure, were favoring the Zionists in their policies.

In 1934 the Arabs formed five political parties, which together went to the high commission asking for the establishment of a democratic representative government, the prohibition of the transfer of Arab land to Jews, and an end to Jewish immigration until a competent committee had determined the absorptive capacity of the land. Again, the administration refused to accept anything that interfered with the Mandate, meaning with the Balfour Declaration. It promised, however, to make another attempt to establish self-governing institutions under the Mandate.

The proposed legislative council would have 28 members, 11 of which would be Muslim, seven would be Jews, and three Christian. The council would have considerable powers, although final policy on immigration should be decided by the high commission. This time the Arabs, though not entirely happy, were ready to talk. The Zionists rejected the proposal and also persuaded Parliament that the power the Arab majority would gain would be inconsistent with the Balfour Declaration.

The Arabs again saw evidences of the strength of the Zionist lobby and maintained, as they had in 1931, that Jewish influence was responsible for the Arabs' not being granted their rights. The representatives of the five Arab parties were invited to London early in 1936 once more to discuss constitutional matters, but developments in Palestine prevented their going. The country was shaken on April 15-16 by major disturbances and the murder of Jews by Arabs and then of Arabs by Jews.

The political parties now gave themselves to forming national committees in all of the Arab towns and villages, and on April 21 they called a general strike. The purpose of the strike was to force an end to Jewish immigration, which in 1935 had reached an all-time high of over 65,000, with an increased displacement of Arab cultivators. The Arabs were now wide awake politically. A Supreme Arab Committee, later known as the Arab Higher Committee, was established with the *mufti* of Jerusalem as president. Christian Arabs were as prominent in the development as were Muslim Arabs in all the political parties.

The Arab Higher Committee expanded the strike, which already paralyzed transport, construction, and shopkeeping, to include refusal to pay taxes. The British, however, seemed not yet to have faced up to the fact that the Arabs were wide awake and that they had legitimate grievances. Another royal commission was appointed "to ascertain the underlying causes of the disturbances," as if these causes were not already known.

Meanwhile, the revolt against the Mandate government and Zionism spread from passive strike to military action in the hills. Pipelines were punctured, roads were mined, railway tracks were torn up, and Jews were murdered. The British brought in two divisions to bring the revolt under control, and before it was over, the official list of casualties listed 314 dead and 1,337 wounded, most of them Arabs. In addition it was estimated that 1,000 Arab rebels had been killed by police, troops, and Hagana forces.

Intervention by Arab Governments

The strike was finally called off by Arab leaders in October, but the end of resistance was not in sight. On the contrary, the year had introduced a new arena of Arab action. In 1936, for the first time, the Palestinian cause brought a reaction from Arab governments outside Palestine. Although they had been sympathetic before, it was not until a change in international status of several Arab states that they intervened.

The Arab states at this point included the independent Kingdom of Saudi Arabia, which had close ties with Britain. The independent Kingdom of Iraq, also in treaty relationship with Great Britain, was ruled by the Hashemites, bitter enemies of the Saudis. The small state of Transjordan, an artificial creation of Britain, was autonomously administered by a Hashemite prince, supervised by Britain. He too was an enemy of the Saudi family. The two republics of Syria and Lebanon were administered by France. Yemen was an independent state, as was Egypt, though the latter was tied to Britain as was Iraq. The stature of Egypt, Syria, and Lebanon were all improved in 1936 by treaties negotiated with Britain and

France. All three states now had greater freedom of action in international affairs.

While a recognized national and international status was thus being achieved, domestic rivalries were bringing ill will to the Arab world, and for a while it seemed that the states would never get together. Emir Abdullah, the Hashemite prince of Transjordan, was aspiring to the establishment of a Greater Syria (Iraq-Syria, Lebanon, Palestine, and Transjordan), according to the British pledge to Hussein, which Abdullah insisted had been postponed but not aborted by the World War I peace settlement. The dissolution of the Mandate, he felt, would bring him and his state the desired fulfillment.

Abdul Aziz Ibn Saud of Arabia was opposed to such a scheme and formed a close relationship with the majority party in Syria. Britain seemed to be sympathetic to Saud's scheme on the assumption that it would make more Arab friends for Britain than would the Hashemite dream. Egypt also supported Saud, hoping itself to become the leader of the emerging block.

All of these rivalries threatened to abort Arab unity, but the Arab rebellion in Palestine gave a new lease on life to pan-Arabism, though not immediately. Iraq, playing up to Britain, twice asked the Arab Higher Committee to call off the strike. The Arab leaders of Palestine responded by saying that they would prefer joint mediation by all the monarchs of all the independent states. Accordingly, the monarchs of Saudi Arabia, Yemen, Iraq, and Transjordan got together and asked the Arabs to call off the strike, promising them that Britain would do justice to the Arab people of Palestine.

The Arabs of Palestine listened and again gave Britain more trust than she had earned. They assumed that Britain would find a solution acceptable to the Arabs. The pressure on the British was relaxed, but the Arab governments were now subjected to constant popular pressure in the form of resolutions, demonstrations, and "Palestine Days" to insist that Britain fulfill its promises.

A Recommendation for Partition

The British solution was anticipated in the findings of the Peel Royal Commission published in June 1937. Peel confirmed that the 1936 revolt was caused by the same factors that had brought about the disturbances in 1920, 1921, and 1933, namely, the Arab desire for national independence and the fear of the Jewish national home. The Commission concluded that the Arab claim to self-government and the Jewish national home were mutually exclusive, a fact that both Arabs and Zionists had known all along. To resolve the conflict, the Commission recommended partition of Palestine, creating a Jewish state in the northern and western regions and incorporating the balance of Palestine into the territory of Transjordan.

The Arab Higher Committee rejected the partition plan and opposed any surrender of Palestinian territory to the Zionists. Some Palestinians close to Abdullah were prepared to accept it. A pan-Arab Conference on September 8, 1937, on the other hand, supported the Arab Higher Committee and declared that Palestine was Arab and its preservation was the duty of every Arab.

The Zionist Congress of 1937, not surprisingly, favored the establishment of the Jewish state, and authorized negotiations. In the meantime the Council of the League of Nations had appointed a commission to submit a partition plan of its own. The result was a report in October 1938 that division was practically impossible without creating a Jewish state in which at least 49 percent of the population would be Arab. Meanwhile the British government also came to the conclusion almost at the same time that the political, administrative, and financial difficulties arising from partition would be so great as to make the plan impracticable.

At that point the British decided to call another London conference to discuss the situation with both Arabs and Jews, the latter represented by the Jewish Agency and other outside Zionist leaders. The Arabs were represented by the Higher Committee and by the governments of Egypt, Iraq, Saudi Arabia, and Yemen. The Arabs refused, however, to meet together with the Jewish Agency, which they had still not recognized. The result was that two conferences, one Anglo-Arab and the other Anglo-Jewish, were held in February and March 1939.

A Concession to the Arabs

At the Anglo-Arab Conference the Arabs demanded an

interpretation of the McMahon-Hussein correspondence of 1915-16. The delegates maintained that Palestine was one of those countries to which independence had been promised. The British conceded that the Arab interpretation had "greater force than had appeared hitherto" but declined officially to accept the view. An Anglo-Arab committee studying the McMahon-Hussein correspondence came to the conclusion

> that His Majesty's Government were not free to dispose of Palestine without regard for the wishes and interests of the inhabitants of Palestine and that these statements must be taken into account in any attempt to estimate the responsibilities which — upon any interpretation of the correspondence — His Majesty's Government have incurred towards those inhabitants as a result of the correspondence.[11]

Unofficially, the British had gradually become ready to admit that the concept of the Jewish national home violated the rights of Palestine Arabs. Another White Paper issued in May 1939 admitted as much when it said that it was not part of the British policy "that Palestine should become a Jewish state." Still trying to appease both sides, the British also insisted that the McMahon correspondence did not form "a just basis for the claim that Palestine should be converted into an Arab state."

The British expressed the hope that within ten years an independent Palestine state, in which both Arabs and Jews would share in the government, could be established and the Mandate withdrawn. On matters of immigration, the White Paper announced a policy that related immigration not only to economic capacity but also to political tolerance. Expressing the view that the commitment of the Balfour Declaration had been fulfilled, the British insisted that henceforth Jewish immigration would be limited to what the Arabs could tolerate.

Now it was the Zionists' turn to be furious, and the 1939 World Congress said that the Jewish people would not acquiesce to a minority status. The Arabs too were critical, but at least they were beginning to see some fruits of their long years of agitation.

In Palestine, meanwhile, the violent hostilities of 1936 were

---

[11] *Report of a Committee Set Up to Consider Certain Correspondence Between Sir Henry McMahon and The Sharif of Mecca in 1915 and 1916*, p. A4.

repeating themselves in 1939, with no less than 3315 incidents of violence reported, including 230 attacks of the police, 130 attacks on Jewish settlements, and 94 incidents of sabotage. Arab and Jewish guerrillas were both in operation. At the end of the year 98 Jews were dead and 159 wounded; the Arabs counted 414 dead and 373 wounded; the British 7 dead and 66 wounded. The military court tried 526 persons, 544 Arabs, and 74 Jews. Fifty-five Jews were sentenced to death.

It was the intention of the British to seek approval for its latest White Paper policy from the Council of the League of Nations, but before it could do so war broke out and the League came to an end. With the results of the war, the situation in Palestine became worse than ever; and the British wanted out more than ever. In the end they were forced to place the problem into the lap of the newly formed United Nations.

9. The Claims of the United Nations

> *The resolution adopted by the General Assembly on November 29, 1947 provided not for simple partition with economic union. It envisaged the creation of an Arab state, a Jewish state, and the City of Jerusalem as a corpus separatum under a special international regime administered by the United Nations.* —Count Folke Bernadotte[1]

The White Paper of May 1939 was believed by the British government to be a step leading toward the solution of the Palestine problem; but whatever potential it may have had for the resolution of the conflict, it was soon overtaken and made of no effect by the arrival of World War II, the ensuing Nazi holocaust, and the resulting developments in both the Jewish and Arab worlds. Consequently, after World War II the big powers determined the future of Palestine through a new international forum, the United Nations.

The war created even more Jewish refugees who wanted to go to Palestine and an even stronger Zionist determination to establish the Jewish national home than had been noted in the 1930s. It also increased Arab nationalism and pan-Arabism with the concomitant desire to have Arabs alone, as individual states or as a union of states, determine the course of events in the Arab world. Months before World War II ended it became evident that the Arab states were destined to occupy a key position in the power politics of the post-war period.

Big Power Involvement

Beyond developments in the Jewish and Arab worlds new

[1] Quoted in *The Middle East Conflict: Notes and Documents 1915-1967*, pp. 50-51.

dimensions appeared in the international power play of the big nations. While Palestine presented Britain with a most unwanted burden, she was by no means ready to give up her interests in the Middle East. Indeed, the 1939 White Paper concessions to the Arabs may be interpreted as an attempt to strengthen Britain's hold on, or access to, the Arab Middle East for its strategic geographic value and its oil resources.

Both of these Middle East assets were also the chief reasons why World War II drew both the United States and the Soviet Union more firmly into the Middle East arena. Both states gave ideological reasons for their interest and involvement, but the practical realities were that no aspiring world power could afford to bypass the geopolitical middle of the earth, around which the whole world seemed to turn, and the holy oil indispensable to the smooth running of the imperial wheels.

The coming of the war in September 1939 had the immediate effect of temporary tranquility in Palestine as both Palestinian Jews and Arabs rallied to the British cause. The Jews were initially recruited for military service by the Jewish Agency, but this arrangement was dropped when the Agency objected to the employment of Jews in military duties outside the Middle East and in military units containing both Arabs and Jews. Thus, only 27,000 of the 134,000 Jewish recruits between the ages of 18 and 40 entered the British services. The more numerous Palestinian Arabs provided fewer than half the Jewish number, though they too served the British cause in significant ways.

The reason for the Jewish Agency's desire to keep the troops close to home can be seen in its great unhappiness with the policies of the British Administration after May 1939. The Zionists were determined not to lose any ground — they rather hoped to gain some — in their movement toward the long hoped-for Jewish national home. Any opportunities in that direction arising from the new situation were to be exploited to the maximum. This meant, among other things, an accelerated buildup of the Hagana (defense) forces. The new access to military equipment and training helped to make this possible. By 1946 Hagana numbered 60,000 men, and all were well equipped.

Parallel to this well-armed Hagana organization were two

splinter military groups, the Irgun Zvei Leumi (National Military Organization) with several thousand members, and the Stern Gang (Freedom Fighters of Israel) with several hundred. The Hagana, as the oldest of the groups, dated back to the nineteenth century. It had functioned as a Jewish police and military force since World War I. All three groups had been importing and manufacturing arms before the war, but the war gave all of them opportunity to increase their strength both quantitatively and qualitatively.

Grievances and the Guerrillas

The Zionists had at least two new grievances to which they were ready to give some military expression. The first was the 1939 limitation on immigration, and the second was the curb on land transfers promulgated in 1940. The 1939 White Paper had actually allowed the immigration of 75,000 additional Jews over a five-year period, meaning 15,000 a year. After 1944 the Arabs were to determine the number of Jewish immigrants to be allowed, if any.

The Zionists, however, were not prepared to accept the immediate reduction and a possible long-term stoppage of immigration, and they prepared to defy the British regulation and the Arab veto by bringing Jewish immigrants in illegally. Economic conditions and security needs being what they were, the British could not allow unauthorized admission. Already in 1940 three passenger steamships with 3554 illegal immigrants on board were intercepted off the Palestine coast.

The Zionists also found the new land regulations unacceptable. The 1939 White Paper had already explained that further transfer of Arab land to Jews would have to cease because of the natural growth of the Arab population and because too much land had already been transferred to the Jews. Too great a landless Arab population had already been created and the existing standard of life for Arab cultivators was already too much threatened. Controls were needed, and these came a year later.

In 1940 Land Transfer Regulations divided Palestine into three zones. In each of these different rules were applied. There was complete prohibition of land transfer in the hilly country and the south of Palestine; and no restrictions at all in certain parts of the coastal plain and the area around Jerusalem. In other areas, including such fertile valleys as Esdraelon and such barren areas as Negev, particular land purchases by Jews required the approval of the Palestine government.

Through the Muslim Supreme Council the Arabs approved the regulations, while the Zionists vigorously opposed them, in spite of the fact that in the first year land purchases proceeded at a level only slightly lower than the average for the previous years. The Zionists claimed, as so often before, that restrictions such as the 1940 regulations were against the Mandate and that the Arabs really were the real benefactors of Jewish expansion. They pointed out that the improvements already carried out in Arab farming were largely achieved by cultivators who had freed themselves of debt by selling some land and using the balance to improve themselves on the acreage remaining.

In any event, the apparent turnabout in policy by the British in 1939-40 had the effect of putting the Jews on the offensive. Guerrilla operations, which had been felt already before 1939, now increased on a noticeable scale. Before the year had passed, the British had discovered a hoard of arms and ammunition in one of the settlements and over eighty Jews were arrested for transporting arms and bombs and otherwise engaging in military maneuvers.

In 1942 the Stern Gang came into prominence with a series of murders and robberies, apparently politically motivated, in the Tel Aviv area. In 1943 Hagana was involved in a widespread theft of arms from British forces in the Middle East. During 1944 Irgun Zvei Leumi was responsible for the destruction of much government property.

Official Jewish spokesmen condemned the outrages perpetrated by Irgun as well as Stern Gang but otherwise did nothing to reduce them. The assassination in Cairo of Lord Moyne, British Minister of State for the Middle East, by Stern could not be undone, and the attempt to assassinate the British High Commissioner outside Jerusalem also had not been prevented.

Zionism in the United States

While the British were trying to curb and control Zionism and give preferential treatment to the Arabs, new support for

Zionism was emerging in the United States. As a result of the war, Zionist headquarters had been transferred from London to New York with the effect that both Jews and Americans in general were affected by the Zionist program. These in turn were to have a profound effect on post-war solutions proposed for the Jewish refugee problem and the Palestine problem.

Until the war, the feelings of American Jews on Zionism were ambivalent. Historical studies dating back to 1869 revealed that many American rabbis and scholars were opposed to Zionism on the grounds that Jews were "no longer a nation but a religious community."[2] Similarly, the American Jewish Committee, declaring its opposition to the Balfour Declaration in 1918, said: "The Committee regards it as axiomatic that the Jews of the United States have been established in a permanent home for themselves and their children."[3]

American Jews had very good reasons for opposing Zionism, explained Julius Kohan, a Jew who for twenty-six years had been a representative in the United States Congress from the State of California. Zionism, he said, created a divided allegiance to two countries and two flags. Moreover, Zionism as a doctrine was in conflict with free institutions. Besides, Palestine could never support the millions of Jews supposedly in danger of persecution.

The United States government also had been quite cautious until the early 1940s, in spite of some earlier action supporting the Balfour Declaration. Throughout the twenties and thirties, the United States regarded the Middle East as belonging to the British political and military sphere, even though American missionary-educational-philanthropic enterprises in the Middle East dated as far back as 1819. Economically, however, there were some involvements in the early 1900s, and the determination to tap Middle East oil seems to have been decisive in involving the United States further. Eventually, American oil companies invested some $2.85 billion in the Middle East, which brought a net annual influx of two billion dollars into the United States.

The growth of Zionism in America helped to give a front-

---

[2] Fadhil Zaky Mohamad, *The Evolution of American Policy in Palestine,* p. 39.

[3] *Ibid.*

line place for Palestine on the American agenda. In 1942 —
Zionists now numbered 200,000 — the international Zionist
Congress was held in New York at the Biltmore Hotel. Its
headquarters was transferred from London to New York, and
the Congress advanced what became known as the Biltmore
Program, defining Zionist aims as follows:

> The immediate establishment in Palestine of a Jewish Com-
> monwealth. The rejection of the British White Paper of
> 1939. Unrestricted Jewish immigration to Palestine and
> settlement in it. Control of immigration and settlement by
> the Jewish Agency. Formation and recognition of a Jewish
> military force fighting under its own flag.

Impressive fund-raising campaigns were initiated to help
implement this program. Already from 1927 to 1942 American Zionists had raised 13 million dollars, at least half of all
the money raised for developments in Palestine by world Jewry.
Those amounts were only a fraction of what was to follow.
Besides direct financial aid, American Jews contributed executive and engineering personnel to help develop industry and
commerce in Palestine. Hundreds of Jews from America, some
of them permanent immigrants, were engaged as builders,
storekeepers, brokers, and in a variety of other business pur-
suits in the crossroads country.

The Refugees and Immigration

After the Biltmore Conference, the Zionist Organization of
the United States pressed at all possible levels for the fulfillment of the announced program. The plight of the Jews in
Europe, which now had become international knowledge, was
used as a basis for appeals in both governmental and nongovernmental circles. Although the full extent of Jewish persecution in Europe and the extermination policies of the Nazis
were not to be revealed until after the war, enough was known
to cause considerable alarm in the West. Later the world
learned that about six million Jews or 63.2 percent of European Jewry had died as a result of the war and Nazi occupation policies in twenty countries. The eastern European countries had suffered the heaviest losses (*see Table 10*).[4]

---

[4] *Encyclopedia Americana,* Vol. XVI, p. 129.

TABLE 10
JEWISH DEAD IN EUROPEAN COUNTRIES
IN WORLD WAR II

Country	Jewish Population in 1939	Total Jewish Dead Number	Percent
Poland	3,250,000	2,850,000	87.7
USSR	3,050,000	1,350,000	44.3
Rumania	850,000	425,000	50.0
Germany	504,000	250,000	49.6
Hungary	403,000	200,000	49.6
Czechoslovakia	360,000	280,000	77.8
France	240,000	120,000	50.0
Austria	175,000	70,000	40.0
Lithuania	155,000	135,000	87.1
Holland	120,000	80,000	66.7
Latvia	95,000	86,000	90.5
Yugoslavia	75,000	60,000	80.0
Greece	75,000	62,000	82.7
Belgium	55,000	30,000	54.5
Italy	57,000	12,000	21.1
Bulgaria	50,000	7,000	14.0
Denmark	6,000	2,000	33.3
Estonia	5,000	4,000	80.0
Luxembourg	3,000	2,000	66.7
Norway	2,000	1,000	50.0
Total	9,530,000	6,026,000	63.2

In the United States and in Great Britain, there was increased agitation for the opening of immigration doors for the Jews. Strangely enough, the doors to be opened were not in the United Kingdom and in the United States but in Palestine. Already in January 1944 the United States Congress expressed itself in favor of unrestricted immigration to Palestine and the establishment of a Jewish state. A more liberal immigration policy for the United States, however, was turned down by Congress, in spite of the repeated appeals by Presidents Roosevelt and Truman.

The British Labour Party, taking a cue from the action

in the United States, passed a resolution suggesting that efforts be made to encourage the Arabs to move out of Palestine and make room for the Jews. Some sectors of the Hebrew press denounced such a strong resolution and expressed the hope that Zionist aims could be achieved without displacing or harming the Arab population.

The 1944 Labour Party resolution, however, reflected the direction of Labour government policy following its election to power in 1945. Encouraged by Labour sentiments, the World Zionist Conference, meeting in London in August, 1945, endorsed the petition regarding the Jewish homeland which the Jewish Agency in Palestine was presenting to the British government. The petition included the following requests:

1. That a decision to establish Palestine as a Jewish State be announced immediately.
2. That the Jewish Agency be invested with all necessary authority to bring to Palestine as many Jews as may be found necessary and possible to settle, and to develop, fully and speedily, all the resources of the country, especially land and power resources.
3. That an international loan and other help be given for the transfer of the first million Jews to Palestine, and for the economic development of the country.
4. That reparations in kind from Germany be granted to the Jewish people for the rebuilding of Palestine, and, as a first instalment, that all German property in Palestine be used for the resettlement of Jews from Europe.
5. That international facilities be provided for the exist and transit of all Jews who wish to settle in Palestine.[5]

The overtures being made to the new British Prime Minister, Clement Attlee, by the Zionist Congress were at the same time being reinforced by messages from President Truman, who was encouraging Attlee to admit 100,000 Jews to Palestine to alleviate the situation in Europe. Truman, it must be said, was much more susceptible to Zionist pressures than Roosevelt had been. Just two months before his death the latter had assured the King of Saudi Arabia that he would make no move hostile to the Arab people.

The Founding of the Arab League

In the meantime, the Arabs had also been encouraged in

---

[5] *Great Britain and Palestine 1915-1945*, pp. 139-40.

their nationalism and pan-Arabism by the British and to a lesser degree by the United States. Both were recognizing increasingly the importance of Middle East oil deposits to the industrial growth of the West. Thus, while the Jews were being encouraged to make Palestine their home, the Arabs were being advised to unify, to modernize, and to remain in close relation with the West.

The British, remembering their pledge to Hussein in 1916 regarding the establishment of an Arab state or a confederation of states, encouraged the Arabs to move in the direction of complete independence. The Arab leaders did not have to be prodded. Egypt, Iraq, Transjordan, Saudi Arabia, and Yemen already had measures of independence, although all stood in some relationship to Great Britain. The next step necessary was to secure also the independence of Syria and Lebanon from the French, and this was accomplished in 1941. The consolidation of pan-Arabism was achieved after two years of negotiations and the formation of the Arab League in Cairo in March of 1945.

External unity might have been achieved somewhat earlier if the rivalries within the Arab world would not have prevented disagreement on Palestine. That Palestine should be an Arab state was assumed, of course, but with which of the Arab power blocks the state would be allied was another question. Abdullah of Transjordan saw Palestine and Transjordan as a nucleus of the Kingdom of Greater Syria to be ruled by the Hashemites. Iraq, on the other hand, saw Arab unity only in terms of a Greater Syria under an Iraqi hegemony, which would exclude Egypt or Saudi Arabian influence. Saudi Arabia was reluctant to accept any situation that would give additional influence either to Iraq or Transjordan. And Egypt was likewise reluctant to accept any growth of power east of the Suez that was not Egyptian in orientation. Eventually, however, the members of the Arab League agreed sufficiently to include some paragraphs on policy regarding Palestine in the pact signed in Cairo. The policy recognized the Arab Higher Committee of Palestine as a voting member of the League and gave its position on Palestine as follows:

> At the termination of the last great war, the Arab countries were detached from the Ottoman empire. These included Palestine, vilayat of that empire, which became autonomous, depending on no other power. The Treaty of Lausanne pro-

claimed that the question of Palestine was the concern of the interested parties, and although she was not in a position to direct her own affairs, the covenant of the League of Nations in 1919 settled her regime on the basis of the acknowledgement of her independence. Her international existence and independence are therefore a matter of no doubt from the legal point of view, just as there is no doubt about the independence of the other Arab countries. Although the external aspects of that independence are not apparent owing to force of circumstance, this should not stand in the way of her participation in the work of the council of the League.[6]

Anglo-American Studies

Meanwhile, the British government under Mr. Attlee was not immediately prepared to follow the suggestion of President Truman that 100,000 immigrant certificates be granted to displaced European Jews for resettlement in Palestine. His Majesty's government, therefore, sought the agreement of the United States to the appointment of an Anglo-American Committee of Inquiry to examine the political and social conditions in Palestine as they related to the problem of Jewish immigration and settlement, the position of Jews in the European countries and the opinions of leading Arabs and Jews.

The committee of twelve members had a time limit of 120 days and began its work in Washington on January 4, 1946. Its unanimous report was signed at Lausanne on April 20 and recommended that the future of Palestine should be based on three principles: 1) that Jews should not dominate Arabs and that Arabs should not dominate Jews in Palestine; 2) that Palestine should be neither a Jewish state nor an Arab state; 3) that the form of government ultimately established should under international guarantees fully protect and preserve the interests of the Christian, Muslim and Jewish faiths in Palestine as a "Holy Land."

Partition of the land, as had been recommended in 1937 as a solution to the Palestine problem, was rejected outright by the committee, since such a measure would only lead to civil strife. The continuation of the Mandate was recommended until such a time as self-governing institutions could be es-

---

[6] *A Survey of Palestine: Prepared in December 1945 and January 1946 for the Information of the Anglo-American Committee of Inquiry,* pp. 15ff.

tablished. To this the Arabs agreed. Then, however, the Anglo-American Committee endorsed practical measures that the Arabs knew militated against the theoretical position that the Jews should not achieve a dominant position. It was recommended, for instance, that the land-transfer regulations of 1940 be revoked and that the Mandate government authorize 100,000 immigration certificates immediately.

President Truman was delighted with the report of the Anglo-American Committee of Inquiry. He expressed pleasure that 100,000 Jews would be admitted to Palestine immediately and that the demands of the White Paper of 1939 had actually been rescinded by the report. The Prime Minister of Great Britain was not quite that enthusiastic. He insisted that the illegal military formations in Palestine be disarmed as a precondition for the admission of 100,000 immigrants.

The report was now given to further examination by British and American officials. Meeting in London during June and July, they came to the conclusion that Palestine should not be partitioned, but rather divided into two provinces, one Arab and one Jewish, with a central government administered by the British High Commissioner. The central government would have exclusive authority in matters of defense, foreign relations, customs and excise, and initially also in domestic law and order. The provinces would have a legislature and an executive, and a wide range of functions including control over land regulations and immigration. The Jewish province should be the entire area on which Jews have already settled, together with a considerable area between and around these settlements.

This arrangement assumed that the Arab province would have full power to exclude all the Jewish immigrants, while the Jewish province would be able to admit as many immigrants as its government desired. These conditions should make possible the immediate admission of 100,000 Jewish immigrants into Palestine and continued immigration thereafter. On July 25, 1946, His Majesty's government approved in principle the policy recommended by this group of British and American officials as a basis for negotiation with both the Arabs and the Jews.

The League in London

The Arab League, meeting in Syria to consider the report

of the Anglo-American Committee, was not enthusiastic about the Committee's conclusions. On the contrary, the League asked the British government to decide the Palestine issue in conformity with the United Nations Charter. The Arab states were assuming, and not incorrectly, that the Charter, with its emphasis on the self-determination of peoples, was in their favor. Consequently, they suggested the calling of a conference to prepare an Arab proposal for the fall session of the United Nations General Assembly.

The United Nations was in 1946 only one year old. A by-product of World War II, the UN was determined to be an effective instrument of international peace and security and to save mankind from the scourge of war. In doing so, the UN resolved to respect, and promote respect for, human rights and fundamental freedoms. However, it was still young and weak, and the victorious powers of World War II, including Britain and the United States, continued to act independently of it in a number of questions, including Palestine.

Since the British government had at various times given pledges to consult the interested parties before reaching a decision on Palestine, the idea of a conference was accepted, and the London Conference of 1946-47 came into being on September 9. However, only the representatives of the independent Arab states and the Secretary-General of the Arab League attended. Neither the Jews nor the Palestinian Arabs accepted the invitation.

The Arab delegates soon made it known that they were in complete opposition to the provinces plan for Palestine. Asked to present their alternative, they outlined a proposal that contained the following main features:

1. Palestine should be a unitary state with a permanent majority of Arabs. Independence would come after a short period of transition (two or three years) under the British Mandate.

2. Within this unitary state, Jews who had acquired Palestinian citizenship (for which the qualification would be 10 years residence in the country) should have full civil rights and equality with all other citizens of Palestine.

3. Special safeguards should be provided to protect the religious and cultural rights of the Jewish community.

4. The sanctity of the holy places should be guaranteed and

safeguards provided for freedom of religious practice throughout Palestine.

5. The Jewish community should be entitled to a number of seats in the legislative assembly proportionate to the number of Jewish citizens in Palestine, subject to the provision that in no case would the number of Jewish representatives exceed one-third of the total number of members.

6. All legislation concerning immigration and the transfer of land should require the consent of the Arabs in Palestine as expressed by a majority of the Arab members of the legislative assembly.

7. The guarantees concerning the holy places should be alterable only with the consent of the United Nations; and the safeguards provided for the Jewish community would be alterable only with the consent of a majority of the Jewish members of the legislative assembly.[7]

The representatives of the Arab states wanted the new government to come into being immediately. The first step would be to establish a provisional government consisting of seven Arabs and three Jews by nomination of the High Commissioner. This government in turn would then arrange for the election of a constituent assembly, and the assembly in turn would within six months draw up a detailed constitution with the above general principles in mind.

Should the assembly fail in its task within the prescribed time, the provisional government would itself promulgate a constitution, and the scheme could then proceed to be implemented even in the face of a Jewish boycott. After the adoption of a constitution, a legislative assembly would be elected and the first head of the independent Palestine state would be appointed, receiving his authority immediately from the High Commissioner.

The Zionists in Basel

The London Conference was suspended to allow certain representatives to attend the Assembly of the United Nations. During this recess the Zionist Congress met in Basel. This Congress was violently opposed to the provincial autonomy plan because it would deny settlement in other parts of Pal-

---

[7] *The Political History of Palestine Under British Administration: Memorandum by His Britannic Majesty's Government Presented in 1947 to the United Nations Special Committee on Palestine*, pp. 15ff.

estine and deny complete autonomy even in the territory al-
located to the Jews.

The Congress also expressed opposition to a United Nations
trusteeship taking the place of the Mandate. As far as the
Zionists were concerned, a further delay in establishing a
Jewish state was totally unacceptable. Unless there was some
immediate movement in that direction, the Zionists could not,
they said, take part in the London Conference. Their own
political aims were expressed in the following terms:

1. The establishment of Palestine as a Jewish commonwealth
   integrated into the structure of the democratic world.
2. The opening of the gates of Palestine to unrestricted
   Jewish immigration.
3. The control of immigration into Palestine to rest in the
   hands of the Jewish Agency, which agency should also
   have the necessary authority for the upbuilding of the
   country.[8]

The Anglo-Arab Conference resumed its work in January
1947, and this time a parallel Anglo-Jewish Conference was
held simultaneously. The British, recognizing how far apart
the Arab and Jewish positions were, made the suggestion that
the British trusteeship be extended five more years in order
to prepare the country for independence, granting a considerable amount of local autonomy during this period. Within
four years a constituent assembly would be elected and, if a
majority of Arab representatives and a majority of Jewish
representatives could reach agreement, an independent state
would be established immediately. If agreement could not be
reached, the trusteeship council of the United Nations would
advise on future procedure.

Since the welfare of Palestine as a whole had to be taken
into consideration, Jewish immigration could not be unlimited
and only 96,000 should be admitted in the first two years of
the trusteeship agreement. These British proposals, however,
were not well received. Both the Jewish Agency and the Arab
delegation, which now also included a representative of the
Palestine Arab Higher Executive, rejected them.

Illegalities in Palestine

In the meantime, Zionist guerrilla activities, acts of terrorism,

[8] *Ibid.,* p. 39.

and sabotage had increased dramatically. An average of two British policemen or soldiers were being killed every day. The targets of the attacks included the central prison in Jerusalem, a coast guard station, the radar station on Mount Carmel, police installations, air fields, and railway lines. Jewish forces also saw to it that illegal immigrants now arriving in large numbers (*see Table 11*)[9] disembarked successfully.

TABLE 11
SUMMARY OF "ILLEGAL IMMIGRATION" TO PALESTINE IN 1946*

Date	Number
January 19	908
March 26	240
March 27	733
May 13	1,662
June 26	1,278
July 2	1,001
July 29	2,760
July 31	497
August 12	1,293
August 13	262
August 15	784
September 3	997
September 22	605
October 19	916
October 31	1,279
November 26	3,914

The peak of terrorism came on July 22, 1946 when a wing of the King David Hotel in Jerusalem was blown up by Jewish terrorists. The Hotel housed the British secretariat and part of the military headquarters, and in the explosion 83 public servants and five other civilians were killed. Two days

[9] Government of Palestine, *Supplementary Memorandum by the Government of Palestine, Including Notes on Evidence Given to the United Nations' Special Committee on Palestine up to the 12 July, 1947*, pp. 50ff.

* Most were forwarded by ships of the British Royal Navy. Apparently what one British law made illegal another made possible.

later the British issued a White Paper on terrorism in Palestine, in which the following main conclusions were recorded:

1. The Hagana and its associated forces working under the political control of prominent members of the Jewish Agency have been engaged in carefully planned use of violence and sabotage under the name of the Jewish resistance movement.
2. The national military organization and the Stern Group had during the preceding eight or nine months been co-operating with the Hagana in certain of these operations.
3. The illegal radio transmitter calling itself the Voice of Israel, working under the general direction of the Jewish Agency, had been supporting the terrorist groups.

Terrorism continued in spite of the accusations, and in February the demolition of an officers' club in Jerusalem cost the lives of 20 persons, including military police and civilians. At one settlement, a week's search uncovered 33 caches of weapons, including 10 machine guns, 325 rifles, 96 mortars, 5,267 mortar bombs, 5,017 grenades, 800 pounds of explosives, and 425,000 rounds of small arms and ammunition.[10]

The Reluctant British Decision

On February 18, 1947, shortly after the failure of the London Conference, the foreign secretary made a speech in the British House of Commons admitting that His Majesty's government was faced with an irreconcilable conflict between 1,200,000 Arabs and 600,000 Jews now in Palestine and that the Mandate had proven itself to be unworkable. The foreign secretary said, in part:

> We have, therefore, reached the conclusion that the only course now open to us is to submit the problem to the judgement of the United Nations. We intend to place before them an historical account of the way in which His Majesty's government has discharged their trust in Palestine over the last 25 years. We shall explain that the Mandate has proven to be unworkable in practice, and that the obligations undertaken to the two communities in Palestine have been shown to be irreconcilable. We shall describe the various proposals which have been put forward for dealing with the situation, namely, the Arab plan, the Zionist aspirations, so far as we have been able to ascertain them, the proposals of the Anglo-

10 *Ibid.*, p. 58.

American Committee and the various proposals, which we ourselves have put forward. We shall then ask the United Nations to consider our report, and to recommend the settlement of the problem. We do not intend ourselves to recommend any particular solution.[11]

The British admission was a signal to the Zionists that they might be in reach of their goal of establishing a Jewish state in Palestine. Terrorism and sabotage thus increased dramatically, as did the arrival of illegal immigrants. In March alone nearly five thousand illegal immigrants arrived, and this rate was continued in succeeding months.

No sooner had the British made their announcement in the House of Commons when the Council of the Arab League met for the seventh time in Cairo, again to discuss the Palestine question. The League declared that the question might very well go to the United Nations but that it should be discussed only on the basis of Palestine's becoming an independent country. More financial support was also given to the Arab Higher Committee, and the League threatened to review Arab economic relations with Great Britain and the United States if these countries would not promote the independence of Palestine on democratic grounds.

When the specially called session of the United Nations General Assembly opened on April 28, the Arab governments of Egypt, Iraq, Syria, Lebanon, Saudi Arabia requested the inclusion of an additional item on the agenda. At that point the agenda included only the British request, namely, "the termination of the mandate over Palestine and the declaration of its independence." The reasons for this request, the Arab governments said, was that the problem before the General Assembly was not the finding of more facts but the establishment and application of certain principles, such as those espoused in the Covenant of the League and the Charter of the United Nations.

These principles, said the League, were inconsistent with the Palestine Mandate and with the Balfour Declaration, which were based on expediency, power politics, local interests, and local pressures. The Arabs also insisted that the problem of the Jews — there were still many Jewish refugees and dis-

---

[11] *The Political History of Palestine,* p. 40.

placed persons in European camps — was a separate problem from that of Palestine.

The United Nations, however, did not see fit to put the Arab request on the agenda. The proposal was soundly defeated, with 15 members in favor, 24 opposed, and 10 abstaining. Instead, the United Nations Committee on Palestine (UNSCOP) was established to study the whole future of Palestine. The committee included representatives from Australia, Canada, Czechoslovakia, Guatemala, India, Iran, the Netherlands, Peru, Sweden, Uruguay, and Yugoslavia.

Another Committee, Another Study

In mid-June UNSCOP arrived in Palestine and conducted 36 meetings as an integral part of its inquiry. The Arab Higher Committee had cabled the United Nations Secretary General that they would not cooperate with the Committee, since it felt that UNSCOP was predisposed toward accepting a Zionist solution. The Arab Higher Committee also made it clear that it was not opposed to giving due consideration to world religious interests; however, these were a separate question from the status of Palestine. The natural rights of the people of Palestine were self-evident on the basis of the principles of the United Nations Charter and need not be subject to another investigation. Again the Committee asked that the issues of Palestine and of the Jewish refugees be separated.

In the minds of the Jews, however, Palestine and the Jewish refugee problem were intimately interwoven. After visiting the refugee camps of Europe, UNSCOP reported seeing posters stating "Palestine — a Jewish State of Jewish People." Large pictorial designs in the camps showed Jews from eastern Europe marching toward Palestine, which was shown in a much larger area than the geographical limits of the Mandate. Children in the various camp schools were being taught detailed historical and geographical knowledge of Palestine.

The UNSCOP report submitted on August 31, 1947 included two proposals. The majority proposal, supported by Canada, Czechoslovakia, Guatemala, the Netherlands, Peru, Sweden and Uruguay, was a plan of partition with economic union. Palestine should be divided into an Arab state, a Jewish state, and the city of Jerusalem, which was to be placed under an international trusteeship administered by the United Nations. The Arab and Jewish states should become independent after a transitional period of two years beginning September 1, 1947, during which time the United Kingdom would progressively transfer the administration of Palestine to the United Nations. The constitutions of the respective states should contain provisions for the preservation of and free access to all the holy places. During the transitional period and for three years, Jewish immigration into Palestine would be permitted, depending upon the absorptive capacity of the country. Such capacity should be determined by an international commission set up for the period of three years and composed of three Arabs, three Jews, and three United Nations representatives.

The minority proposal, supported by India, Iran, and Yugoslavia, included a plan for a federal state that would comprise an Arab state and a Jewish state, with Jerusalem as its capital. The federal state would have full authority with regard to national defense, foreign relations, immigration, currency, taxation for federal purposes, foreign and interstate waterways, transport and communications, copyrights and patents. The Arab and Jewish states would enjoy full powers of local self-government and would have authority over education, taxation for local purposes, the right of residence, commercial licenses, land permits, grazing rights, interstate migration, settlement, police, punishment of crime, social institutions and services, public housing, public health, local roads, agriculture and local industries.

The UNSCOP report was submitted to an *ad hoc* committee on the Palestine question, who debated it vigorously from October 4-16. During the debate, seventeen proposals were submitted to the committee including those of the Jewish Agency and the Arab states.

The Zionist Lobby

The Zionists were enthusiastic about the majority plan because it fully accorded with their aspirations for a Jewish state, even though they would like to have seen this state larger than recommended by the partition plan. However, they were prepared to accept it as "the indispensable minimum." The rest would come later.

The Arab governments rejected both the majority and minority plans outright, because in their opinion they both

violated the Charter of the United Nations and the democratic right of a people to self-determination. They declared
that they were in favor of an "independent unitary state em-
bracing all of Palestine in which the rights of the minority
would be scrupulously guarded."[12] Supported by the World
Zionist Organization, the Jewish Agency was most aggressive
in promoting its point of view and supplied the United Nations and its members with volumes of documentation to support its claims for the establishment of a Jewish state in the
whole of Palestine. The Jewish appeals were based on what
was called "the agony of the Jews" in Europe, as well as the
plight of Jews in Muslim lands, the Balfour Declaration, the
League of Nations Mandate and the findings of the Anglo-
American Palestine Committee. The Agency also submitted
that the land of Palestine could support many thousands, if
not millions of people, and that the potential for Jewish mass
immigration into Palestine was very large. Besides, Palestine
would contribute to the welfare of the entire Arab world.
The economic achievements of the Jews in Palestine to date,
which were considerable, were presented as evidence of the
capacity of both Palestine and the Jews. On the land already
under cultivation, Palestine could easily settle 2,800,000 persons, and the water resources were such that millions of additional *dunams* could be irrigated to support additional thousands. So said the Agency.

Much sympathy for the Zionist cause was now apparent in
America. The plight of the Jews in Europe now resulted in
an attempt to redress earlier wrongs occasioned by European
anti-Semitism. The American conscience wanted to do right
by the Jews, as the British had done in the previous century
by promising a homeland to the Jews. Just as British Christianity provided support for English interests in Palestine and
the Middle East in the nineteenth century, so American Christianity now became the ideological and emotional wellspring
of support for the Middle East aspirations of America in general and of Zionism in particular.

The Christian Palestine Committee

Most of the Christian support for Jews and Zionism and

---

[12] Leila S. Kadi, *Arab Summit Conference on the Palestine Problem,
1936-50; 1964-68,* pp. 44-45.

much of the Zionist message to Christians were channeled through the American Christian Palestine Committee (ACPC). The exploitation of Christian sympathy for the Zionist cause had begun immediately after the extraordinary Zionist conference in New York's Biltmore Hotel in 1942. Field workers were dispatched across the nation to build local chapters of what was then known as the American Palestine Committee, the forerunner of the ACPC.

By 1948 the American Zionist Emergency Council was spending up to $150,000 annually for work among non-Jews, meaning Christians, and local Zionist Organizations of America chapters were exhorted to provide their Christian Zionist neighbors with funds, clerical services, and moral support. The goal was "to crystallize the sympathy of Christian America for our cause, that it may be of service as the opportunity arises."[13]

Christians by the tens of thousands rallied to the support of the American Christian Palestine Committee, believing that the destiny of the Jews was of immediate and urgent concern to the Christian conscience. The Zionists reminded the Christians that the Old Testament supported the return of present-day Jews from their exile to their national home in Palestine. It was not difficult to convince many that the cause of Zionism was scriptural, because hundreds of Christian teachers and preachers were associating Christian fulfillment with the return of the Jews to Palestine.

The increase of ideological and emotional support for the Zionist cause made it relatively easy for the Zionists to translate empathy into favorable public opinion and political support, and American decisions in turn affected the positions of other nation states. President Truman later admitted the pressure of the Zionist leaders, and in his memoirs he said:

> I do not think I have ever had as much pressure and propaganda aimed at the White House as I had in this instance. The persistence of a few of the extreme Zionist leaders — actuated by political motives and engaging in political threats — disturbed me and annoyed me. Individuals and groups asked me usually in rather quarrelsome and emotional ways, to stop the Arabs, to keep the British from supporting the

[13] Humphrey Walz, *The Story of the American Palestine Committee*, p. 3.

Arabs, to furnish American soldiers, to do this, that, and the other.[14]

The President was opposed in his leanings toward the Zionist cause by a number of close colleagues, including Secretary of State Dean Acheson, who did not believe that Palestine was a solution to the Jewish refugee problem nor that America's best interests would be represented by following the Zionist line. In his memoirs he explained his position as follows:

> ... The number that could be absorbed by Arab Palestine without creating a grave political problem would be inadequate, and to transform the country into a Jewish state capable of receiving a million or more immigrants would vastly exacerbate the political problem and imperil not only America but all Western interests in the Near East. From Justice Brandeis, whom I revered, and from Felix Frankfurter, my intimate friend, I had learned to understand, but not to share, the mystical emotion of the Jews to return to Palestine and end the Diaspora. In urging Zionism as an American government policy they had allowed, so I thought, their emotion to obscure the totality of American interests.[15]

In spite of the opposition, President Truman was "sucked in," to use Acheson's words, and thereafter he himself exerted pressure on members of the United Nations or had such pressure exerted in his name. Secretary of Defense James Forrestal claimed in his diary that the methods used to get votes in the General Assembly "bordered closely on to scandal"; and Sumner Welles, a former Undersecretary of State, wrote:

> By direct order from the White House, every form of pressure direct or indirect was brought to bear by American officials upon those countries outside the Muslim world that were known to be either uncertain or opposed to partition. Representatives of intermediaries were employed by the White House to make sure that the necessary majority would at length be secured.[16]

Other Jewish leaders, however, were deeply troubled by the Zionist program both before and after the UN decision. A conference of American rabbis had announced, in what became known as the Pittsburgh Platform, that Jews were "a

---

[14] Sami Hadawi, *Palestine Before the United Nations,* p. 77.

[15] *Present at the Creation,* p. 169.

[16] Hadawi, *loc. cit.*

religious community" and not a nation.[17] The American Council of Judaism likewise vigorously opposed the establishment of "a national Jewish state in Palestine or anywhere else" and dissented "from all these related doctrines that stress the racialism, the nationalism, and the theoretical homelessness of Jews."[18]

Others, like Rabbi Isserman, expressed the belief that political Zionism was "a liability to prophetic religion" and that the return of the Jews to Palestine as a fulfillment of prophecy was not a Jewish but a Protestant idea.[19] The Jewish biochemist I. M. Rabinowitch foresaw that "a Jewish state in Palestine meant war" and that the alleged sanctuary for Jews "could readily become a death trap."[20] Others like Morris Cohen identified Zionism with tribalism, while men like Yehezkel Kaufmann saw in political Zionism "the ruin of the soul."[21]

Some Jewish leaders clearly saw how unacceptable and unadaptable a Jewish state must be to the Arab world. *New York Times* publisher A. H. Sulzberger expressed the belief that Arabs could easily accept as many as 350,000 Jewish refugees but that they could never make room for a Jewish state.[22] Jabir Shibli explained the Arab viewpoint that a Jewish state would be a misfit in the Middle East thus:

> Palestine is the heart and center of the Arab world, extending as it does from the Red Sea to the Mediterranean. Palestine is the keynote state of the coming Arab union. Its settlement by Jews would be equivalent to the occupation of Pennsylvania by France or Russia. Palestine is the only bridge between the 20 million Arabs of western Asia and the 40 million Arabs of northern Africa. Its conversion into a Jewish state would sever the Arab world and prevent its unification. It is no wonder that the Arabs are determined at any cost to keep Palestine in the Arab fold.[23]

All of these warnings, however, did not discourage Zionists

---

[17] *Papers on Palestine III: A Collection of Articles by Distinguished Jews Who Oppose Political Zionism*, p. 66.

[18] *Ibid.*, p. 64.

[19] *Ibid.*, p. 59.

[20] In a speech before the Canadian Club in Montreal; *ibid.*, p. 62.

[21] Michael Selzer (ed.), *Zionism Reconsidered.*

[22] In a speech before the Mitzpah congregation, Chattanooga, Tennessee; *ibid.*

[23] *Ibid.*, p. 44.

in America or in Palestine, and the Zionist movement advanced, to use the words of Rabbi Elmer Berger, "like the march of a ruthless Goliath."[24]

While the Zionists were presenting their case inside and outside the United Nations directly and indirectly, the Arabs too were making a last attempt to impress the world community with their position. Strangely enough, they did not exploit the economic power represented by their petroleum resources to obtain their objectives, and in the end they lost out.

The Decision to Partition

When the president of the General Assembly in the United Nations called for a vote on the recommendations of the *ad hoc* committee on November 29, 1947, the result was 33 in favor of the majority partition plan with economic union, 13 against, and 10 abstentions. The two-thirds majority was obtained only by some remarkable lobbying. At the last moment eight doubtful members were persuaded by the partition lobby. The eastern European Communist countries at this point were very much sympathetic to the Jews, because it was in eastern Europe where so many had died at the hands of the Nazis. One newspaper correspondent commented:

> The general feeling among the delegates was that regardless of its merits and demerits and the joint support given by the USSR and the USA the partition scheme would have been carried in no other city than New York. ... The strength of the Jewish influence in Washington had been a revelation.[25]

Those who voted in favor of partition were Australia, Belgium, Bolivia, Brazil, Byelorussian SSR, Canada, Costa Rica, Czechoslovakia, Denmark, Dominican Republic, Ecuador, France, Guatemala, Haiti, Iceland, Liberia, Luxembourg, the Netherlands, New Zealand, Nicaragua, Norway, Panama, Paraguay, Peru, Philippines, Poland, Sweden, Ukrainian SSR, Union of South Africa, USSR, United States of America, Uruguay and Venezuela. Voting against were Afghanistan, Cuba, Egypt, Greece, India, Iran, Iraq, Lebanon, Pakistan, Saudi Arabia, Syria, Turkey and Yemen. Those who abstained included Argentina, Chile, China, Colombia, El Salvador, Ethi-

---

[24] *Ibid.,* p. 66.
[25] George E. Kirk, *A Short History of the Middle East,* p. 222.

Map 9 — *Palestine According to United Nations Partition Plan*

opia, Honduras, Mexico, United Kingdom, and Yugoslavia.

After the partition resolution had been passed, the Jewish Agency for Palestine indicated its acceptance, while the Arab Higher Committee and the Arab delegates from Arab countries said that they would oppose the implementation of the partition plan. Their reasons were those given many times before. They believed that the plan would be unworkable and that it would bring perpetual war to the area. They also believed that the United Nations had no jurisdiction to partition countries and that the action was illegal, undemocratic, and contrary to the principle of self-determination contained in the Charter.

The Arabs also objected to the nature of the partition itself. The partition resolution allotted the proposed Jewish state 56 percent of the total area of Palestine at a time when Jewish ownership of land did not exceed six percent of the total area of the country and only nine percent of the area of the proposed Jewish state (*see Map 9*). Besides, the Jewish portion of the land, except for the Negev desert, was better than the Arab portion, which consisted largely of arid and mountainous regions with little irrigation possibilities and very sparse cultivable areas. Perhaps the greatest objection lay in the fact that the Jewish state would include within its territories as a permanent minority almost as many Arabs as Jews (*see Table 12*).[26]

According to the partition resolution passed by the United Nations General Assembly, the independent Arab and Jewish states and the special international regime for the city of Jerusalem (*see Map 10*) should come into effect two months after the evacuation of the armed forces of the Mandatory power, but in any case not later than October 1, 1948. The British set August 1 as the date for their final withdrawal of Mandatory power. With that announcement, both the Jews and Arabs determined that their cause would win, and in the ensuing contest the Jews pressed their claim most forcefully and most successfully.

---

[26] See UN General Assembly Resolution No. 181(11), November 29, 1947; Hadawi, *op. cit.,* p. 81.

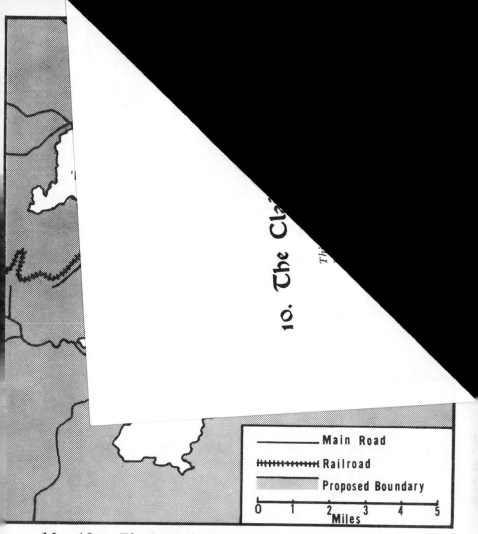

Map 10 — *The Jerusalem International Zone*

TABLE 12
SUMMARY OF UN PALESTINE PARTITION PLAN

State	Land-Area		Population	
	Sq. Miles	Percent	Jews	Arabs
Jerusalem	67	.65	100,000	105,000
Arab	4,476	42.88	10,000	725,000
Jewish	5,893	56.47*	498,000	497,000

* Including large desert area, the Negev.

...ims of Israel

...rty years of struggle under the British Mandate, fifteen years of heartache over the plight of Jewry in Hitler's Europe, and two thousand years of longing for a homeland had ended. Civilization . . . had invested the Jewish people with nationhood. —Frank Gervasi[1]

The last remaining legal obstacle to the creation of a national Jewish state had been removed by the United Nations Partition Resolution, but there were other problems to be overcome. Foremost of these was the unwillingness of the Palestinian Arabs and the Arab states to recognize this international authorization of a new state. As they saw it, the legalization of Israel meant dehumanization for the Arabs. Thus it happened that the United Nations, far from solving a problem, created a situation that resulted in three major wars in twenty years, none of which solved the problem.

Preparations for Statehood

Jews throughout the world hailed the United Nations decision with joy, and there was dancing in the streets of Tel Aviv and Jerusalem, but there was also a strong awareness that many problems lay ahead. Chaim Weizmann, who later became the first president of Israel, recognized that Arabs would not easily accept the loss of their political independence, but he expressed the belief that they would feel themselves "largely compensated for by what they gain in other respects."[2]

---

[1] *The Case for Israel*, p. 76.

[2] *The Jewish Case: Statements and Memoranda: Before the Anglo-American Committee of Inquiry on Palestine as Presented by the Jewish Agency for Palestine*, p. 27.

Other Jews like Ben-Gurion, the first Prime Minister of Israel, promised that Arabs and other non-Jewish neighbors would be treated on "the basis of absolute equality as if they are Jews," but then he added a disclaimer reminiscent of earlier British vacillation between the two viewpoints:

> When we say Jewish independence or a Jewish state, we mean Jewish country, a Jewish soil, Jewish labor, we mean Jewish economy, Jewish industry, Jewish sea. We mean Jewish language schools, culture; we mean Jewish safety, security, independence, complete independence as for any other people.[3]

In Palestine itself specific preparation for the establishment of the Jewish state had been in progress even while the UN was still debating the Palestine question. The Jewish community had for years already been organized into a quasi-government with its own health, educational, social, and military defense services. An Elected Assembly, a quasi-parliament, had been functioning for some time, and its cabinet, the National Council of Executives, was together with the Jewish Agency administering those aspects of communal organization not attended to by the British.

The administration was efficient, because "within the Jewish community there was a large body of individuals trained and experienced in European government, the mandatory offices, and the Jewish national institutions."[4] Given the Zionist goal and the human resources to engineer its achievement, it is not too surprising that the Agency and the Executives were ready for the UN decision. Plans had been drawn up for the maintenance of essential government services after the departure of the British. Plans had been laid for a constitution and a legal code for the new Jewish state.

As the UN announced its decision, the Elected Assembly decreed the total mobilization of Jewish manpower. Hagana was converted into a regular army; and all possible efforts, both legal and illegal, were now made to increase Jewish immigration, with special attention to the immigration of the young. Military preparedness was attended to in other ways as well, as Fred J. Khouri has observed:

> Jewish as well as non-Jewish veterans of Allied armies —

---

[3] *The Jewish Case*, pp. 66-72.
[4] Don Peretz, *Israel and the Palestine Arabs*, p. 6.

pilots, engineers, naval experts, and the like — were hastily recruited. Arms and military equipment were desperately sought from various sources. New Jewish villages in strategic areas were hurriedly set up.[5]

The Palestinian Arabs, on the other hand, were much less equipped and ready for the end of the British administration. They had no quasi-government and few elected administrators. They had no experience in self-rule, though their national sentiment was strong. Thus their reaction was similar to what it had been in the past thirty years. While the Jews rejoiced on November 29, 1947, the Arabs demonstrated and started a general strike. Fighting broke out in Jerusalem, Haifa, Tel Aviv, and Jaffa, and this fighting spread. In two months (from December 1, 1947 to February 1, 1948) there were nearly three thousand casualties, the majority of them Arabs (1,462). The Jews had lost 1,106 and the British 181.

The United Nations meanwhile was helpless to ameliorate the strife between the two communities. A decision to implement peace in Palestine had been made, but implementing it peacefully was quite another matter. The Palestine Commission, which was set up to implement the resolution, could not get the Arab Higher Executive to cooperate at all, and the British were also less than enthusiastic about partitioning Palestine. Britain even announced that she would not share her power with the Commission. The British would leave Palestine on May 15 and the Commission could enter only two weeks before that. The result was that only one representative of the Commission entered Palestine, and there was very little he could do except to prepare a number of reports.

The first special report of the Palestine Commission of February 24, 1948, advised the UN that the Arabs were and would be resisting the partition resolution by force and that no peaceful implementation was in sight. By that time the US State Department had also come to the conclusion that the partition plan was unworkable and that the US should take steps to have the partition proposal reconsidered.

President Truman, however, was of a different mind. On March 19 the US took the position that the UN might enforce a temporary trusteeship after the departure of the British; the Zionists, however, did not approve of that idea, and

---

[5] *The Arab-Israel Dilemma*, p. 59.

soon they were doing all in their power to block the trusteeship plan and threatening to use force to prevent trusteeship in the same way that the Arabs were threatening to use force to prevent partition.

Military Developments in Palestine

In Palestine itself military developments had already overtaken the political and diplomatic activities at the UN. Whenever it appeared that partition would be implemented, the Arabs resisted with attacks and raids on Jewish centers, and whenever it appeared that the UN was leaning toward the repeal of the partition resolution, the Zionist community intensified its military efforts to occupy as wide an area of the Holy Land as possible.

The Zionists were operating on the assumption that "force of arms, not formal resolutions" would determine the issue, and that the *fait accompli* would finally be decisive. Accordingly, the war of independence, as David Ben-Gurion called it, concentrated on gaining full control of various cities and Arab localities.[6] At least 18 such attacks or occupations were reported by the *New York Times* between December 2, 1947 and May 8, 1948. The worst of these attacks was on April 9 when Irgun and Stern Gang soldiers entered Deir Yassin, a village near Jerusalem, and massacred 250 men, women, and children. Such actions had the intended effect of panic among the Arabs, and by May 15, the date of the end of the British administration, some 200,000 Arab refugees had left Jewish-occupied territory.[7]

The Jews, fresh from their terrifying European experience, also felt Arab pressure and believed once more that they were fighting for their survival. In Jerusalem the Arabs were cutting off water and food supplies to the 1,700 Jews in the Jewish quarter of the Old City and to the 100,000 Jews in the New City. Convoys of supplies were ambushed, and in one attempt to reinforce the Hadassah Medical Center on isolated Mount Scopus 77 men and women lost their lives, including a young scientist engaged to be married to David Ben-Gurion's youngest daughter.

[6] From speeches by David Ben-Gurion quoted in Fayez A. Sayegh, *The Arab-Israeli Conflict*, p. 14.

[7] John H. Davis, "Deir Yassin and the Arab Exodus," *The Arab Case*, II:10 (April 1969), p. 74.

All of this, of course, strengthened Ben-Gurion's determination not to have independence postponed, and the Jews of Palestine found in him their Winston Churchill. He ordered every *kibbutz* and settlement manned, fortified, supplied, and defended — Jerusalem was to be defended at any cost — and, as Gervasi has written, "suddenly no Jewish male was too old to fight or too young to die."[8] By Ben-Gurion's own admission, however, the Arabs had acted with restraint:

> Until the British left, no Jewish settlement, however remote, was entered or seized by the Arabs, while the Haganah captured many Arab positions and liberated Tiberias and Haifa, Jaffa and Safed. . . . So, on the day of destiny, that part of Palestine where the Haganah could operate was almost clear of Arabs.[9]

The Proclamation of Independence

The moment of destiny was midnight May 14, 1948, the time of the termination of the British Mandate. The UN Partition Resolution had decreed that partition should not go into effect until two months later, on July 15, assuming that the Palestine Commission had not yet become effectively functional. On May 14 the UN General Assembly met to vote on the plan to appoint a UN Mediator (the vote was 37 to 7 with 16 abstentions) to reexamine the situation and to promote a peaceful adjustment of the future situation of Palestine.

The Zionists, however, presented the UN with the accomplished fact. One hour before the UN General Assembly convened, the Jewish Agency announced that the new State of Israel had been proclaimed. Shortly after the press was advised that President Truman had given full recognition to the new state sixteen minutes after the official proclamation in Tel Aviv. The "proclamation of independence" read in part:

> The Land of Israel was the birthplace of the Jewish people. . . .

> Exiled from the Land of Israel, the Jewish people remained faithful to it in all the countries of their dispersion, never ceasing to pray and hope for the return and the restoration of their national freedom.

> . . . In the year 1897, the First Zionist Congress, inspired by Theodore Herzl's vision of the Jewish State, proclaimed the

---

[8] *Op. cit.,* pp. 86-87.
[9] *Rebirth and Destiny of Israel,* pp. 530-531.

right of the Jewish people to national revival in their own country.

This right was acknowledged by the Balfour Declaration of November 2, 1917, and re-affirmed by the Mandate of the League of Nations. . . .

The recent holocaust, which engulfed millions of Jews in Europe, proved anew the need to solve the problem of the homelessness and lack of independence of the Jewish people by means of the re-establishment of the Jewish State. . . .

In the Second World War the Jewish people in Palestine made their full contribution to the struggle of freedom-loving nations against the Nazi evil. . . .

On November 29, 1947, the General Assembly of the United Nations adopted a Resolution requiring the establishment of a Jewish State in Palestine.

It is the natural right of the Jewish people to lead, as do all other nations, an independent existence in its sovereign State.

ACCORDINGLY WE, the members of the National Council, representing the Jewish people in Palestine, and the World Zionist Movement, are met together in solemn assembly today, the day of termination of the British Mandate for Palestine; and by virtue of the natural and historic right of the Jewish people and of the Resolution of the General Assembly of the United Nations.

WE HEREBY PROCLAIM the establishment of the Jewish State in Palestine, to be called "Medinat Israel" (The State of Israel).

WE HEREBY DECLARE that, as from the termination of the Mandate at midnight, the 14th-15th May, 1948, and pending the setting up of the duly elected bodies of the State in accordance with a Constitution, to be drawn up by the Constituent Assembly not later than the 1st October, 1948, the National Council shall act as the Provisional State Council, and that the National Administration shall constitute the Provisional Government of the Jewish State, which shall be known as Israel.

THE STATE OF ISRAEL will be open to the immigration of Jews from all countries of their dispersion; will promote the development of the country for the benefit of all its inhabitants; will be based on the principles of liberty, justice and peace as conceived by the Prophets of Israel; will uphold the full social and political equality of all its citizens, without distinction of religion, race or sex; will guarantee freedom of religion, conscience, education and culture; will safeguard the Holy Places of all religions; and will loyally uphold the principles of the United Nations Charter.

THE STATE OF ISRAEL will be ready to cooperate with the organs and representatives of the United Nations in the implementation of the Resolution of the Assembly of November 29, 1947, and will take steps to bring about the Economic Union over the whole of Palestine.

We appeal to the United Nations to assist the Jewish people in the building of its State and to admit Israel into the family of nations.

In the midst of wanton aggression, we yet call upon the Arab inhabitants of the State of Israel to preserve the ways of peace and play their part in the development of the State, on the basis of full and equal citizenship and due representation in all its bodies and institutions — provisional and permanent.

We extend our hand in peace and neighbourliness to all the neighbouring states and their peoples, and invite them to cooperate with the independent Jewish nation for the common good of all. The State of Israel is prepared to make its contribution to the progress of the Middle East as a whole.

Our call goes out to the Jewish people all over the world to rally to our side in the task of immigration and development and to stand by us in the great struggle for the fulfillment of the dream of generations for the redemption of Israel.

With trust in Almighty God, we set our hand to this Declaration, at this Session of the Provisional State Council, on the soil of the Homeland, in the city of Tel Aviv, on this Sabbath eve, the fifth of Iyar, 5708, the fourteenth day of May, 1948.[10]

With the Israeli Proclamation of Independence, full-scale fighting broke out. The armed forces of the surrounding Arab governments moved into Palestine. Explaining the action to the United Nations Secretary-General the Arab League noted that until May 15 the British had been responsible for law and order, peace and security, and that whereas Zionist forces had already occupied such cities as Jaffa and Acre, assigned to the

---

[10] *Israel Yearbook, 1950-51,* pp. 50-51.

Arab state by the UN, they feared for the whole of the proposed Arab State of Palestine.

The League also insisted that the unilateral proclamation of the State of Israel was juridically invalid for two reasons: 1) the majority (Arabs) rather than the minority (Jews) should determine by democratic vote the future of Palestine upon termination of the Mandate, and 2) the Jewish state was not, in any event, entitled to exist until two months after July 15.

The Palestine War

For the Jews, on the other hand, the action of the Arab governments was a threat to their very survival, even though they must have known that the armed forces of the Arab states were little prepared. Between them, the five nations most involved (Egypt, Iraq, Syria, Transjordan, Lebanon) had no more than 80,000 troops of varying qualities. Of these they dispatched at most 25,000 to assist the Palestinian Arab liberation forces. These forces, it might be added, included some 7,000 Arab volunteers from outside Palestine. All were poorly trained, poorly organized, and poorly led.

The Provisional Government of the State of Israel, on the other hand, had a military manpower of some 60,000 in Hagana and several thousand in Irgun and Stern Gang, and all of these were integrated into a single armed force in June. While exceeding the Arabs in trained manpower resources, the Israelis lacked weapons. But on May 15, 30 shiploads of arms from Europe were on their way — some had already arrived — and some Jewish factories were quickly converted to military production.

The Arabs lacked the engineering and industrial capacity of the Jews, and they also had the disadvantage of long lines of communication. The greatest strength of the Israelis, however, probably was their effective intelligence, their able leadership, and the high motivation of their entire population. In the end, the Palestine War of 1948 was to the Israeli advantage. Not only did they increase their land area, but their armed forces and arms increased substantially.

One week after inconclusive fighting, the United Nations Security Council adopted a resolution calling upon all governments to cease their fighting, and a second more effective directive was issued another week later. Fighting was again re-

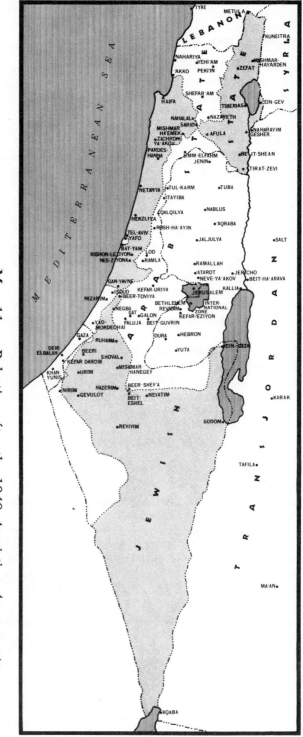

Map 11 — *Palestine after the 1949 Armistice Agreements*

sumed for nine days on July 9, but then the opposing parties accepted a cease-fire. The Swedish Count Folke Bernadotte was appointed mediator for the United Nations, but on September 17, 1948, before his task was completed, he was assassinated by men who wore the uniform of the Israeli army. The United Nations demanded that Israel bring the assassins to justice, but they could not be found. To the Arabs, Bernadotte remained a saint and a martyr because his report urged the immediate return of the Arab refugees to their homes.

In November, the Security Council called upon the parties in the conflict to conclude an armistice, and one by one the Arab countries signed separate armistice agreements with Israel, as a result of which Israel came into control of about 8,000 square miles of territory, or 77.40 percent of the total land area of Palestine, instead of the 56.47 percent allotted to the Jewish state under the partition plan (*see Map 11*). The new territory included much of Galilee as well as new Jerusalem; the internationalization plan for that city having been defeated, they insisted that the conclusion of the armistice did not mean the recognition of Israel. A state of war, they said, still existed until a permanent settlement was reached. Each agreement included the proviso:

> It is also recognized that no provision of this Agreement shall in any way prejudice the rights, claims, and positions of either party hereto in the ultimate peaceful settlement of the Palestine question; the provisions of this Agreement being dictated exclusively by military, and not by political, considerations.[11]

As the remaining part of Arab Palestine was annexed by Jordan, Israel established Jerusalem as her capital and applied for admission to the United Nations. The first application had been rejected in December 1948 because Israel had not fulfilled the requirements of the UN, meaning withdrawal from the territory assigned to the proposed Arab state and from the international zone of Jerusalem. On May 12, 1949, Israel was admitted, however, after signing the Lausanne Protocol of the UN Palestine Conciliation Commission. By that signing, Israel committed herself to observe the resolutions of the UN, specifically with respect to wrongly held territory and evicted refugees, of which there were over 700,000. These refugees rep-

---

[11] Sami Hadawi, *Palestine in Focus,* p. 53.

resented three-fourths of the Arab population in Israeli-controlled territories.

The Building of a State

The victories in the Palestine War gave the Israelis additional incentives to develop their national community, which already had many of the attributes of a modern democratic state. The intense nationalism of pre-war years was many times strengthened. As soon as the fighting subsided, Israel proceeded to establish and develop its national institutions. The first elections for the Constituent Assembly were held on January 25, 1949, and 120 representatives of 12 parties were elected to the Knesset (Parliament).

The large number of parties reflected the diversity of thought and background of the people in Israel, whose founders were determined that it should be a democratic state with freedom of speech. While all parties were pro-Israel, they differed in the intensity of their Zionism, in their economic policies, and in their relations to the Arabs. The Herut Party, for instance, representing the dissolved Irgun, held extreme views on capitalism and expansionism. They wanted control of all of Palestine. At the other end of the continuum were the Communists, who wanted complete equality of the Arabs. In between these two extremes were the large socialist labor parties, as well as other groups.

As time went on new political formations and alignments appeared, as old ones disappeared and new splinters or new parties emerged. By 1969 even the Communists had split into two groups. Generally, the political mood shifted to the right as Israel found itself endlessly at war with its neighbors.

While there was considerable factionalism in the new state, it was prevented from getting out of hand by the fact that all the parties received some of their funding from the Jewish Agency. Furthermore, dissension was greater within and among the Arab governments. The military defeats had dealt such a blow to Arab pride and self-confidence that internal instability and unrest resulted. Discontent with existing economic, social, and political conditions was also mounting. These dissatisfactions produced a military coup in Syria in 1949, the assassination of King Abdullah in Jordan in 1951, and the overthrow of King Farouk in Egypt in 1952.

Israel also benefited from the rivalries between and among the various states. Transjordan had annexed the part of Palestine not conquered by Israel, and King Abdullah saw his vision of a Greater Syria being fulfilled. But the Arab League denounced this annexation, and under Egypt's leadership an All-Palestine government was organized in the Gaza strip.

The legislative measures that were passed in the first two years of the State of Israel had far-reaching implications for its development. Free and compulsory education for all children was initiated. A conscription law required all youths, both male and female, to undergo at least two years of compulsory military training and service. Economic laws assumed a planned economy that aimed at control of all vital goods and services.

The Ingathering of the Exiles

Perhaps the most significant of early measures was the aggressive promotion of immigration into Israel, referred to by the Jewish Agency as "The Ingathering of the Exiles." The Law of the Return gave every Jew in the world the right to immigrate into Israel and to settle there permanently, and the Nationality Law provided for the acquisition of Israeli nationality immediately upon the return.

The machinery for bringing in new immigrants was, of course, already in existence, but this had to be adapted to a rapidly changing situation and to a growing volume. During the three years between May 15, 1948, and May, 1951, some 600,000 Jews entered Israel (see Table 13),[12] as compared with 452,157 during the previous 29 years of British Mandatory rule. Jewish population thus more than doubled in less than four years. The gigantic operation has been described by J. Hodess as follows:

> The task of "ingathering" undertaken by the Jewish Agency would have been enormous if the immigrants had come from only a few countries; but to direct and arrange transportation from 52 or more countries of persons with different habits of life and speaking diverse languages in three and one-half years necessitated world-wide machinery involving offices and representatives in Poland, Czechoslovakia, Romania, Hungary, Italy, France, England, Belgium, Holland, Switzerland, Sweden, Spain, Portugal, Morocco, Tunis, Tripoli. Emissaries,

[12] From Israel Office of Information, published in The Middle East— A Political Economic Survey, 1954, p. 299.

medical missions, arrangements for a luggage service, harbour storage, etc., all had to be provided.[13]

TABLE 13
JEWISH IMMIGRATION TO PALESTINE (1948-51)

Source		Number
America & Unspecified:		22,307
Africa:		92,999
Egypt	16,467	
Libya	30,942	
Tunisia-Morocco-Algeria	45,006	
Others	584	
Asia:		237,377
Iran	21,784	
Iraq	123,265	
Turkey	34,294	
Yemen	45,040	
Others	12,994	
Europe:		331,592
Bulgaria	37,253	
Czechoslovakia	18,731	
Germany & Austria	10,756	
Hungary	14,301	
Poland	106,136	
Romania	117,910	
Yugoslavia	7,644	
Others	18,861	
TOTAL		684,275

Until 1948, 90 percent of the Jewish immigrants had been from Europe, but in the first three to four years after statehood had been proclaimed this dropped to 50 percent, the other 50 percent coming from Asia and Africa. After 1948 the position of the Jews in Arab countries underwent a considerable change. The Arab world was no longer a preferred haven for the Jews as had been the case for centuries.

This was true for several reasons. A number of Arab countries were undergoing major social revolutions, which made conditions difficult for the propertied minorities, regardless

---

[13] *Israel Yearbook, 1952-53*, p. 42.

of their religion or race. In addition, the attitude of many Arabs to the Jews in their midst changed as the Zionists established the State of Israel, which they saw as a wedge in the Arab world. The increasing economic and political discomforts felt by the Jews made them much more open to the "ingathering" program being vigorously promoted by the Jewish Agency.

The first major transfer of Jews from Arab lands was from May, 1949 to September 1, 1950, when 45,000 Yemenite Jews were airlifted to Israel in the famous "magic carpet" operation. This was followed by the ingathering of 49,500 Iraqi Jews, again by special airborne operation. In all, over 300,000 Jews from Muslim lands, most of them Arabic in language and culture, arrived in Israel between 1949 and 1951.

Absorption and Economic Expansion

If immigration was a major achievement, absorption was a no less formidable task. While the exodus of 750,000 Arabs had left many openings for as many immigrants and more, not all of the newcomers could be assimilated into the labor force. Thousands of the immigrants were children, thousands more were old or sick, and many of these had to be housed in temporary camps manned by three thousand officials.

Immigration and absorption required vast monetary resources, since many of the immigrants came penniless, being European victims of the war. Also, most of the Jews leaving Arab countries were forced to leave most of their assets behind. However, the task of the State of Israel was made easier by three kinds of resources: 1) the contributions of the Jewish Agency averaging about $100,000,000 a year (1946-47) and coming mainly from the US; 2) properties left behind by the Arabs (more will be said on this matter later); and 3) reparation payments by the West German government.

Israel demanded one billion dollars from West Germany and a half billion dollars from East Germany, these being collective claims on top of the $175,000,000 already granted to half a million individual Jewish claimants. The final negotiated settlement committed West Germany to pay nearly one billion for goods and services assisting in resettlement and rehabilitation over a period of years. Israel, on the other hand, agreed to give preference to German commodities and services and also to consider the agreement as a final settlement, though the claims of individual Jews were not to be affected thereby.[14]

In addition to the material resources, Israel had an abundance of human leadership potential, and this was being rapidly expanded by western-type universities and technical schools. The resources facilitated the absorption of the immigrants in agriculture and industry. Nearly 500 new villages were established in Israel's first twenty years, as were numerous industries. From both agriculture and manufacturing there were substantial exports so that Israel's gross national product grew by an annual average of nine percent.

Economically and culturally, the new State of Israel was indeed impressive. Thousands of acres of land were being reclaimed. Millions of trees were being planted. New crops were being introduced. Many miles of frontier roads were being built. Not only was Israel developing her own land, but before long she was also assisting in training and development programs in Africa, Asia, and Latin America.

Jerusalem — The New Capital

The rapid expansion of Israel's population (*see Table 14*)[15] and the advance of her economy was as irritating to the Arabs as it was a source of pride and joy for the Jews. Although the Arabs had signed armistice agreements, these agreements only meant the end of military operations and not the recognition of Israel, certainly not the assent to all that Israel was doing in the name of her alleged sovereignty.

TABLE 14
POPULATION AND JEWISH IMMIGRATION
1948-1966

| Period | Immigration | Population at end of period | | |
		Jews	Non-Jews	Total
1948	101,828	758,702	120,000	878,702
1949	239,576	1,013,871	160,000	1,173,871
1950	170,249	1,202,992	167,101	1,370,094
1951	175,095	1,404,392	173,433	1,577,825
1952	24,369	1,450,217	179,302	1,629,519
1953	11,326	1,483,641	185,776	1,669,417

[14] *Ibid.*, pp. 112-116.
[15] *1968 Facts About Israel*, p. 60.

| Period | Immigration | Population at end of period | | |
		Jews	Non-Jews	Total
1954	18,370	1,526,009	191,805	1,717,814
1955	37,478	1,590,519	189,556	1,789,075
1956	56,234	1,667,455	204,935	1,872,390
1957	71,224	1,762,741	213,213	1,975,954
1958	27,082	1,810,148	221,524	2,031,072
1959	23,895	1,858,841	229,344	2,088,685
1960	24,510	1,911,200	239,200	2,150,400
1961	47,638	1,981,700	252,500	2,234,200
1962	61,328	2,068,900	262,900	2,331,800
1963	64,364	2,155,500	274,600	2,430,100
1964	54,716	2,239,000	286,400	2,525,600
1965	30,736	2,299,100	299,300	2,598,400
1966	15,730	2,344,900	312,500	2,657,400

The changes that were being effected in Jerusalem were one major point of contention. The UN Partition Resolution had intended for the city to be internationalized, but during the Palestine War Israel had seized the new western section of the city while Transjordan occupied the smaller and older eastern sector containing most of the holy places. The armistice agreement between Israel and Transjordan accepted the situation as it was, since neither side was much interested in internationalization. There continued to be pressures for internationalization, however. The pope wanted it, as did Orthodox and Armenian church leaders; and the USSR and other states favoring partition wanted the provisions for the Holy City implemented. Accordingly, the UN set up a Conciliation Commission for Palestine, whose duties among other things were to draw up proposals for an international regime for Jerusalem. In due course, the Commission recommended, however, that the Arab and Jewish sectors remain intact but that a UN commissioner for Jerusalem be appointed to ensure demilitarization and neutralization of the Holy City.

But the Jews were in no mood to neutralize or allow an international commission with authority over their sector of the city. Before 1948, the Jews had reluctantly relinquished their claim to Jerusalem, if only they could achieve statehood, but now they were determined not to retreat one foot from the sovereignty achieved, especially in Jerusalem, the most desired part of the national homeland.

Some verbal concessions were made by Israel when she sought UN membership, for a condition of this membership was for Israel to allow internationalization. Shortly after Israel was admitted, however, she again opposed internationalization and proceeded to move more and more of her governmental agencies to Jerusalem. The Knesset held its sessions in Jerusalem, and on January 25, 1950, it announced that Jerusalem had been the capital since the first day of independence. The Hashemite Kingdom of Jordan, as Transjordan was now called, was also opposed to any changes in the status quo, and eventually (in 1959) the Old City was proclaimed by Jordan as its second capital, though the central government remained in Amman.

Additional efforts were made by the UN, and the western powers refused for a while to move their embassies from Tel Aviv to Jerusalem. However, after the Soviet ambassador presented his credentials in Jerusalem in December of 1953, the US, Britain, and France soon followed suit.

Many Border Clashes

The status of Jerusalem after the 1949 Armistice Agreements was only one of the problems remaining. There were Arab-Israeli tensions at many places along the border. The earliest incidents were largely caused by individuals or groups with innocent motives. Bedouin tribes, who for centuries had freely moved through the Negev and other parts of Palestine, were suddenly told that they were trespassing, and Arab refugees seeking return to their villages to harvest crops, visit relatives, or claim some movable properties were told that they were infiltrators and treated as such by Israel.

Other incidents arose because of inadequately marked demarcation lines. Some of these borders cut Arab villages off from their fields. The teams of the United Nations Truce Supervisory Organization (UNTSO), established in 1949, were unable to prevent all incidents, especially as provocative Israeli patrols and poorly disciplined Jordanian police themselves crossed the lines.

The governments on both sides at first took certain measures to prevent border incidents, but beginning in 1951 Israel developed "a deliberate and official policy of retaliation," though full responsibility for these assaults was not assumed until 1955. By that time Prime Minister David Ben-Gurion was openly contending that only superior force and "two-for-one" retaliation policies would keep the Arabs from infiltrating, meaning returning to their homes. As Fred J. Khouri has established with well-documented reports:

> In practice, Israel frequently went beyond the principle of "an eye for an eye" and sought to inflict many more casualties on the Arabs than she had originally suffered.
>
> For example, on October, 1953, in reprisal for the murder of an Israeli woman and two children, Israeli military forces attacked the Jordanian village of Qibya, killing forty-two men, women, and children and injuring 15 other persons. . . . From the period of January 1, 1955 through September 30, 1956 UNTSO reported the following verified casualties: 496 Arabs killed and 419 injured compared to 121 Israelis killed and 332 injured.[16]

Israeli attacks served a variety of purposes. They ensured a flow of financial and political support from world Jewry. They helped to strengthen national unity in Israel, and, at a time when unity was by no means to be taken for granted, Israeli political pressures were such that especially in election years more and larger reprisal raids were necessary.

The Sinai War

Sometimes the so-called retaliations were attempts to end Arab boycotts and blockades and to force Arab governments to come to terms with Israel. The economic boycott had its origin in a 1945 decision of the Arab League to boycott all Zionist firms in Palestine, and this was expanded after Israel became a state. Egypt, for instance, made it impossible or difficult for ships dealing with Israel to use either the Suez Canal or the Gulf of Aqaba. This handicap became one of the most impelling reasons for the Israeli invasion of the Sinai in October 1956.

At that time Britain and France also had their grievances against Egypt, especially after President Nasser nationalized the Suez Canal Company in July 1956. Other developments in that year forged a closer alliance between the western powers and Israel, while the Soviet Union was beginning to align her-

---

[16] *Op. cit.,* pp. 187-188.

self with the Arabs. France had energetically been supplying Israel with arms, and this had led Nasser to seek arms from the United States. When such aid was not forthcoming in the desired amount, Nasser turned to the Soviet bloc for help and at the same time he recognized China. The US was so incensed that Secretary of State John Foster Dulles suddenly withdrew the US offer to finance the Aswan Dam, and so Nasser turned to the USSR also for aid on that project. In further retaliation, he nationalized the Canal, offered to compensate company shareholders, and announced that Canal revenues would be used to help pay for the dam.

An 18-nation conference, convened in London by the US, sought to set up an international authority to administer the Canal, but Egypt rejected the proposal as a continued infringement on her sovereignty. Britain and France were enraged, not least of all because both countries were already smarting from the decline of their power positions elsewhere in the world.

The moment was ripe for Israeli action against Egypt, and in October the government decided to initiate a preventive war against Egypt. Since Nasser had largely withdrawn his Sinai forces to protect the Canal against British and French intervention, the Israeli troops were able to make a deep thrust toward Egypt. At that point the British and French ordered both forces to withdraw ten miles from the Canal so that they could "protect it." They ended up bombing Egyptian air fields and other military targets.

Israel had hoped that the US, engaged as it was in an election campaign, would not antagonize Jewish voters, but President Eisenhower could not support Anglo-French-Israeli action. Instead, he took the initiative in calling a meeting of the UN Security Council, which in turn called for a Special Emergency Session of the General Assembly. A resolution introduced by the US called for prompt withdrawal behind armistice lines of the Israeli forces, and the vote passed overwhelmingly with only Britain, France, Israel, Australia, and New Zealand voting against it.

Pressures were also brought to bear on Britain and France with the result that they accepted a cease-fire on November 6. Israel reluctantly agreed to a cease-fire on November 8. Subsequent resolutions demanded immediate and unconditional withdrawal, which took until March 8, 1957 to complete.

In the meantime, the UN passed a Canadian resolution setting up a United Nations Emergency Force (UNEF) to help keep the peace between the Egyptian and Israeli border. However, the peace was at best an uneasy one. Israel refused to allow UNEF troops on her soil because this would infringe on her sovereignty, and Egypt insisted on the right to have UNEF removed if she so chose, and such a choice was made in 1967.

The 1967 June War

For several years after 1957 the Israeli borders with her Arab neighbors were quiet, but then the minor incidents and border conflicts increased, both in number and intensity. Each new incident between Israel and Egypt, Israel and Jordan, or Israel and Syria increased hatred and fear among both Arabs and Israelis.

The unresolved refugee question remained a festering sore as Israel refused to abide by a series of UN resolutions relating to the refugees. Jordan for her part refused free access to the Jewish holy places in the Old City — Israel complained that Jewish sites were being desecrated — and interfered also with the cultural and humanitarian institutions on Mount Scopus. Both acts were in contravention of the armistice agreement. Egypt continued to interfere with Israeli shipping in the Suez Canal and the Gulf of Aqaba, these having been two provisions which the Israelis had obtained assurances for from both the UN and the US.

Early in 1967 the hostile attitudes and acts on the part of both Israelis and Arabs led to another major crisis and the six-day military confrontation known as the June War. The events leading up to it included sharp confrontations between Syria and Israel. Syria supported Palestinian refugee commando activities, and Israel continued to send tractors to cultivate disputed lands in the demilitarized zone. On April 7 there was a major clash when Syria fired on what she said was an armed tractor in disputed territory and what Israel said was an unarmed tractor on Israeli lands. Israel responded with a large-scale reprisal action, and it was only with great difficulty that UNTSO could arrange a cease-fire.

The April incident had important consequences. The Syrian military alliance with Jordan and Egypt of 1956 came into play, and Arab solidarity appeared to be greater than ever.

In Egypt Nasser felt political pressures from both without and within, and on May 16 he began to move large numbers of troops into the Sinai. A few days later he requested that the UNEF troops be withdrawn, and on May 22 he closed the Gulf of Aqaba to Israeli ships. Israel complained about the UNEF withdrawal, but unlike Egypt, Israel had never accepted UNEF on her soil in the first place. Nor did Israel invite UNEF to locate on her side of the border at this time.

Similarly, Jordan's King Hussein was being pressured to do more for the Palestinians, who constituted two-thirds of Jordan's population. On May 30 he traveled to Cairo and signed a five-year mutual defense pact. Meanwhile, the UN Secretary-General U Thant had convened a session of the Security Council where the Arab-Israeli conflict became a war of words, with the Soviet Union now providing full backing for the Arabs, while the US stood behind Israel, committing herself to support the political independence and territorial integrity of that nation.

As the crisis deepened in the Middle East — and it appeared in the West that the Arabs were about to push the Jews into the sea — Christian leaders who had been opposing American intervention in Vietnam now called for intervention on behalf of Israel. Sponsoring a three-quarter-page advertisement in the *New York Times* on Sunday, June 4, men like John C. Bennett, Martin Luther King, Reinhold Niebuhr, and Robert McAfee Brown called for "moral responsibility toward the Middle East" in view of the fact "that Israel is a new nation whose people are still recovering from the horror and decimation of the European holocaust." Majdia D. Khadduri has written:

> That Israel took the offensive in the war only increased the pressure on Christian leaders for moral support. In city after city, representatives of churches were called on to share the platform at meetings and rallies with rabbis and public officials and to affirm that Israel's cause was just. . . . This is nothing new. Over the years pro-Israeli interests have systematically cultivated the Christian clergy. . . . Clergymen were offered free trips to the Holy Land. . . .[17]

American Christian support for Israel could not, from Israel's point of view, have been more timely. On June 3 the

---

[17] Majdia D. Khadduri (ed.), *The Arab-Israeli Impasse*, p. 182.

cabinet had approved a massive military action, on June 4 the advertisement appeared, and on June 5 Israel once more initiated a "preventive war" and once again made full use of the element of surprise. Devastating air attacks were launched on military airfields in Egypt, Syria, Jordan, and Iraq. All of these were in a state of complete unpreparedness, and there was little evidence that the Arabs had been ready for a big push.

With unchallenged control of the air, Israeli armor and mechanized infantry took the offensive and in a few days they conquered the Gaza Strip, the Sinai, Jordan's West Bank, and the Golan Heights in Syria. Meanwhile, the UN Security Council was in session calling for a cease-fire. With most or all of her immediate military objectives achieved, and under pressure from the UN to cease hostilities forthwith, Israel agreed to a cease-fire on June 11.

A Victory Without Fruit

For Israel the June War had been an overwhelming victory and for the Arabs a most humiliating defeat. While Israel had 679 soldiers killed and 2,563 wounded, the Arabs had lost far more, both civilian and military casualties. But in spite of Israel's triumph none of the basic issues in the dispute were settled. The Arab states were only temporarily defeated, and their defeat now united them more than ever. The war brought Hussein and Nasser together, and Saudi Arabia as well as other oil-rich Arab states were helping Egypt in the economic crisis resulting from the closing of the Suez. The big powers were more committed than ever. The USSR was determined to rearm the Arabs, and the United States was more than ever linked to Israel.

Most important of all, the War had created many new refugees on Israel's borders, and brought within her own occupied territories 540,000 Palestinian Arab refugees and another 500,-000 Jordanians, Egyptians, and Syrians. Hatred against Israel was greater than ever and there was even danger that the approximately 314,000 Israeli Arabs in Israel proper, who had until then not been a major security factor, would now become restless.

At first Israel gave the impression that she had no permanent interest in the occupied territories, but the Old City of

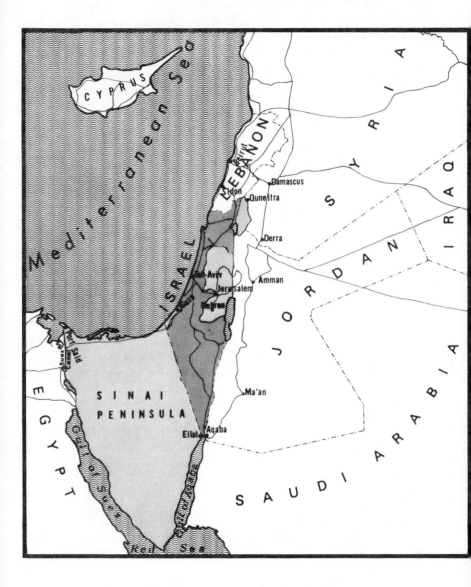

Map 12 — *Palestine after the June War of 1967*

Jerusalem was annexed on June 29 and developments in the other territories likewise suggested permanent intentions. While Israel took these actions, as she said, in the interest of security, her insecurity was really greater than ever. On three fronts (Egypt, Jordan, and Syria) and sometimes five (Lebanon and internally as in Gaza) there were positions to hold and borders to be guarded (*see Map 12*). By the end of 1969 the attacks and counterattacks of pre-June War days had increased in frequency as well as magnitude.

The UN Tries Again

In the meantime, the United Nations had again worked out a peace formula as best it could and commissioned its representative, Gunnar Jarring of Sweden, to mediate, reconcile, and implement. The peace resolution commissioning the representative was passed by the UN Security Council on November 22, 1967, just one week before the 20th anniversary of the partition resolution.

The new plan asked Israel to withdraw its forces and to provide a just settlement for refugees. The Arabs, on the other hand, were asked to guarantee freedom of navigation through international waters as well as the sovereignty, territorial integrity, and political independence of Israel. Said the resolution:

The Security Council,

Expressing its continuing concern with the grave situation in the Middle East,

Emphasizing the inadmissibility of the acquisition of territory by war and the need to work for a just and lasting peace in which every state in the area can live in security,

Emphasizing further that all member states in their acceptance of the Charter of the United Nations have undertaken a commitment to act in accordance with Article 2 of the Charter.

1. *Affirms* that the fulfillment of Charter principles requires the establishment of a just and lasting peace in the Middle East which should include the application of both the following principles:

(i) Withdrawal of Israeli armed forces from territories of recent conflict;

(ii) Termination of all claims or states of belligerency

and respect for an acknowledgement of the sovereignty, territorial integrity and political independence of every state in the area and their right to live in peace within secure and recognized boundaries free from threats or acts of force;

2. *Affirms further* the necessity (a) for guaranteeing freedom of navigation through international waterways in the area; (b) for achieving a just settlement of the refugee problem; (c) for guaranteeing the territorial inviolability and political independence of every state in the area, through measures including the establishment of demilitarized zones;

3. *Requests* the Secretary General to designate a special representative to proceed to the Middle East to establish and maintain contacts with the states concerned in order to promote agreement and assist efforts to achieve a peaceful and accepted settlement in accordance with the provisions and principles in the resolution;

4. *Requests* the Secretary General to report to the Security Council on the progress of the efforts of the special representative as soon as possible.[18]

The resolution appeared to suggest the best possible way to peace with minimum compromises on either side. However, there was no way to begin. Israel insisted on talking directly with the Arabs before making any move, and the Arabs insisted on withdrawal from occupied territories and the return of refugees before talking. Israel insisted from June 29 on that the issue of Jerusalem and other matters were not negotiable, and so the Arabs were even less disposed to coming to the conference table.

Since the powers in the Middle East themselves were not moving toward peace and since the UN also lacked the potency to achieve a settlement, the Big Two (USSR and US) or the Big Four (also France and Britain) were meeting in 1969 in search of a peace formula. Their major handicap, however, was their lack of credibility. By that time all of the powers had switched sides at least once, and if the United States had not switched sides, she had, at one time or another, been engaged in arming both sides.

The United States, more than any other big power, appeared to hold the key to a Middle East settlement, but when at the end of 1969 she urged Israeli withdrawal from occupied

---

[18] UN Security Council Resolution No. 242 (1967).

territories and the repatriation of refugees, Israel denounced her as she had earlier denounced the talks of the Big Two and the Big Four. For the United States, the strong reference to the priority need for a settlement of the refugee problem was a new emphasis. Along with most of the world she was coming to the conclusion, somewhat belatedly, that at the heart of the Middle East problem was the injustice done to the Palestinian Arabs in the process of providing in Palestine a new homeland and statehood for the Jews. Several months later, however, the main focus again was on armaments, as both the USSR and the US became militarily more involved than ever, and the solution to the Middle East conflict seemed farther away than ever.

11. The Claims of the Palestinians

The Palestinians seek only the right to live in peace in the land that is their home. When the Israeli leaders relinquish their narrow, chauvinistic aims and recognize the fundamental rights of the Palestinians, a compromise will be possible and peace will return to the Land of Peace.
— Karin Hatuoum[1]

A good case could be made for concluding our historical summary with a focus on the Arab states vis-à-vis Israel or on the growing involvement of the super-powers, inasmuch as the Middle East problem consists of several layers of conflict. However, it is necessary at all times for the historian to address himself to the most fundamental forces at work. It is the present writer's assessment, further to be clarified in the final chapter, that the most basic confrontation in the Middle East is not between the United States and the Soviet Union or between Egypt and Israel, but rather between Israel and the Palestinians.

A Count of the Palestinians

At the end of the 1960s it was necessary to speak of two groups of Palestinians, those inside of Palestine and those outside of Palestine, a total of nearly three million people (*see Table 15*). Those inside of Palestine could also be divided into two groups: the approximately 314,000 Arabs who resided within the borders of the State of Israel as established by the 1949 Armistice Agreements and the approximately 992,000 who came under Israeli occupation as a result of the June

---

[1] "Existence of Palestinians Key Issue in Middle East," *The Arab World,* XIV:5-6 (May-June 1968), p. 2.

War as can be seen from Table 16.[2] More will be said about these later.

While the number of Palestinians remaining inside of Palestine numbered in excess of 1,300,000, the total Palestinian population was more than doubled by those outside the country, as can be seen from Table 17.[3]

TABLE 15
SUMMARY OF LOCATION OF ALL PALESTINIANS

Location	Number
In Israel (1967)	314,000
In Occupied Territories (1967)	992,000
Outside Palestine	
Registered by UNRWA (1969)	1,123,278
Outside Palestine	
Not registered by UNRWA (1969)*	400,000
Total	2,829,278

* As reported by Arab Information Office in Canada, with the qualification that figures are somewhat arbitrarily arrived at.

TABLE 16
NON-JEWISH POPULATION IN THE STATE OF ISRAEL AND OCCUPIED TERRITORIES AFTER 1967 WAR

In Israel		In Occupied Areas		
By Religion		By Location		By Religion
Muslim	223,000	West Bank	596,000	Muslim	956,000
		(Jordan)	(60,000)*		
Christian	58,500	Gaza Strip	356,000	Christian	30,000
		(Egypt)	(175,000)*		

* In refugee camps, according to Israeli figures.

---

[2] *Facts About Israel,* p. 52.

[3] Based on *Report of the Commissioner-General of the United Nations Relief and Works Agency for Palestine Refugees in the Near East,* July 1, 1968 to June 30, 1969, and on estimates of Arab Information Center, Ottawa, Ontario. See also *Twice in a Lifetime,* p. 4.

Druzes,	31,000	Northern		Druzes	6,000
etc.		Sinai	33,000		
		(Egypt)			
		Golan			
		Heights	6,400		
		(Syria)			
Total	314,500	Total	992,000	Total	992,000

TABLE 17
PALESTINIANS OUTSIDE OF PALESTINE IN 1969

Country	Registered by UNRWA	Not Registered by UNRWA*	Total
Jordan	489,762		
Egypt	307,714		
Lebanon	171,517		
Syria	154,285		
In almost all Arab countries		400,000	
Total	1,123,278	400,000	1,523,278

* As estimated by Arab Information Office, Ottawa.

Of the total, over 1,300,000 were classed as refugees according to the registrations of the United Nations Relief and Works Agency for Palestinian Refugees in the Near East. More than half of these refugees were outside the country (*see Table 18*).[4]

TABLE 18
PALESTINIAN REFUGEES REGISTERED WITH UNRWA
(As of July 1, 1968)

Country	In Camps	Not in Camps	Newly Displaced Refugees	Total
Jordan				
East Bank	82,139	213,816	193,807	489,762
West Bank	73,903	197,893	—	271,796

[4] *Ibid.*

Total	156,042	416,709	193,807	761,558
	(240,020)[1]	(482,667)	—	(722,687)
Egypt	195,446	112,268	—	307,714[2]
(Gaza)	(205,723)	(111,053)		(316,776)
Lebanon	86,459	85,058	—	171,517
	(82,930)	(77,793)		(160,723)
Syria	27,151	127,134	—	154,285
	(24,151)	(120,239)		(144,390)
Total	465,098	736,169		1,395,074
	(552,824)	(791,752)		(1,344,576)

Notes: 1) Figures in parentheses are as of June 1, 1967, i.e. before June 1967 hostilities.

2) This figure includes about 40,000 refugees still reported in Gaza, but who have left since the hostilities to live in various countries.

The Exodus and Its Causes

The exodus of Palestinians from their homelands took place in two major stages. The first was in 1947 and 1948, when around 700,000 Palestinians left their homes.[5] The second was in 1967, when 150,000 of these original refugees were displaced a second time, and another 150,000 Palestinians, 100,-000 Syrians, and 35,000 Egyptians became refugees for the first time.[6]

The first exodus in 1947-48 in itself consisted of several phases. About 30,000 higher-class Arabs, mainly from Haifa and Jaffa, remembering the bloody skirmishes in the 1930s, left immediately after the UN General Assembly Partition Resolution on November 29, 1947. In doing so, they expected to return, as they did in the 1930s, after calm had been restored.

This time, however, they could not return. The loss of these key people in the Arab community left a leadership vacuum, and, as the fighting spread and intensified, other thousands of frightened Arabs left their homes. After the Irgun and

---

[5] The United Nations Economic Survey Mission in December of 1949 estimated that 726,000 Palestinians had fled their homes, and 652,000 of these were in need. See United Nations document A/Ac .25/6, Part I, p. 22.

[6] *Twice in a Lifetime.*

Stern Gang massacre at Deir Yassin on April 9, 1948, Arabs throughout the country "were seized with limitless panic and started to flee for their lives," according to Menachem Begin, the commander of the Irgun forces.[7] By May 15, some 200,-000 Palestinians had already become refugees.

After Israel proclaimed its statehood and the Arab armies joined the irregulars in opposition to the partition of Palestine, the Arab exodus gained considerable momentum. By the time of the second truce in the middle of July only about 170,000 Arabs remained in Israel.

Israel maintained that the cause for the flight of so many Palestinians was that Arab leaders wanted it that way. According to Israel, Arab leaders had given such orders for three reasons: (1) to clear the roads and villages for the advance of the regular Arab armies; (2) to demonstrate the inability of Jews and Arabs to live side by side; and (3) to disrupt services at the end of the Mandate and thus make impossible the peaceful formation of the Jewish State.[8]

The Arab claim, reported by Khouri, was that Israeli authorities "used both military force and psychological warfare to compel as many Arabs as possible to leave their homes."[9] In the western world, the Israeli viewpoint concerning the refugees was the one that was most promoted and most believed. Thus, only after 1967 did it become clear that only one side of the story had been heard. As John H. Davis, the former Commission-General of UNRWA reported:

> General Glubb has pointed out, voluntary emigrants do not leave their homes with only the clothes they stand in, or in such hurry and confusion that husbands lose sight of wives and parents of their children. Nor does there appear to be one shred of evidence to substantiate the claim that the fleeing refugees were obeying Arab orders. An exhaustive examination of the minutes, resolutions, and press releases of the Arab League, of the files of leading Arabic newspapers, of day-to-day monitorings, of broadcasts from Arab capitals and secret Arab radio stations, failed to reveal a single reference, direct or indirect, to an order given to the Arabs of Palestine to leave. All the evidence is to the contrary; that

---

[7] *The Revolt: The Story of the Irgun,* p. 164.

[8] *The Arab Refugee Problem, How It Can Be Solved: Proposals Submitted to the General Assembly of the United Nations,* p. 19.

[9] *The Arab-Israeli Dilemma,* p. 124.

the Arab authorities continuously exhorted the Palestinian Arabs not to leave the country. . . . Panic and bewilderment played decisive parts in the flight. But the extent to which the refugees were savagely driven out by the Israelis as part of a deliberate master-plan has been insufficiently recognized.[10]

Considering the Israeli point of view it could hardly have been otherwise. The entire Zionist scheme of establishing a state dominated by Jews would have faltered without the Arab eviction. In the Jewish State, authorized by the UN, the Arab population would have been almost equal to that of the Jews — 495,000 to 498,000. Within the boundaries established by the Armistice, the Arab population, without the exodus, would have been 892,000 compared to 655,000 Jews.

As it was, the immediate interests of the Zionists could not have been served better than by the departure of the majority of the Arabs. The Jews became a decided majority. Some 350 Arab villages lay vacant for the arrival of thousands of Jewish immigrants, and the refugees left behind two-thirds of the cultivated land acquired by Israel. The value of all abandoned Arab property in Israel was conservatively estimated by the United Nations at $336 million.[11]

Relief and Repatriation Attempts

The 700,000 displaced Palestinians placed an enormous burden on the neighboring Arab states, and they did what they could to help the refugees. However, the task was too great for the meager resources of the young and relatively poor Arab states, who appealed to the UN for help. Count Bernadotte, the UN Mediator, initiated an emergency relief action under the UN Director of Disaster Relief, but his main attention was given to refugee repatriation as the best relief of all. He appealed to Israel to receive the refugees on the promise that the UN would screen them and eliminate potential security risks, but Israel refused precisely on grounds of security.

When repatriation did not become immediately possible, the UN on December 19, 1948 authorized the appointment of a Director of UN Relief for Palestine Refugees, approved emergency funds of five million dollars, and asked member

---

[10] *The Evasive Peace,* pp. 56-57.
[11] "Progress Report of UN Conciliation Commission for Palestine Covering Period January 23 to November 19, 1951," General Assembly Official Records: Sixth Session, Supplement No. 18 (S/1985).

states to provide an additional $32,000,000. A year later, when the refugee problem was still unsolved, the UNRPR was succeeded by UNRWA, the UN Relief and Works Agency for Palestine Refugees, which was authorized to spend up to $54,900,000 on a relief and works program during an initial 18-month period.

The United Nations was still assuming that the refugees would be repatriated. Count Bernadotte had established the right to repatriation as one of the seven basic premises for peace. He successfully asked the UN to establish a Conciliation Commission, which would have as one of its functions the supervision and assistance of repatriation and rehabilitation of the Arab refugees, or the compensation for property lost of those who would choose not to return. Said the Third General Assembly of the UN:

> ... the refugees wishing to return to their homes and live at peace with their neighbors should be permitted to do so at the earliest practicable date, and that compensation should be paid for the property of those choosing not to return and for loss of or damage to property ... the Conciliation Commission to facilitate the repatriation, resettlement, and economic and social rehabilitation of the refugees and the payment of compensation. ... [12]

The resolution set forth the UN policy toward the Arab refugee. It became the basis for most statements that define UN relations to the refugee problem, and it has been cited at each regular session of the General Assembly since 1948. Still bitter over the Partition Resolution, the Arabs at first were not enthusiastic about any UN action, but by early 1949 they became strong advocates of UN implementation of the refugee resolution.

Israel refused to act until the Arab states would conclude a peace settlement, and the Arab governments in turn insisted on repatriation before there could be any negotiations. The result was a complete stalemate on the question of repatriation, except for the reunification of some 40,000 Arabs with their families. Arab leaders maintained that this action was insignificant in that at least 35,000 of the number were Pales-

---

[12] UN General Assembly Resolution 194 (III) "Palestine—Progress Report of the UN Mediator" (December 11, 1948).

tine Arabs, who left their homes during the height of the 1948 conflict but remained within the area that is now Israel.[13]

As early as one month after the declaration of independence, Israeli Prime Minister Ben-Gurion took the position that no refugee should be returned, and the promotion of immediate and large-scale immigration was intended in part to make a return impossible. In other words, the policy of the *fait accompli* was pursued also in this area. Early in 1949, western and UN officials became quite impatient with Israel, and in a strong note to Ben-Gurion on May 29, 1949, President Truman expressed his "deep disappointment at the failure" of Israel to make any concessions on the refugee issue, "interpreted Israel's attitude as dangerous to peace," insisted that "tangible refugee concessions should be made now as an essential preliminary to any prospect for a general settlement," and threatened that "the United States would reconsider its attitude toward Israel."[14]

The pressure from the United States caused Israel to modify her position, but two of her own suggestions proved unacceptable to the Arabs, the United States, and the UN Conciliation Commission, and nothing came of them. The first was an offer to return the refugees of the Gaza Strip in exchange for sovereignty over the area. The second offer suggested a return of 100,000 refugees, provided Israel could choose the place of their resettlement and the Arab states would consent.

Other efforts were made to get Israel to accept repatriation, but in July 1950 Israel announced that she was no longer bound by former offers regarding the return of Arab refugees since "the context in which that offer was made had disappeared." Four months later Abba Eban told the UN Ad Hoc Political Committee:

> As months and years passed without any agreement from the neighboring states to negotiate a peace settlement, the possibility of any substantial restoration of the conditions existing before the war steadily diminished, in the eyes of all qualified observers. Life had not stood still. It had moved forward with headlong speed. A vacuum does not endure.[15]

---

[13] Davis, *op. cit.*, p. 62.
[14] Khouri, *op. cit.*, p. 127.
[15] Quoted in Schechtman, *The Arab Refugee Problem*, p. 40.

Compensation and Resettlement

The UN resolutions not only provided for repatriation, but also spoke of resettlement and compensation for lost or damaged property of those who were unable or unwilling to return. As already indicated, the Arabs left behind substantial holdings. These included whole cities like Jaffa, Acre, Lydda, Ramleh, Baysau, and Majdal, 388 towns and villages, and large parts of 94 other cities and towns. Some 10,000 shops, businesses, and stores were also left behind. Eight percent of Israel's total land area represented land abandoned by the Arab refugees, and fruit produced on Arab lands provided nearly 10 percent of Israel's foreign currency earnings from exports in 1951.[16]

Israel's attitude to Arab properties was determined not only by security and social considerations but also by economic factors, for "during its formative years the new state's economy hovered constantly on the brink of bankruptcy."[17] The funds provided by world Jewry through the Jewish Agency, the German reparation payments, the grants-in-aid from the United States government, and other foreign loans supplemented very handily the native Jewish resources; yet they were insufficient.

The fields, orchards, vineyards, shops, factories, and businesses left behind by the Arabs, therefore, were made to order for the new Jewish immigrants, who needed shelter, food and employment; and the Israeli government readily turned to these new resources to meet its own emergencies. In December 1948 the office of the Custodian of Abandoned Property was established by Israel. It was his task to be in charge of all movable and immovable property belonging to, controlled by, or even occupied by "absentees," who were described as follows:

> ... any owner who on November 29, 1947, was a citizen of Lebanon, Egypt, Syria, Saudi Arabia, Transjordan, Iraq, or the Yemen; or who on that date was in any part of Palestine not Israel or Israel-occupied territory; or who on that date was a citizen of Palestine and had left his normal place of Palestine without a certificate exempting him from the status

---

16 Peretz, *Israel and the Palestine Arabs*, p. 143.
17 *Ibid.*, p. 141.

of absentee. Also defined as absentee was any company, partnership or association if at least half its members were absentees or if at least half its capital belonged to absentees.[18]

In other words, the Custodian was placed in charge of all property that Arabs were not bodily present to claim as their own as of November 29, 1947. While this ordinance was promulgated before the large flight of refugees and initially applied only to nonresident owners or resident owners temporarily abroad, it reflected the attitude of Israel and the eagerness with which it reached for accessible Arab real estate. Israel's finance minister stressed that the Israeli legislation was patterned on that of Pakistan and India following partition in that part of the world in 1947 with resultant vast exchanges of population.

While properties legally belonged to the absentees, the Custodian used them for incoming refugees. By July 1950 at least 170,000 persons, mostly new immigrants, had been housed in premises under the Custodian's control, and 7,800 shops and stores and offices had been sublet to new arrivals. After November, 1949, the Custodian operated under a new bill affecting the property of all persons who had fled, meaning all refugees in addition to the absentees. This new measure also permitted the Custodian to sell the property to a State Development Authority at prices not less than 80 percent of the value.

Israel's Resistance

These resources, it was at first assumed by some Knesset members and other leaders in Israel, would be used to compensate the Arabs. But compensation was at first hindered by disagreement in Israel itself and then by disagreement on the method of compensation between Israel and the Arab states. Israel insisted that "any funds that it agrees to defray for compensation be credited to the integration fund instead of being dissipated in individual payments." Compensation, in other words, was to be paid in a lump sum to an agency of the UN.

This procedure was rejected outright by the Arab League, which demanded that compensation be paid the refugees in-

---

[18] Schechtman, *op. cit.,* p. 96.

dividually by those persons in Israel "who have robbed them of their property." Damage to property was also to be paid, as well as a rental fee for the use of the property in the interim period.

As an agreement on compensation was delayed, Israeli absorption of Arab property continued through the sale of such property according to the latest ordinance and the policies of the Development Authority. Through these policies not only the property of absentees and refugees was being absorbed but also land belonging to Arabs still in Israel. The latter often came under the jurisdiction of the Custodian or the Authority for security reasons or the development of Jewish collectives under the Land Acquisition Law. In this way some 30,000 Arabs legally residing in Israel lost access to part of their lands, though some of it was rented back to them on a yearly basis.

In 1951 the approach of the Israeli government hardened even more than before, when Arab Iraq set up a Custodian of Jewish Property with power to control the properties of the departed Iraqi Jews. One hundred thousand of these Iraqis were now in Israel, and their 15,000 influential members of the intellectual, professional, and capitalist class became a powerful pressure group. In their opinion the property abandoned by Jews in Iraq was about equal to that abandoned by Arabs in Israel. Their argument was persuasive, and from that time on Israelis frequently suggested that the books could be closed on refugee repatriation and compensation, inasmuch as a fair exchange of population and property had been effected.

The Iraqi Jews and Israel may have considered this a fair deal, but for the Palestinians now located mostly in UNRWA refugee camps justice had by no means been done. Through UNRWA, the Arab League, and sympathetic governments they continued their efforts in the desired direction, but every passing year made either repatriation or compensation more difficult.

After 1956 Israel linked any further consideration of compensation to the abandonment by the Arab states of their economic boycott against Israel. The only concession made by Israel was the partial release of some $7.5 million of the total held in Arab-blocked accounts, as well as the contents of some safety boxes, a tiny fraction of the total of abandoned Arab property.[19]

Attempts at Resettlement

As both repatriation and compensation were delayed, various efforts to settle Palestine refugees in Arab lands were made, this also having been a provision of the UN General Assembly's basic resolution in 1948. Support by some UN member states for resettlement was vigorous already in 1949. The appointment in that year of an Economic Survey Mission had resettlement as part of its goal. The Mission was headed by Gordon Clapp, a former chairman of the board of the Tennessee Valley Authority.

The Conciliation Commission and the Clapp Mission assumed that if economic problems could be resolved political tensions would be eased. Clapp proposed a program of public works in the countries where the refugees were situated. This program was calculated to improve the productivity of the areas while continuing relief until all refugees could be absorbed. The proposals were reflected in the name of the new agency established as a result and to which we have already been introduced, namely: the United Nations Relief and Works Agency for Palestine Refugees in the Near East (UNRWA).

The initial $59 million fund was supplemented by $30 million in 1950, and in 1951 a three-year program costing $200 million was approved — $50 million for relief and $200 million for reintegration. Relief was to be progressively reduced until it would amount to only $5 million in 1954. The hope of the UN was that there would be a gradual transfer of responsibility from UNRWA to the Arab states when the refugees would already be largely self-supporting.

However, for both the Arab states and the Palestinian refugees the assumptions of the Clapp Mission were false. To them economic factors were not the most important. The development projects were viewed with suspicion, and to support them, the Arabs believed, would undermine the right of the refugees to return to their homes in Palestine. No progress was, therefore, made on the major development schemes, and at the end of 1954, the target date for ending relief, only 8,000

---

[19] "Sixteenth Progress Report," United Nations Conciliation Commission for Palestine; UN Document A/3835, June 18, 1958.

refugees had been made self-sufficient and less than $10 million had been used on "works" of the UN agency.

Politics in the Arab World

The Arab states on the whole had their own political reasons, apart from the humanitarian considerations, for wanting the Palestinians repatriated. The refugees posed internal economic, social as well as political problems for such host governments as Lebanon, Jordan, and the United Arab Republic (meaning Egypt and Syria) especially after 1958.

In Lebanon the 126,485 Palestinians represented 8.4 percent of the country's population. These refugees, mostly Muslims, were threatening to upset the delicate balance between almost evenly divided Christians and Muslims in the country, with the Muslims challenging the Christians for control. The Lebanon government, therefore, did not grant political rights to Palestinians, who were granted only residence visas and who had to hold special identity cards. Work permits were also difficult to obtain, although many Palestinians worked.

The United Arab Republic granted most civil rights to Palestinians — that is, they had access to the courts —but political rights were not granted. In the Gaza Strip (25 miles long and 5 miles wide), really a vast refugee camp under Egyptian military control and not included in the 1958 UAR union, the movement of Palestinians was severely restricted, as it was under the four-month Israeli occupation in 1956-57. An elective Legislative Council was formed in 1958, but all actions of the council were subject to the approval of the Egyptian Governor-General.

Only in the Hashemite Kingdom of Jordan, both East Bank and West Bank, did Palestinians enjoy full citizenship with voting rights. For Jordan there really was no alternative since the bulk of Palestinian refugees were in Jordan; and, added to the West Bank Palestinians, they constituted more than one-half of Jordan's 1.6 million population.

The citizenship status of Palestinians was unaffected by the federation of Jordan and Iraq in 1958, but it tended to reduce their considerable political power in Jordan. The refugees were also adversely affected by the power play between the United Arab Republic and the Iraqi-Jordan federation, since the Palestinians in the federation tended to be pro-Nasser, and their politics were more anti-Israel than Jordan's.

The Works of UNRWA

In the absence of repatriation and resettlement, the Palestinian Arabs remained the wards of UNRWA and the international community. This does not mean that the host governments did not assume responsibilities. On the contrary, by 1968 Jordan, Egypt, Syria, and Lebanon had spent more than $100 million in direct assistance for health services, education, campsites, housing, roads, and security.

Nor were the refugees themselves negligent or irresponsible as has been frequently insisted and commonly believed in the West. The evidence is to the contrary, according to UNRWA Commissioner-General John H. Davis:

> Following the upheaval of 1948, virtually all able-bodied male refugees who possessed skills needed in Arab countries or, for that matter, elsewhere, found jobs almost immediately and became self-supporting and have never been dependent on international charity. This group comprised some 20% of the total working force which left their homes in Palestine in 1948-1949; for the most part they were persons from the urban sector of Palestine, their good fortune being that the world needed the skills which they possessed.[20]

It was difficult, however, to provide employment opportunities for Arab farmers, for in the vicinity of the camps there was little available arable land. The Arab countries themselves had a surplus of peasants, given the then available land resources and the exploding population. The Arab population in the camps burgeoned. More than 500,000 new refugees were born in less than twenty years, increasing the registered refugee population to 1,395,074 by July 1, 1969.

The exact number of Palestinian refugees away from their homeland has always been a debatable figure. In the first place UNRWA never registered all of them, and in 1969 Arab Information Offices estimated, as has already been pointed out, that this unregistered sector of the Palestinian population had increased to about 400,000, admitting that this figure was somewhat arbitrary.

Some uncertainty also arises from the fact that UNRWA

---

[20] Davis, *op. cit.*, pp. 62-63.

was confronted by inevitable duplicate and false registrations. Allowances and adjustments were made for these annually for a total of some 58,000 from 1950 to 1968. Even so it knew that its rolls might be further inflated by some concealment of refugee deaths. But UNRWA could not rectify the situation because no census could be undertaken without the permission of host countries and refugee leaders.

In general the Arabs tended to exaggerate the numbers of refugees entitled to relief, and Israel tended to minimize them, the latter estimate usually falling some 300,000 short of Arab estimates. In the Gaza Strip, however, which Israel held from November, 1956 to March, 1957, the UNRWA figures were not challenged by Israel.

It should also be said here that the total UNRWA registration of 1,395,674 (1969 figure) included only 806,366 full-ration recipients. Half-ration recipients numbered 13,466 while babies registered for services numbered 326,185. The registered refugees receiving no rations or services numbered 148,004 while others receiving only partial services totaled 101,053.[21]

The cost of the services to the refugees in 64 camps (*see Map 13*) including food, shelter, medical and welfare services, and education for the refugee children was covered by special governmental and nongovernmental grants to UNRWA, averaging less than $40 million a year after 1950. Even so they were difficult to raise annually, in spite of the fact that food costs were kept at an average of seven cents a day per refugee.

About 70 percent of the UNRWA support came from the US, with the United Kingdom and Canada standing second and third as contributors. The Soviet Union and its allies have never contributed to the support of the refugees, and only with its realignment with the Arabs in 1957 did the USSR begin to demand repatriation and compensation. The lack of UNRWA funds presented this agency with the constant need to keep its services at a minimum and occasionally even to cut back.

In spite of its meager resources UNRWA performed a gigantic service for the refugee population. Death rates and

[21] Report of the Commissioner-General of UNRWA, July 1, 1968-June 30, 1969. General Assembly: Twenty-Fourth Session, Supplement No. 14 (A/7614), p. 63.

Map 13 — The Location of UNRWA Refugee Camps

sickness were kept below the average in the Arab world. General education, vocational and teacher training, as well as university education were provided for nearly half a million young people.

The Desire and Determination to Return

What UNRWA could not do was to make the Palestinians happy. Almost all continued to express their desire to return. The feeling that injustice had been done increased rather than diminished with the passing of time. The Palestinians continued to hope and assume that the Arab governments would help them to go back as they said they would and that the UN would also facilitate the return, which it said annually was the right of the refugees. Palestinian feeling and frustration was well expressed before the UN Special Political Committee by a Christian Arab doctor in exile, Izzat Tannouns, as follows:

> I happen to be a Christian Arab of Christian parents born in Palestine. My home is in Jerusalem where I lived all my life. I am not permitted to go back by the Israelis, not because I declared war on any country, not for occupying other people's homes; and not for persecuting the Jews, but for the simple reason that I was not born a Jew. While American Jews, Austrian Jews and even Arab Jews can go and occupy my home today I cannot do so because I am a Christian. The Jewish faith is the only valid visa to go and live in Israel today. Did you ever conceive that this could take place in this twentieth century, the century of the Declaration of Human Rights, the era of religious tolerance? I had the honor to tell this committee last year and I will tell it again this year, that my home is only 300 yards away from the armistice line and my clinic is on the other side of the road. ...I see people in them, people coming and going but I cannot move an inch forward. If I do I will be killed and my body will be labeled "guilty of the Criminal Act of Arab infiltration." This infiltration, Mr. Chairman, into one's own home, land, farm, and country has been the cause of the death of hundreds of my countrymen by people who, only a few years ago, were total strangers to the land. Moreover, this home of mine is being offered to any Jew in the world, be he from Warsaw, Tokyo or the West Indies, if he will condescend to go and take it. The Palestine Arab refugee problem is the transplantation of one people of one faith in the place of other people of other faiths through the force of arms. It is the problem of religious discrimination. ... How

can we improve the political atmosphere to begin peace talks of any kind if we are still prevented from reaching our homes? The mere discussion of "right of return" will be a "psychological road block" to a solution. . . . It is the duty of the United Nations before it is too late to place the Palestine problem in its proper perspective.[22]

With the June War of 1967 the attitude of the Palestinians changed dramatically. They now saw that the world had not prevented the complete takeover by Israelis of their land, which they knew all along had been part of the Zionist plan. Indeed, they assumed after 1967 that the Greater Israel called for even more territorial acquisition in East Bank Jordan, Lebanon, and Syria.

Again, the UN General Assembly passed a resolution asking Israel to allow the new 1967 refugees to return to their homes in the occupied area. Eighty-five percent of those 245,000 who had fled to the East Bank of Jordan filled out applications asking to return, but only about 15,000 were admitted by Israel.

Although the Palestinians had been organizing, training, and dispatching groups before 1967, the *fedayeen* movement now gained strength dramatically. The desire and determination to return to their homelands was finding an enthusiastic military expression. So strong had the movement become that the politics and military strategy of the Arab states was by 1969 almost completely dominated by the Palestinian determination to have justice done. Yasir Arafat, the leader of Al-Fatah, the strongest of the Arab commando movements, was attending Arab summit conferences and generally being treated like a hero and head of state.

The liberation movement also had its supporters in Israeli-occupied territories, so that Israel's security problem had a new dimension for that reason after 1967. There was now a real possibility that Al-Fatah, some Arab states, and the Arabs in occupied territories would rise up to crush the State of Israel, as they had threatened to do since 1948.

In the interests of her security, Israel was, therefore, conducting almost daily jet raids across the Suez and the Jordan. The Syrian region too was being bombed and strafed, and Lebanon, which in 1969 gave more operating freedom to Al-Fatah, was likewise threatened.

---

[22] Quoted in *Middle East Newsletter,* III:5-6 (September 1969), p. 14.

Inside Israel and the occupied territories security was being tightened. Land was being seized, Arabs were being evicted, and buildings were being demolished all in the name of security. Arabs were constantly being searched, and neighborhood punishment (meaning demolition of houses) was in 1969 instituted where neighbors were believed to have withheld information about commando activities.

As in the past, so in 1969 Israeli retaliation, however, was producing exactly the opposite of the intended effect. Instead of suing for peace the Arabs were preparing for the inevitable war with Israel. While they knew that Israel's military superiority might win her another round or two they were confident that in the long run the victory would be theirs. Meanwhile, the UN and the big powers stood by increasingly helpless as hate and hostilities in the Middle East escalated to a point of no return.

The return that most peacemakers were seeking was to the status quo before the June War of 1967. Others, however, knew that the promise of Middle East peace had been destroyed already in 1947 with the UN Partition Resolution and before that by the Balfour Declaration of 1917. But even the return to 1967 had become impossible, and peace was nowhere in sight.

12. The Claims of God

I look forward, and my people with me look forward, to a future in which we will help you and you will help us to develop the land which is close to both our hearts. . . .
—Prince Feisal[1]

Peace can come only if Israel and Ishmael can feel that they are brothers.   —Juda L. Magnes[2]

The foregoing historical review has revealed the prominence of God or gods in the minds of men in the long history of the Middle East, and so it is desirable and perhaps even necessary that we return to that theme once more as a way of seeking the best possible understanding of the problem and the most helpful insights relative to its resolution. In so doing, we will not produce a theological treatise but rather continue with the historical method, albeit with some theological intent on the assumption that North American Christians will in all likelihood be reading this book first and most.

I. THE CHRISTIAN INVOLVEMENT

This audience has been chosen as a primary target for several reasons. First is the fact that many works for general audiences have been written and published in recent years. Second is the belief that it is precisely the Christian com-

[1] Letter from Prince Feisal (later Feisal I, King of Iraq) of the Arab Delegation to Felix Frankfurter, of the Zionist Delegation in Paris, March 3, 1919. For complete text see Maurice Samuel, *Light on Israel*, pp. 46-47.

[2] Statement by Dr. Juda L. Magnes, president, Hebrew University, upon his resignation from the United Jewish Appeal because of its refusal to do anything about the Arab refugees. See Alfred M. Lilienthal, *There Goes the Middle East*, p. 266.

munity which needs the longer historical view, the broader theological perspective, and a more creative international political concern. Third is the knowledge that the theology and politics of Christians have had in the past, and may have in the future, a profound effect on western policies with regard to the Middle East.

Some Distinct Handicaps

Having expressed this optimism about the Christian role, it is necessary to recognize first of all that the Christian community comes to the Midde East situation with some very distinct handicaps. The first of these is a rather sad record of past involvement, which appears to have had the character of imperialism. One needs only to review the policies of the various rulers of various empires who in one way or another contributed to the Middle East conflict — the emperors of Rome and Byzantium; the popes of the Crusades; the tsars of Russia; Napoleon of France; Wilhelm of Germany; Balfour, Churchill, and Attlee of Britain; Wilson, Truman, *et al.,* of the United States.

All of them wanted to establish order in the Middle East, all of them explicitly or implicitly in the name of God. All of them had the direct and indirect benefit of Christian advisors. And all of them contributed to the present mess in the unfortunate middle of our world.

The future Christian contribution to the resolution of the Middle East conflict must be and can be of a different order than what has been in the past, but the historical record will remain a handicap. The effects of the Crusades, or of the French imperial protection of Latin Christians, or of British imperial intervention, to name only a few examples, are with us to the present day. As the Jordanian paper *al-Manar* reminded us in 1964:

> Our memories and experiences of Christians of the West are completely different [from those of the East]. They include the memory of Lord Allenby planting his sword in the Mount of Olives in Jerusalem and boasting "Now end the Crusades!" They include the memory of General Gourand putting his foot on the tomb and exclaiming "We have returned, O Saladin!"[3]

---

[3] Quoted in A. J. Arberry (ed.), *Religion in the Middle East,* Vol. 2, p. 585.

Apart from the regrettable role that Christians have played in relation to the ambitions of their nation states, they have a special handicap with respect to Arabs, particularly Muslim Arabs, and to Jews. Both of these peoples are Semites. The historical record shows a great deal of Christian hostility toward Arabs and Jews, both of whom have been related to the anti-Christ. Both have experienced Christianity at various times and places as anti-Semitic. Both have been the targets of rather imperialistic Christian conversion attempts, and only recently have relationships been described as "conversations." As a bitter communication from Israel, addressed to the West, recently reviewed the Christian approach to the Jews: "Your inquisitions, pogroms, expulsions, the ghettos into which you jammed us, your forced baptisms. . . ."[4]

Understandably, therefore, both the Jews and the Arabs are not easily ready to listen to Christian proposals for the resolution of the Middle East conflict. Any suggestion to the Palestinian commandos that they lay down their arms, so as not to threaten the security of the Jews, quite properly produces the rejoinder: "It was largely your arms that drove us into the desert" and "where were you during the 20 years that we were relatively pacifistic waiting for justice to be done without our resort to arms?"[5] The "Hymn of Hate" of a Palestinian Arab writing about his occupied homeland expresses Arab disappointment with the Christian West equally directly:

> If Jesus could see it now,
> He would preach *jihad* with the sword!
> The land in which He grew
> Has given birth to a million slaves.
> Why does he not revolt,
> Settle the account, tooth for tooth and eye for eye?
> In spite of all His teachings,
> The West's dagger is red with blood.
> O apostle of forgiveness!
> Dazed by calamity, I do not know the answer:
> Is it true you lived to suffer?
> Is it true you came to redeem?

---

[4] "A Letter to the World from Jerusalem," *New York Times* (October 19, 1969), p. E9.

[5] "Philip Kamel" of Al Fatah in conversation with the author, Amman, Jordan, June 13, 1969.

O apostle of forgiveness! In our misfortune
Neither forgiveness nor love avail.[6]

Similarly, the Jews are apt to respond with their own criticisms to every Christian suggestion that Israel give its attention to justice for the Arabs. They are quick to charge that Christians have always been ready to talk justice to Jews, but always reluctant to offer justice to Jews. Even more disarming is the frequently heard accusation that the Christian critique of Zionism or Israel's doings is but a thinly disguised anti-Semitism. We say disarming, because every Christian in the West would rather be called by any other name than anti-Semite, for anti-Semitism is associated in minds of all the world with the worst evil of all, the Nazi holocaust. Zionists know this and use very effectively the subtlest hints of anti-Semitism to intimidate even the mildest critics. Unless the Christian remembers that criticism of a Jewish state or the Jewish people is not necessarily anti-Semitism, and that all Christians are not guilty of genocide any more than all Jews are guilty of deicide, he is, indeed, handicapped. Unless he can accept the past failures of Christians with humility and then rise above them with courage there will be very little for him to say or do.

Some Definite Assets

The Christian comes to the Middle East conflict, however, not only with severe handicaps but also with distinct assets, which permit him to disregard, refute, or overcome the blame which is so easily directed his way. These assets, like the liabilities, are related to both sides of the conflict.

On the one hand are the conversational relationships that Christians and Jews have established in the West, particularly since World War II. In numerous cities in North America and in a variety of ways, Christians and Jews have engaged in useful dialogue and common social action projects. Indeed, Christians in America have in the twentieth century helped Zionism to achieve the goal of establishing a national homeland in the same way that British Christians in the nineteenth century prepared the way for the acceptance of the Zionist dream. And in the 1967 June War, the majority of Christians in North America accepted and promoted the popular inter-

---

[6] Kamāl Nāsir, "Hymn of Hate," quoted in Arberry, *op. cit.*, p. 586.

pretation that little David (Israel) had once more defeated the giant Goliath (the Arabs) with the help of God, the weekly *Christian Century* magazine being one of the very few exceptions.

The analogy of David and Goliath was incorrect because it was Israel and not the Arabs that had military superiority; but that is, for the time being, beside the point. The point is that Israel enjoyed nearly universal Christian empathy in North America in 1967 as in 1947, and Zionist condemnation of its Christian critics for the sins of the past are only fractionally relevant. As North American Christians went to battle against the enemies of the Jews in Europe in World War II, so their hearts, rightly or wrongly, were on Israel's side in the most recent confrontation with the Arabs. A record of anti-Semitism is, therefore, only one side of the coin, and maybe not even the complete side at that, the other side being a strong element of pro-Semitism, vis-à-vis Israel.

This strong western inclination toward Israel is, of course, well known by the Arabs, which means that western Christian liabilities are by that fact substantially increased in the Arab world. However, even there Christians are not without advantages, for they do have a strong bridge to the Arabs through the large and virile Christian Arab community in the Middle East. The western church is tied together with those Christians in the World Council of Churches and various other fraternal relationships, fellowships and endeavors. Admittedly and regrettably, the western Christian community has been too ignorant and too unrelated too long to this sizable and significant Arab Christian community; but all this has changed, as with the Jews, in recent years.

Christianity's center position, historically speaking, among the three monotheistic faiths originating in the Middle East may be another asset, inasmuch as the Christian religion is in position to converse with both Judaism and Islam. The position is crucial in terms of influence in both directions and can serve both to enlighten and darken. That the western Christian influence has often been negative has been documented by Merlin Swartz when he says: "We in the West must remember, however, that we have little right to stand over either the Arabs or the Jews in superior, patronizing judgment, for the root of the current dilemma is precisely that both Arabs and Jews have learned too much and too well from the West."[7]

Much to Learn and Unlearn

Swartz was specifically referring to the deity-sanctioned religious nationalisms and holy wars that Jews and Muslims have learned from Christians. But if there has been one kind of learning there is no reason why there should not also be another kind. Regrettably, Christians have had, all their pretense to the contrary notwithstanding, very little to teach both Jews and Muslims. To make maximum use of their present conversational opportunity, therefore, Christians themselves will first of all have to do the most learning and, we might add, unlearning. History and historical theology suggest the need for modifications, if not reversals, of Christian thought in a number of areas, for there have been serious distortions.

1. *The God whom Christians have named has not always been the highest God.* The Crusades probably remain the best classic example of mistaking the misguided ambitions of religious zealots for the highest mandate of the highest God, but the same can be said of many lesser Christian crusades both before and after. It is a fact of human cultural history that man's thoughts and deeds have too often been implicitly accepted as the highest expression of the divine will.

Indeed, if it should be suggested that God's promise to Abraham was in large measure the normal ambition of an enterprising and devoted Fertile Crescent patriarch, who attributed the calls within him to God, history would offer some understanding for that position. Similarly, the slaughterings by the children of Israel, allegedly authorized by God, were dictated not by the highest God but by God reduced to a tribal deity in the minds of Israel, whom they called the Lord God of Israel.

Christians too have done this more often than not, and gone forth to battle with the Russian, French, British, German, and American gods. However, if they want to be light in a dark world, they will have to seek a higher God. Without such a God, Christians cannot possibly make a contribution toward peace in the Middle East. Nor do they have anything to say to Muslims or Jews whose Allah and Yahweh have sometimes

---

[7] "The Position of Jews in Arab Lands Following the Rise of Islam," unpublished paper, January 12, 1969, p. 28.

— not always — demanded a higher morality and been a higher God than the Christian deity.

2. *The Christ the Christians have named or deified was not always the divine Christ.* In the third and fourth centuries Christians felt it necessary to defend their faith by expressing its cardinal doctrines in creedal form. The motives for this defense were quite noble, but the consequences were disastrous because the manner of defending the statements often became a denial of the very Christ they confessed.

At the time that Christians began in their creeds to uphold the deity of Christ, they began in their deeds what the divine Christ would least have tolerated. He who expressed his divinity by dying for his enemies now had to observe how his followers persecuted his enemies in the name of deity. Anti-Christs were identified on every hand, among the Jews, Muslims, and Communists, and the Christ who came to save the anti-Christian world as a suffering servant carrying a cross, now went out to save himself as a crusader with creeds and swords.

Christians wondered why Muslims and Jews could not accept this Christian Messiah. They were obviously expecting too much. How could Jews and Muslims accept him whom the Christians were themselves not fully accepting? Jews and Muslims, of course, have been equally guilty, for they too did not accept the messiahship or the highest moral insights of their own religions.

3. *The chosen people the Christians have identified were not always the 'chosen' people.* The earliest and also the later clashes between Jews and Christians were largely due to the religious rivalry arising out of the claims of both groups to be the chosen people. In the process both distorted the concept. The Jews claimed to be chosen just because they were Jews, and the Christians claimed to be chosen just because they were Christians. In the eyes of God, both probably lost their chosenness to the degree that they insisted on it, in the way they insisted on it, and that is why he turned to raising up children from the stones in the desert. As John the Baptist, so called, explained to his racist contemporaries:

> You brood of vipers! Who warned you to flee from the wrath to come? Bear fruit that befits repentance, and do not presume to say to yourselves, "We have Abraham as our

father"; for I tell you, God is able from these stones to raise
up children to Abraham (Matt. 3:7-10).

Christians have claimed chosenness both for themselves
and, at the nationally convenient moments, for the Jews. They
have also applied it wrongly to their national communities,
thus contributing to racist nationalisms and *Herrenvolk* (master
race) concepts, particularly in Britain, Germany, and the
United States. Chosenness does not depend on race. There is
no chosenness where chosenness or potential chosenness is
denied to others. There is no chosenness where there is no
choosing. Nor are there any people of God where the Lord
is not God.

4. *The holy land and places named by the Christians were
not always holy land and holy places.* As the history reports,
the early Christians were not preoccupied with holy soil and
holy sites. They did relate God to nature, but they saw this
relation as equally applicable to all places. Palestine was
sacred by association, but pilgrimage was not a necessary
duty of the church, and its imperatives about Jerusalem were
valid and applied to all cities everywhere. Christians felt called
to make the entire world a holy place, and, as The Epistle to
Diognetus said: "Every foreign land is their fatherland and
every fatherland a foreign land."[8]

This position or attitude changed with Constantine and his
successors, and Christians adopted the pagan practice of giving sacramental significance to particular sites. The bloody
Christian crusades, the religious political pilgrimages, the ex-
cessively commercialized tourism, and western efforts to in-
ternationalize Jerusalem, when the old internationalization of
colonialism was fading, are all a consequence of a misplaced
preoccupation with holy places.

And unholiness was also a consequence. The partition of
Palestine made the Holy Land unholy in the same way that
the original division into two Hebrew kingdoms had unholy
consequences. Holiness is not primarily where Jesus once
walked but where he is walking today, not where he once
bled but where he is bleeding today and where he is coming
alive today.

Christians, especially western Christians, should renounce
their legal and spiritual claims to any holy places in Palestine,

---

8 Quoted in Arberry, *op. cit.,* p. 376.

turn all their outposts, their hostels and garden tombs over to the natives, and proclaim to all the world that Christ and Christianity are not dependent on them for meaning or for survival. This act of renunciation could help other religions to reconsider their excessive preoccupation with the holy places and with their holy acts of religion, and to return once more to the essence of true religion:

> Bring no more vain offerings; incense is an abomination to me. New moon and sabbath and the calling of assemblies — I cannot endure iniquity and solemn assembly. Your new moons and your appointed feasts my soul hates; they have become a burden to me, I am weary of bearing them. When you spread forth your hands, I will hide my eyes from you; even though you make many prayers, I will not listen; your hands are full of blood. Wash yourselves; make yourselves clean; remove the evil of your doings from before my eyes; cease to do evil, learn to do good; seek justice, correct oppression; defend the fatherless, plead for the widow (Isa. 1:13-17).

5. *The so-called kingdoms of God, identified by Christians, have not always been the kingdom of God.* The social order of the early Christians emphasized spirituality and universality. Their kingdom was different and larger than any kingdoms of the world. The kingdom of God represented relationships and had goals that transcended earthly kingdoms. Caesar and his empire, they believed, represented a loyalty too limited.

This attitude too changed with Constantine, in whose mind the empire of the Caesar and the kingdom of the Christ became almost synonymous, and that thinking carried over to Christians. Subsequently they became some of the most avid religious nationalists that European and North American states have known. After Constantine it was inevitable that Christians should attempt to establish a "Kingdom of Jerusalem" somewhere, if not in Jerusalem (though that possibility was not destroyed with the failure of the Crusades) then in Rome (where a kingdom has been established), or in Moscow (the Third Rome), Berlin (headquarters for the millennial Reich), Paris, London, or Washington.

These latter kingdoms extracted from the Christians attachments, loyalties, and sovereignty acknowledgments that were intended for the kingdom of God. The results were the warring nationalisms of the nineteenth and twentieth centuries, which

Christianity nurtured and supported. The religious intensity of Arab or Jewish nationalism is, as Merlin Swartz has reminded us, the contribution of the western Christian states. To expect transcendence in Judaism and Islam is to expect more than Christians themselves have achieved. Therefore, if Christians hope to make a contribution to long-term peace they will have to rethink and reverse themselves on the kingdoms in favor of a world federalism and the greater kingdom of God.

6. *Most, if not all, of the holy wars were unholy wars.* Muslims are not the only religious people who believe in *jihad* or holy war. The Christians have fought many holy wars, many more than the Arabs, and all the present military action in the Middle East proceeds on the assumption that God or gods have sanctioned or even demanded it.

But a holy war is really a contradiction in terms. Christians have always believed that the *jihad* was incompatible with God. The Muslims had a similar conviction about the Christians' crusades. These crusades were against Allah, not for him. Similarly, the Jews have recognized only their own wars as holy, no matter how bloody they once were or how flaming they are now. What all three religious peoples have not recognized is that their own wars are as unholy as all the rest, and peace will not come to the Middle East until they apply to their own wars the condemnation they usually reserve for other wars.

Christianity must renounce the concept of holy warfare, first for themselves and then for the Jews and Muslims, if they are going to make any contribution to peace.

7. *The Bible that Christians have read was not always the Word of God.* Christians will have to restudy their holy book, for all their misrepresentations of God, Christ, chosen people, holy places, kingdom, and holy wars, have been read out of the Bible. How this can and does often happen and how the poetic literature of the Bible lends itself to various uses can be seen from a 1969 advertisement in the *New York Times Magazine* for Sabra, a liqueur imported to North America from Israel.[9] Introducing the ad were the words of Isaiah 27:6: "And Israel shall blossom and bud, and fill the face of the world with fruit."

---

[9] Advertisement, *New York Times Magazine* (November 9, 1969), p. 110.

Even the most prophecy- or nationalist-minded interpreter of the biblical literature would agree that such a literal application of Isaiah's poetry represents a complete misreading of the prophet. But why should the words not apply to liqueur, if words have been similarly misapplied to racism, nationalism, militarism, and Zionism — all of which have turned out to be a much stronger drink for Judaism and the Middle East than Sabra will ever be to the world?

Some biblical scholars, seeking to understand the ancient and modern events in the Middle East, have brought together all the references in the Bible to Jerusalem, Zion, Israel, promised land, etc., and constructed from them elaborate schemes of prophetic fulfillment. What these schemes overlook is that the same words either in biblical or extrabiblical usage did not always have the same meanings and could not always be equated. Zion, Jerusalem, and Israel, for instance, sometimes mean literal-historical places, but often they are used poetically and symbolically to communicate universal moral and spiritual truths.

Christians should remind themselves that the various prophetic schemes that have had credence within the Christian community all arose in specific political contexts in which Christ and anti-Christ were related to the political powers of the day struggling against each other.[10] The schemes changed with the changing of the powers. At the moment many Christians see Christ allied with America and Israel and the anti-Christ with Russia and the Arabs. One would think that before such a scheme is taken too far one would at least consult Arab and Russian Christians whose devotion to Christ, as well as their national feelings, have at least as much validity as those boasted in the West.

This is not to say that there is no prophetic content in the Bible, but the prophecy has been of a different order than has been commonly understood. The prophetic direction of the scriptural message is toward the universalization not the tribalization of God, toward racial inclusiveness rather than exclusiveness with respect to the chosen people. The promised land is extended rather than narrowed. Its people are increasingly known for their moral righteousness rather than

---

[10] For one of the most recent attempts see Wilbur M. Smith, *Israel/Arab Conflict and the Bible*.

for their military might. "Jerusalem" becomes the eternal city of God and of man rather than the temporal city of a nation or tribe. To read the Bible in the other direction, as it were, is to misread it and to contribute to the Middle East conflict rather than to resolve it.

Some Specific Problems

There are many specific problems one could discuss. We shall consider a few of these in order to illustrate how necessary the rereading actually is. One problem has to do with the intended beneficiaries of the land of promise. The normal answer, of course, is that the promise was given to Abraham and his sons. But who are these sons? There are two broad interpretations: the literal-physical interpretation and the symbolic-spiritual interpretation.

If the literal interpretation is to be followed, there still are two possibilities. In the first place, Muslim and Christian Arabs see themselves, at least to a considerable extent, as descendants of Abraham through Ishmael (the first son of Abraham) or Esau (the other son of Isaac), and thus as having a claim to the promise. It may be said that Ishmael was excluded in preference for Isaac, but Arab Christians can present a good scriptural case for including Ishmael.

If the descendants of Ishmael are not to be included, then, according to the literal interpretation, one would still be forced to ask whether modern Jews are the descendants of Abraham, Isaac, and Jacob. Earlier in this narrative it has been suggested that many of the modern Jews are by no means racial descendants of Abraham's family and that the modern Jew by Jewish definition is a Jew because of his mother. Racially the Arabs may be more purely Abrahamic than the Jews, although one must not forget that Arabs too are racially a heterogeneous group.

If one follows the spiritual interpretation, there also are several possibilities. In the first place, the spiritual sons of Abraham can include all those Jews, Muslims and Christians who are identified with the monotheistic religions based on Abraham. In a more specific spiritual sense, Christians have seen the new community founded on Christ as the new Israel. Whatever emphasis is followed, Abraham's "descendants" are those of likeminded faith rather than those of similar flesh.

Once the true "descendants" of Abraham have been identified, the geographical dimensions of their inheritance can be seen in a different light. The land promised to Abraham and his descendants, it has been said, extends from the Nile to the Euphrates (Gen. 15:18). These references to borders, however, have symbolic rather than literal meaning, and one should recognize that for Abraham they represented the normal limits of his world's geography. His vision for a promised land was worldwide.

If one gives the passage in Genesis a literal interpretation, it presents two problems. If, on the one hand, one applies it to the Land of Israel, it follows that the State of Israel must expand, as most Arabs think it intends. To them, of course, such further military advance is unthinkable and humanly unjustifiable. On the other hand, if one applies the promised land to all of humanity as one should, because even Abraham's dream envisaged blessing for all nations, then the Nile-to-the-Euphrates land is much too narrow.

For Abraham, it must also be remembered, the promise of blessing had as much to do with the revealing of a higher god as it had to do with the sighting of new land. Besides, the promise was as much a promise given as a promise received. There was no promise without a covenant, and the moment Abraham heard "to your descendants will I give this land" he also understood "walk before me, and be blameless" (Gen. 15:18). All of this means, of course, that it is foolish to talk about promised land purely in terms of acreage or territory as it is to talk of chosen people in terms of flesh or race, or as it is to talk of God's coming society in terms of a particular hill or buildings, such as the city that once belonged to the Jebusites.

Some Significant Conclusions

What does all this mean? Does it mean that Palestine is not the promised land and that Jerusalem is not the Holy City? Does it mean that the Jews are not the chosen people, nor are the Christians and the Muslims? The answer to all of these questions is both yes and no.

The answer is certainly no if we consider all of these matters in a legalistic way. There are no chosen people and no promised land anywhere in this world without a covenant with the highest God, and this includes stewardship, justice, righteousness, and morality. There is no holy city, no matter how many holy places there may be for any number of religions, if God does not dwell there in spirit and in truth.

There also is no just claim to any land where such a claim means a denial of a similar claim to one's fellowman. America does not belong to white Americans if it does not also belong in an equal way to Indians and Negroes. Palestine does not belong to the Jews who are now there if it does not also belong to the Arabs who once were there, and it does not belong to these Arabs if it doesn't also belong to those Jews.

Thus to minimize the present status of the land of promise and the qualifications of all the self-chosen chosen people is not to say that Palestine cannot or should not or will not be a land of promise in the twentieth century. The Middle East is still a land and water bridge between three major continents. It still is the place where the three major monotheistic faiths have their roots and symbols. Palestine and Jerusalem are still a focal point for much of humanity. This land can flow with milk and honey. Its foremost city can be the source of truth and righteousness.

One can, therefore, sympathize with the late Jewish philosopher Martin Buber, whose hope for Israel was that it will offer to the world a new way of life and that Jerusalem may yet become a substitute for other world capitals such as Moscow and Washington. The Lord knows how badly the world needs the model for a new way of life and a new Jerusalem, "a Zion radiating its righteousness across the whole world."[11] The Jews, who have given and still give much to the world, could once again contribute to such an alternative, as could the Arabs, whose genius is blessing the world in ways too numerous to mention. Christians, who discovered in Jesus the way, the truth, and the life, may also not be excluded. Now, however, one can only say "a plague on all your houses." Unless the Judaism of present-day Israel and Israel itself undergoes a transformation, unless also Islam experiences a conversion, and unless Christianity is reintroduced to the true Christ, there will be no chosen people and no promised land.

If there will be, we will probably find them in another place. In the same way that God can raise up children unto Abraham from stones, he can find his chosen people today where he will. He can create a promised land where he will, and he can turn

---

[11] Buber, *To Hallow This Life,* p. 174.

any hovel of a village into his holy Zion. As things stand at present, neither Jerusalem, Moscow, Berlin, London, Paris, Cairo, Rome, or Washington is receptive to the establishment of his holy hill.

II. THE CONFLICT SITUATION

Now that we have discussed some aspects of the Christian involvement and identified some of the rethinking that is necessary if Christians are to make a real long-term contribution to peace in the Middle East, we may look at the situation itself and then consider some more specific responses. These responses, it must be emphasized, will have real significance only in the context of the new heart and the new frame of mind set forth above. The prophecy that most needs to be fulfilled among Christians as well as among Jews and Muslims is the one that came through Ezekiel: "A new heart will I give you, and a new spirit I will put within you; and I will take out of your flesh the heart of stone and give you a heart of flesh" (Ezek. 36:26).

The Gravity of the Situation

In our look at the situation, then, we must first acknowledge that the Middle East confronts the world with a conflict of the gravest proportions. As horrible and problematic as are the war in Southeast Asia and the recent civil war in Nigeria, one could visualize these conflicts ending without engulfing the entire world. The Middle East conflict, on the other hand, shows no signs whatsoever of coming to an early end.

The traditional kind of ending to conflict, a decisive but regionally contained military finish, is not possible for the foreseeable future. Israel can and probably will win additional "six-day wars" over the Arabs, but it cannot possibly crush them. Both Arab humanity and geography are too large for such a victory, and Arab stubbornness is too great for an easy surrender. By military measures the Arabs have been "defeated" several times, but they have not acknowledged defeat and bowed to the victor. Consequently, the victor in the Middle East is helpless.

The Arabs, on the other hand, cannot in the near future overcome Israel. Although the West tends to overemphasize Arab disunity, disorganization, and inefficiency, it is undisputed that Israel is strong in all those areas in which the Arabs are weak. Thus the Arabs too are not in military position to end the conflict, if a military end to it can be visualized at all.

Even if one side or the other could at this time attempt a final military decision, there would be so much opposition from world public opinion that the attempt would be severely handicapped. Indeed, the opposition would be so great that big-power intervention would be the undoubted result, and this in turn would lead to a conflagration of unprecedented magnitude. The word Armageddon would not be too weak to describe the ensuing holocaust.

Such an international disaster will indeed be the end of the Middle East conflict, if peace is not established soon. Unless some agreements are reached between the contesting parties, it is just a question of time before the time bomb in the middle blows up the entire world. Before that happens we face a shorter (perhaps a decade) or longer (perhaps a century or more) period of intermittent warfare with the hot conflicts becoming increasingly hotter and the cooling off periods increasingly shorter. All of these wars and the final war may be viewed as a judgment of God on all that man did to cause the conflict and on all that he failed to do to avoid it.

Sometimes the situation appears to be so grave, the trends so irreversible, and the causal factors so deeply rooted that little can be done, it seems, to avoid the ultimate catastrophe. Yet, we cannot give up hope that man will yet judge himself, recognize his wrongdoing, reverse the trends, and make peace with his fellowman. With an Israeli writer, we can express both realism and optimism:

> I am an optimist. I believe that nothing in history is predetermined. History in the making is composed of acts of human beings, their emotions and aspirations.
>
> The depth of bitterness and hatred throughout our Semitic Region seems bottomless. Yet it is a comparatively new phenomenon, the outcome of the recent clash of our peoples. Nothing like European anti-Semitism ever existed in the Arab world prior to the events which created the vicious circle.
>
> We have seen, in our times, Germans and Frenchmen co-operating, if not loving each other, after a war which lasted for many hundreds of years and whose bitter fruits are deeply imbedded in both German and French culture. We are witnessing today the beginnings of an American-Soviet alliance

which would have been unthinkable only a dozen years ago.[12]

The Heart of the Conflict

Before there can be a beginning in the desired direction, however, there must be a clear recognition of what factors or causes are central to the Middle East conflict. We must, therefore, return to the claimants and their claims, and identify the basic or what we might call prior claims. The following layers in the conflict require consideration:

> The United Nations
> The Super-Powers — US and USSR
> The Arab States and Israel
> Judaism, Christianity, and Islam
> The Palestinian Arabs and the Israelis

The several layers or dimensions in the Middle East conflict complicate the issue exceedingly, but it is most important that we assess the situation as it is at the beginning of the 1970s. Where we begin determines where we come out. What central focus we give to the problem has bearing on the focus of our solution. How close we come to the source of the cancer may determine the success of treatment and surgery.

Our reference to the United Nations is not to be seen as running parallel with the listing of other parties to the conflict, yet we may not pass this power structure by. Ideally, the UN is the indispensable arbiter and mediator in the conflict, giving its ear to all parties in the dispute and making decisions on the basis of the UN Charter and established international law. The UN has been in the past, and will need to be in the future, a neutral police force to enable orderly implementation of the international will. In the meantime, the relief agency of the UN (UNRWA) is providing essential, though minimal, services to the refugee community, and those programs should be undergirded.

The United Nations is by no means ideal or perfect as an instrument of international law, order, and justice, and it too stands under the judgment of God. Indeed, the UN may have made some very fundamental mistakes in its early years with respect to the Middle East. But the UN represents a step — at present the world's biggest and best step — in the direction

---

[12] Uri Avnery, *Israel Without Zionists: A Plea for Peace in the Middle East,* pp. 212-213.

of the vision of Isaiah, who saw the nations of the world sur-
rendering their sovereignty in favor of a higher authority and
a superior will:

> It shall come to pass in the latter days that the mountain of
> the house of the Lord shall be established as the highest of
> the mountains, and shall be raised above the hills; and all
> the nations shall flow to it, and many peoples shall come,
> and say: Come, let us go up to the mountain of the Lord ...
> they shall beat their swords into plowshares, and their spears
> into pruning hooks; nation shall not lift up sword against
> nation, neither shall they learn war any more (Isa. 2:1-4).

The United Nations has difficulty living up to its own ideal
role, because, like its predecessor, it tends to be used by the
big powers to their advantage. In the same way that the League
of Nations did the will of France and Britain, so the United
Nations largely represented the will of the victorious European
and North American nations of World War II, particularly
in its early years.

The position of these nations, for instance, prevailed over
the legitimate will of the indigenous Middle East peoples and
nations in 1947. Even the idea of the internationalization of
Jerusalem, advanced in 1947 and again in 1967 as a good way
of recognizing the universal interest in and character of this
famous city, was a western idea, which could be traced back
to the early nineteenth century, when the British wanted and
needed an outpost in Jerusalem.

The western nations have always reached eagerly for every
opportunity to have political, religious, commercial, or military stations all over the world; and, as the colonial era passed
in the Middle East, internationalization appeared to be a good
way to accommodate the continuing western interest. To the
Arab world, however, internationalization of a city belonging
to them was an idea as bad and as unacceptable as the internationalization of London, Paris, and Washington would have
been to the British, French, and Americans, respectively.

Powers, States, and Religions

This leads us to consider more specifically the involvements
of the big powers. There are at least four, though the earlier
interests of Britain and France, which reached their recent
peak in the Sinai-Suez War of 1956, have now definitely given

way to the two super-powers, the United States and Soviet Union. Since 1967 there has been a tendency to look upon these two nations as the main causes of the conflict and also as the only solutions. Late in 1969 some Arab states announced that they looked upon the United States as their number one enemy. Similarly, the Israelis have frequently blamed Communist interference in the Arab world for the lack of a peace settlement.

The two big powers are obviously committed to the Middle East, and their presence both as cause and solution to the problem, should not be underestimated. But neither should it be overestimated, as has frequently been the case. In spite of the interests of both the United States and the Soviet Union, the Middle East conflict cannot and should not be reduced simply to another US-USSR confrontation.

Nor should it be identified purely as a struggle over boundaries between Israel and the respective Arab states, as is frequently done by the popular press. The various Arab states are, of course, in a state of war with Israel, especially those who claim territory that Israel now occupies, namely: Egypt (Sinai and Gaza), Jordan (West Bank), and Syria (Golan Heights). Yet, one could visualize all of these states making separate peace treaties with Israel after certain border adjustments, if the territorial conflicts were not overlaid by a more basic quarrel. After all, they all did sign separate armistice agreements in 1949.

Beyond the quarrel over territory, the Arab states and Israel, respectively, symbolize the conflicting cultures of two peoples. But as serious as the disparity between the two is, it is not at the moment the fundamental issue which is firing their respective nationalisms, and we must take a closer look at what is really burning.

The oil on the fire has sometimes been identified as religion, and consequently the conflict has been seen as a war between Judaism and Islam. Islamic appeals for a holy war following the 1969 burning of the Al-Aksa mosque in Jerusalem and Jewish reaction to the Arab maltreatment of the holy places of Judaism lend some support to this theory. And it is true that both sides appeal to holy literature and other sacred symbols in support of their causes.

Yet it would be a mistake to see the Middle East problem primarily as a religious war in the sense of an Islam-Judaism confrontation, and that for several reasons. In the first place, the Arab world is not all Islamic. There are many Arab Christians in Egypt, Palestine, and Lebanon who feel exactly as their Muslim Arab brethren do. Secondly, not all the Islamic world is Arabic, and non-Arabic Asian and African Muslims do not enter into the Middle East problem with the same intensity, if they enter it at all, as do the Arabs. Finally, Judaism as a religion does not appear to be a primary motivator with a large majority of Israeli Jews.

Two Peoples, One Land

The Middle East conflict at its core is not another US-USSR confrontation, not a test of military muscle between Nasser and Dayan, and not a quarrel between Muhammad and Moses. Rather it is a contest for control of the same parcel of land (Palestine) by two peoples, namely, the Jews (mostly of European origin) and the Palestinian Arabs. Both of these peoples have been terribly wronged in the past.

To be sure, both have won the support of, and been sponsored by, one or more of the big powers. Both have appealed to their religious heritage for direction, strength, and legitimacy. And, to the extent that the Arab states have spoken and fought for the Palestinian cause, the struggle has taken on the shape of a contest between sovereign Arab states and the State of Israel. But at its root, the quarrel results from the incompatible claims of two peoples for the same parcel of land. Both call it their homeland. To the Jews, who have gained it, the new name for the homeland is security. For the Arabs, who have lost it, it could very well be called justice. For both, the land, in addition to justice and security, spells fulfillment.

The Jewish need for security, of course, goes back to the European experience of many centuries of second-class citizenship and persecution. Whatever the Jews themselves may have contributed to the discrimination, persecution, and extermination policies of which they were the target, there can be, and must be, no doubt about the fact that they have been terribly wronged. It should never have been necessary for the various European states to pass special laws giving Jews the full rights which were theirs by birth. To the extent that history made special laws necessary, they should never have been delayed until the middle of the nineteenth century.

These rights, having been granted, should not have been rights only on the law books but also in the hearts and minds of the people. France, England, and the United States should not have found it necessary to find a home for the Jews outside of their own countries, while they themselves had still not fully accepted Jews or welcomed their persecuted brethren from elsewhere in the world.

In eastern European countries the bloody pogroms can never be excused no matter how well the national historians may succeed in explaining them. And Germany's "final solution" for the Jews in the twentieth century is an injustice and horror too great to describe in words. Admittedly, many Jews too were not without social guilt, but that is quite beside the point in the light of the wrongs that were done against them by European populations and their rulers, most of whom supposedly enjoyed the enlightenment of the Christian faith.

As the Christian nations in Europe and America recognized, belatedly, the wrong that had been done, they tried to make amends by redressing the wrongs committed against, and winning the favor of, the Jews. These efforts in turn produced the church theologies and the national and international policies that granted to the Jews their own territorial state in the twentieth century.

In the process of serving the Jews, the western peoples worked out once more, perhaps subconsciously, their traditional hostilities against Islam and the Arab, no longer by overt crusades against him, but by ignoring him and treating him as a non-entity. One might say that an old anti-Semitism directed against the Semitic Jews now became a new anti-Semitism directed against the Semitic Arabs. As the old anti-Semitism terribly wronged the Jews so the new anti-Semitism terribly wronged the Arabs.

No six million Arabs were exterminated, but their humanity was bitterly offended as slowly but surely several million were pushed into the desert and kept there, not by gas ovens but by the fire bombs of napalm. The surprising and shocking part was that the survivors of the gas ovens were now the administrators of the fire bombs. As Arnold Toynbee has written:

> The Jews knew from personal experience what they were

doing; and it was their supreme tragedy that the lesson learned by them from their encounter with the Nazi Gentiles should have been not to shun but to imitate some of the evil deeds that the Nazis had committed against the Jews.[13]

An Injustice Against the Arabs

This then is the central problem of the Middle East: the attempt to redress a wrong committed against the Jews produced a similar wrong against the Palestinian Arabs. The very promises made by the big powers and the United Nations that gave the Jews their homeland denied the Arabs theirs. The acts of the Zionists that restored the Jews robbed the Arabs. The tragedy of the robbery was compounded by the fact that the victims of the new Jewish self-assertion were not the guilty-of-persecution Europeans, but the relatively innocent Arabs, who for centuries had, with few exceptions, provided a haven for certain homeless and insecure Jews.

But this is not to say that the Arabs were in no way responsible for the human tragedy that befell the Palestinians. Absentee Arab landowners, who disregarded the rights of tenants as they sold their land for material gain, and ambitious Arab rulers, who were hungry for personal power and resisted the social revolution so needed in the Arab world, must share some of the blame for the maltreatment of the Palestinians.

The biggest abusers by far, however, were the British, the Zionists, the Americans, and the French, followed by the Russians. The big powers felt that if they pushed out another big power, namely, the Ottoman empire, they were free to do with the area as they pleased after the manner of former empires. Sharing the blame with the western powers are their Christian communities, who lacked the respect due the native Middle East populations and their faiths at the most crucial times.

The Zionists, encouraged by the stance of the Christians and the policies of Christian nations, promoted dreams and visions that discounted the native population, much in the same way that European immigrants to North America through the years discounted the humanity of the native Indian and Eskimo populations. The Zionists did not ask about the rights

---

[13] Quoted in Hadawi, *Palestine in Focus*, p. 53.

of the Arabs. The League of Nations allowed itself to be blinded by the Zionists and the big powers, which had material interests in the Middle East, all on the assumption that the Arabs were not aware, mature, alert, capable, or even there.

To this very day, some Zionists deny the presence of over 650,000 Arabs at the time of the Balfour Declaration, and even' those whose presence is acknowledged are written off as homeless Bedouins without territorial rights or as bastard descendants of the previous conquerors.[14] As late as 1969 Israeli Prime Minister Golda Meir denied the existence of Palestinians:

> How can we return the occupied territories? There is nobody to return them to. . . . There was no such thing as Palestinians. . . . It was not as though there was a Palestinian people in Palestine considering itself as a Palestinian people and we came and threw them out and took their country away from them. They did not exist.[15]

The Palestinians patiently endured the nonrecognition of their humanity and its basic rights at a time when the rights of the people around the world were being recognized, and when all the colonies were being decolonized. Considering the wrong done against them, their passivity and endurance was remarkable, even when we acknowledge that their political and military handicaps left them little other choice.

It is wrong, therefore, to say today that the Palestinians understand only the language of force. Their taking up arms is much more an indication that the Zionists and the big powers understand only the language of force. For twenty years, from 1947 to 1967, the Palestinians were relatively pacific, waiting for the Arab states to do what they said they would be doing, and waiting for the United Nations to implement its resolutions. When all of these failed, the Palestinians organized themselves and turned to arms as a way of achieving the recognition and the dignity they had long been asking for.

We must recognize, therefore, that the Palestinian struggle for the liberation (as they call it) of their homeland is at

---

[14] Yaakov Morris, Director of Information, Israeli Department of Foreign Affairs, in a Jerusalem lecture in the presence of the author, June 19, 1969.

[15] From speeches by Israeli Prime Minister Golda Meir on March 8, 1969 and June 15, 1969, quoted in *The Middle East Newsletter*, III:5-6 (September 1969), p. 1.

the root of the current problem. It is this cause which is now dominating the politics of the Arab states. It is this cause that has won massive support, not only from Arab states but also from several of the bigger powers like the Soviet Union and to a lesser degree France and to a still lesser degree Britain.

Israel's greatest security problem is not now (if it ever was) any one of the Arab states or all of them together but rather the Palestinians and their commandos seeking a return to their homeland. In this return they are demanding and receiving the support of the respective Arab states. Admittedly, some of these states, as they cooperate, have very much in mind their own power interests and border grievances, but in the Middle East conflict these are secondary to the more basic Palestinian cause.

That Palestinian cause will remain a cause as long as injustice is continued. The western powers have, ever since World War I, proposed Middle East solutions that bypassed or minimized the injustice. They hoped, no doubt, that the Palestinians would adjust to the new order of things in the same way that millions of displaced Europeans adjusted to new situations. But the Middle East injustice would not be adjusted away, and for the westerner to demand that unwilling Arabs adjust to injustice was only to perpetuate the injustice.

As a child of refugee parents who fled the Bolshevik Revolution and made a new home in Canada, this writer too wonders why the Palestinians did not express readiness to resettle. Otherwise, however, he is in no moral position to make the suggestion that they do, partly because the western immigration door is no more open to them than it was to the Jews in the 1930s and 1940s. But how can justice now be done to the Palestinian Arabs without once more threatening the security of the Jews? Admittedly, the situation is complex, but it is not so difficult that nothing can be done.

III. THE CONTRIBUTION TO PEACE

Many peace plans have been advanced by many people at various levels of authority in the last two decades, all to no avail it appears; and one must be a little foolish, a little presumptuous, and a little courageous to make additional suggestions. Most of what remains to be said is not new, being simply a reinforcement of what has already been advanced by others, including the former Commissioner-General of UNRWA, John H. Davis. Speaking about the "evasive peace," he suggested the following guidelines:

> The policy adopted must hold forth real promise of bringing an end to conflict, which means that it must be both equitable and possible of implementation; it must bring justice to the Arab people for the grave wrongs that they have endured that Israel might exist, and protect their rights and their way of life for the future; and it must protect the people in Israel against wrongful acts and persecution and, in so far as possible, preserve for them their traditional way of life. Also, it is imperative that the welfare of the people be put above that of institutions and states when the two are in conflict. As a general guide, past United Nations resolutions should prove helpful, since their weakness has never been their content but their lack of implementation. Furthermore, the members of the United Nations have already reached agreement on them.[16]

Some Policy Alternatives

What can western Christians do toward that end? The most important contribution has already been dealt with at length, namely, adopting for themselves and offering to the world new ideas about God, the Messiah, chosen people, holy places, the kingdom, holy wars, and promised land, for it is the old ideas — the distortions of Christian faith — that have brought so much tragedy. In other words, let the Christians, first of all, accept their Messiah and become Christians, and they will have made their most important contribution to peace.

The new spirituality will, of course, require outlets in a new policy. This policy will have to go beyond the two that Christians have always supported, almost without reservation: preaching and shooting. It may seem incredible, but between these two extremes Christians have had difficulty visualizing and supporting other strategies.

Let us, therefore, propose two others between the two extremes. The one, which we will call "prophesying," has often been disparagingly called "getting involved in politics," and many conservative Christians have rejected it because it was too realistic and not sticking close enough to the gospel. The other, which we can call "cross-bearing" or "peace-making,"

---

16 *The Evasive Peace,* p. 102.

has been rejected, usually by the same people because it was not realistic and practical enough as, for instance, was shooting.

Prophecy and Public Opinion

Essentially, prophesying has to do with the bold proclamation of the will of God in very practical and relevant terms in high places and low places. Adapted to the modern situation it has to do with giving God a chance at mass public opinion. It requires confronting the decision-makers at all levels with respect to the priority claims of God, with righteousness, justice, security, and peace. It means getting involved in politics the way the Old Testament prophets involved themselves with wayward Israel, the way Muhammad involved himself by challenging the idolatry with the concept of one God, and the way Jesus involved himself when he announced a new kingdom.

Admittedly, the prophetic role requires much insight and wisdom (a political position, if you will), and courage. But if Christians could begin to prophesy to each other first, and then to their societies and to their nation-states, they would gradually prepare the way for the purest kind of prophecy coming from the church at its most authoritative levels to the highest decision-makers in the world, meaning the superpowers and the United Nations. Eventually, they might even prophesy to Judaism and Islam, but this could only be done if Christians were prepared also to hear Jewish and Muslim prophets. But what may be the substance of the prophetic proclamation, of the Christian injection into public opinion? In general and basic terms the ground has already been covered in the first part of this chapter, but let us now be somewhat more specific:

1. *Justice for the Palestinian Arabs.* There can and should, first of all, be a full recognition in the West that a great injustice has been done to the Palestinian Arabs and that mostly by the West. This admission, if it were full and sincere, would itself do much to relieve the pressure in the Middle East. A verbal admission of course must be followed by some meaningful action. But to begin with, let British, French, American, and Canadian Christian people admit themselves and persuade their governments to admit the repeated violation of the human rights of Palestinians.

Secondly, let Christian people help the Palestinian Arabs

tell their story to the world. They have tried to tell the West by themselves since 1919, but they were weak and handicapped, and western ears were learning to respond less and less to simple pleas for justice and more and more to massive propaganda onslaughts and the noise of firearms. It is regrettable that the Palestinian Arabs are now learning the propaganda and military games, but they have turned to this undesirable way of communicating not because they could not communicate another way but because the West would not listen any other way. If Christians would give a fair hearing and fair telling to the Palestinian story, the Palestinians would feel less need to communicate with hijackings and bombings.

A third requirement of prophecy is to prevent further expulsions. Early in 1970, more and more Arabs in the occupied territories were being made homeless in the name of Israeli security, while Jewish immigrants were being received at the rate of 150 a day. The 1969 totals were near the 60,000 mark, one of the highest yearly totals. Whatever rights to Palestine these European Jewish immigrants may have, they surely do not transcend the rights of the Palestinian Arabs who are already there and those who are waiting to return from beyond the river. The most elemental prophecy that Christians could give is that which has already been given to Israel by one of its own leaders:

> Nothing frightens the Arabs more than the idea of the Ingathering of the Exiles. There arises before Arab eyes the spectre of a wave of Jewish immigration, bringing to Israel another ten million Jews, overflowing its narrow frontiers and conquering Arab states, evicting the inhabitants and grabbing land for innumerable new *kibbutzim*. There is something ludicrous in the present situation. Zionist leaders, including Prime Minister Eshkol, make visionary speeches about millions of Jews who will soon arrive on the shores of Israel, fulfilling the prophecy of Zionism. To an Israeli audience, knowing the reality, this is the sort of wishful thinking by which an antiquated regime tries desperately to preserve its obsolete slogans. Yet, to millions of Arabs these speeches sound like definite threats to Arab existence, threats made even more terrible by Israel's manifest military superiority.[17]

Fourth, while preventing further expulsions of and injustices

---

[17] Avnery, *op. cit.,* pp. 162-163.

to Arabs is a difficult task, the return of those who have been away from their homes, most of them out of the country for over twenty years, is vastly more complex. Their country is still there, but it is no longer what it once was, and in most, if not all, instances their homes are no longer waiting for them. Physically, however, the country is in position to receive them just as easily as it can accommodate any number of Jews.

The least that can be done and should be done is to affirm with the United Nations that the Palestinian Arabs have a right to return or to receive reparations, whichever may be their preference, and to facilitate such return and reparations. We should not say to the Arabs, as we have so frequently in the past, that they should give to the Jews a small share of the vast Arab geography. The Palestinian Arabs had only Palestine, and we might as well say to the Rhodesian blacks that they should resettle to some other part of the vast black continent and leave a little sovereign territory for the whites. That is the language of imperialism, not of justice.

The Arab states and Palestinian commandos may, of course, not be excluded from the requirements of justice. They may for themselves not see any alternatives, but they should at least be reminded that guerrilla activities have already started a vicious circle of terror and counter-terror that will bring additional, perhaps unprecedented, miseries to the Palestinian people. Al-Fatah may claim to be liberating the Arab people but it could very well also spell their end as a nation. The prophecy must draw attention to this possibility.

2. *Security for the Jews.* This is an issue as great as injustice for the Arabs, and surely God is as much concerned about the one as about the other. We must understand the Jews of Israel. They came to Palestine in search of security. In Europe and other parts of the world they had been most insecure. Most of the immigrants had relatives who were sacrificed to Hitler's final solution. Now as they are confronted by what they perceive as a threat to their physical survival, they are responding as we would all respond. No people can face the prospect of genocide a second time in a generation.

It has been said in the Middle East that the Arab threat to push the Jews into the sea is only propaganda. We must understand the Arab and his language, we are told, because to him the deed has been accomplished when the word has been spoken. Granted that there is some truth to this observation on Arab culture, the prophetic word should include a response to such threatening language. When an Arab voices threats he is responsible not only for what they mean to him, but also for what they mean to his enemies. God does not want the Jews pushed into the sea any more than he wants the Arabs pushed into the desert. Thus, the Christian prophecy must seek the restraint of the Arabs, both as states and as Palestinian commandos.

Moreover, we must probably also give attention to the continuing insecurity of Jews in Eastern Europe, even if that insecurity is not as great as Zionist propagandists would have it.[18] We should make sure that in the United States and Canada they will always find a warm welcome and security. It would be wrong to suggest that these too go to Palestine, because we have already concluded that security for Jews in Palestine means injustice for the Arabs there, and that in turn means insecurity for the Jews.

The Jews who have already made Palestine their homeland have a right to stay there, but it would be difficult to accept further immigration until the requirements of justice to the Arabs have been met. Surely, Palestine belongs more to the Palestinian Arabs in exile who want to return than to the eastern European Jews who have never been there.

It has been said that the security of the Jews as a people depends on the sovereignty of Israel as a state. Indeed, that sovereignty was allowed by the international community on the assumption that it meant security. That assumption, however, is becoming increasingly questionable as time goes on. To the Palestinian Arabs security for Jews and sovereignty for Israel were always two separate questions. They were always prepared to guarantee the former but never to accept the latter.

Consequently, they opposed Jewish immigration to the extent that it pointed to the establishment of a Jewish state. When the Zionists insisted, as they still do, that the security of their people and the sovereignty of the state were one and the same thing to them, then they also began to mean the same thing to the Arabs. At that point the Arabs began to say that the destruction of Israel as a state could require that the

---

[18] See Peter Worthington (for five years a *Toronto Telegram* correspondent in the USSR), "Jews in the Soviet Union: The Truth Behind Zionism's Gigantic Distortion," *Issues*, XXL:3 (Autumn 1967), pp. 1-22.

Jews as a people be driven into the sea, just as the creation
and expansion of the state required the driving of the Arabs
into the desert.

This will not happen soon, but eventually it could happen.
In the long run an Israeli state is as insecure in the Arab
world as white regimes are insecure in Africa. All who are
interested in the security of the Jews in Palestine are, therefore,
obligated to prophesy to them about the sovereignty that does
not fit, the state sovereignty that militates against Jewish security. Not to do so will mean once more to share in the
guilt of Jewish insecurity.

Support for this point of view is to be found not only in
a proper analysis of the current situation but also in a review
of the ancient kingdoms of the Hebrew people, as well as
some contemporary Jewish leaders. As one Jewish historian
has reminded us:

> The throne of Israel was a precarious post, offering the ruler
> an average occupancy of 11 years. Altogether nine separate
> dynasties rose and fell during the 212-year period of its
> monarchy, one dynasty lasting as little as seven days. Few
> of the 19 kings who occupied the throne died of natural
> causes.[19]

The Israel of the twentieth century is in many ways politically
and militarily stronger than the kingdoms of old, but the perils
from without are also much greater. And were there no perils
from without, the divisive perils within would loom large, because Zionism has within it the seeds of its own destruction,
as much as did the Kingdom of Solomon. For Israel to depend
for the security of the Jews on chariots and horsemen seems
as foolish now as then.

Some Jewish leaders inside and outside of Israel have themselves recognized the dangerous character of the present State
of Israel and called for its de-Zionization. Essentially, they have
reiterated the warning given by the late Henry Morgenthau,
prominent American Jew and Senator, who foresaw the tragic
consequences of Zionism already after World War I. Having
been sent to eastern Europe by President Wilson to investigate
the plight of Jews he was fully acquainted with "the indigni-
ties and outrages to which he had been subjected." But he
did not see Zionism as a "way out of this morass of poverty,

---

[19] Max I. Dimont, *Jews, God, and History*, p. 53.

hatred, political inequality, and social discrimination." Instead:

> Zionism is the most stupendous fallacy in Jewish history. . . .
> The very fervor of my feeling for the oppressed of every
> race and every land, especially for the Jews, those of my
> own blood and faith, to whom I am bound by every tender
> tie, impels me to fight with all the greater force against this
> scheme, which my intelligence tells me can only lead them
> deeper into the mire of the past, while it professes to be
> leading them to the heights. Zionism is . . . a retrogression into
> the blackest error, and not progress toward the light.[20]

The president of the World Jewish Congress since 1951 and
former president of the World Zionist Organization, Nahum
Goldman, likewise questioned the earlier assumptions of Zionism. Writing early in 1970, he suggested that if the State of
Israel was to bring security to the Jews as people, it would
as a minimum have to become a different state, militarily
neutral, territorially less ambitious, and politically more re-
specting of Arab rights and Palestinian aspirations:

> The history of the Zionist movement, as of many others,
> proves that the greatest real factors in history in the long
> run are neither armies nor physical, economic, or political
> strength, but visions, ideas, and dreams. These are the only
> things which give dignity and meaning to the history of
> mankind, so full of brutality, senselessness, and crime. Jew-
> ish history certainly proves it: we survived not because of
> our strength — physical, economic, or political — but because
> of our spirit.[21]

Related to the question of security is the question of morality in the context of sovereignty. As we have already seen, the
State of Israel is in the nature of an exclusivistic state, again
comparable in kind if not degree to the white regimes in Africa.
It has proved itself repeatedly to be expansionist. Both of these
facts together mean the inevitable subordination of other peoples in the contravention of the UN Charter, of the best in Judaism, and of the rights of humanity.

Justice and security for all the peoples who are in Palestine
and who have a right to return cannot lie in the rule of one

---

[20] *Papers on Palestine III: A Collection of Articles by Distinguished
Jews Who Oppose Political Zionism*, p. 66.

[21] Nahum Goldman, "The Future of Israel," *Foreign Affairs*, XLVIII:
3 (April 1970), p. 459 (pp. 441-459).

group over the other, but rather in the equal participation of all in the government of the total area. Jews can and will find their security if they share their sovereignty, and Arabs can and will find the highest form of justice if, as they return from the desert, they lay down their arms and abandon the notion of pushing the Jews into the sea. Both of these messages to both parties must be part of the Christian prophecy.

On both sides we hear people saying that justice (meaning return) for the Arabs or that security for the Jews (meaning that they should stay) are impossible. If they are indeed impossible then we must face the ultimate fact that survival is impossible and that Armageddon is inevitable. But if survival is desirable and necessary, and if it is to be made possible, then compromise must also be possible. In some ways this will be more difficult in 1970 than it was in 1920, but in some ways it can be easier, because the passing of time has made it more necessary than ever, as both sides are beginning to recognize.

3. *Restrain the Powers and Boost the UN.* How is survival possible? How can the minimal necessary requirement (a fraternal federation of Jewish and Arab states within the land area of Palestine) or the maximal desirable requirement (a single state in which both peoples are equal and secure) be achieved?

It can only be achieved if both parties agree to such a development, and the willingness itself must come by peaceful means. This rules out the usual kind of intervention by the super-powers, which is now advocated by an increasing number of people. There is very little in the imperial history, which we have reviewed, which encourages direct big-power roles as real solutions to regional problems. In their own minds, the big powers may be pursuing the claims of God — and they usually persuade most patriotic-religious folk that they are — when in reality they are working out the claims of empire or the claims of the imperial god, whom they call God.

Both of the present super-powers involved in the Middle East have persuaded themselves and their partners and are trying to persuade the rest of the world that their claims are of the highest order. One speaks of the defense of human freedom and the other of human liberation from imperialism. Both slogans are about as close to claiming to act in the name of God as one can get. Neither is much different from any of the empires that have preceded it. Both use high-sounding phrases to hide selfish imperial intentions.

Rather than increasing big-power intervention, the will of God, as historically revealed, lies in big-power extrication. The best solution the United States and the Soviet Union can contribute is to cease being part of the problem, which they are as they pursue their economic and strategic interests, as they supply arms to both sides, and as they get in the way of the United Nations, or prevent it from playing its role in the conflict. This is not to say that the big powers must isolate themselves and withdraw from world problems, but unless intervention can be more creative and unselfish, withdrawal would be far better.

The United Nations, as has already been indicated, also has it weaknesses, but it is humanity's best step in the direction of achieving peace among the states who need to surrender some of their sovereignties to this higher cause. So let the big powers throw their moral and material weight behind the United Nations, and let the Christians prophesy to that end. As the pen is mightier than the sword, so the prophecy can be much more helpful than the military power to which states too easily resort too quickly.

Christians as Peacemakers

The prophetic contribution to peace does not end, or perhaps even begin, with the spoken word, as important as that word may be for the direction of public opinion and national policy. The bold word must be accompanied, as it always has been in the best of the Jewish, Christian, and Muslim traditions, by the sacrificial deed. And this can mean many things, such as the usual varieties of philanthropy for Jews and Arabs.

The present Middle East conflict, however, calls for the deed that goes beyond the ordinary and the usual. It calls Christians back to the central theme of their faith, namely, that of a man laying down his life for his friends and his enemies. This is precisely the role to which Christians are being called in today's world.

The Middle East situation confronts us with the historical fact that many Jews and Muslims have died or sacrificed their rights on behalf of Christians. Christians can now make a con-

tribution to peace only if they become willing to die and sacrifice on behalf of Israelis and Arabs. And this does not mean
going to war on their behalf on either side. Indeed, it is time
for Christians to leave all their guns at home. But it does
mean entering the arena of war on both sides and sharing
the insecurity that the conflict brings. We have in mind an
unarmed peace force, consisting of well-trained, well-motivated,
fearless, strong, and loving young men and women who would
in one way or another absorb the insecurity, fear, and even the
blows arising from the conflict.

They would stand by and help the Palestinian and Jordanian
farmers as they braved the Israeli jets to cultivate their acreage in the Jordan and other valleys. Similarly, they would
stand with the Israeli *kibbutzim* and other settlements being
shelled by the Arabs. They would search out and defuse bombs
in the market places. They would also help Arabs to dig
shelters, warn them of approaching jets, and stand with them
in air raids.

To many people such a proposal is undoubtedly the height
of unrealism, but it is only unrealistic because it has rarely
been tried. It could at least be as realistic and effective as
policies now being pursued. Many details and technicalities
concerning this new strategy would, of course, have to be
worked out, but all of this should not prevent Christians from
expressing their willingness to enter the conflict at its physically
most dangerous points in order to point the way to security
and justice. With today's idealistic and sacrifice-minded young
people, finding enough volunteers would probably be the least
problem to worry about.

This approach has application not only to the Middle East
but also to other parts of the world, where we might see its
relevance more clearly. Take Southeast Asia, for instance. In
the spring of 1966 President Johnson pledged his country to
an assistance program amounting to one billion dollars to
harness and develop the water resources of the Mekong River
which begins in China and flows through Laos, Thailand, Cam-
bodia, and Vietnam. It seemed to be a very generous offer, but
in the light of the thirty billion dollars annually expended
since then in military activity, it was a pittance.

Yet, if that one billion dollars would have been applied
and if all the thousands of Christian Americans who went to
Vietnam would have left uniforms and guns at home, and

instead gone with overalls and spades to work on that Mekong project under UN auspices, Vietnam and the world would be much, much different today. Not much imagination or prophetic insight is required to conclude that in all probability: many less Americans and Vietnamese would be dead today; the Southeast Asian economy would be in better shape; the political situation would be sounder and stabler; Chinese and Russian influence would be weaker; and American society would be healthier at home and have much greater respect abroad.

We must learn the lessons of Vietnam and begin to apply them to other parts of the world where we still have opportunity. As far as the Middle East is concerned, European and North American Christians should leave all their weaponry and hostility at home and persuade their governments to do likewise. For Christians, the holy lands could attain their greatest holiness yet, if they could find, like Christ, a way of willingly, innocently, and sacrificially bearing on their bodies the blows of a warring world. In the shedding of their blood they would find their holiest ground. In the laying down of their lives they would find their most exalted chosenness. In their equal concern for Jew and Arab they would bring all, including themselves, closer to the Father. They would, in fact, be establishing the everlasting kingdom of peace of which the prophets spoke and for which the whole world continues to hope.

Bibliography

I. Books and Documents

Acheson, Dean. *Present at the Creation: My Years in the State Department.* New York: Norton, 1969.

Albright, William Foxwell. *From the Stone Age to Christianity: Monotheism and the Historical Process.* Baltimore: Johns Hopkins, 1957.

Angus, Jacob Bernard. *The Meaning of Jewish History.* Toronto: Abelard-Schuman, 1963.

Annual Report of the Secretary-General on the Work of the Organization, June, 1968-June, 1969. United Nations General Assembly: 24th Session. Supplement No. 1 (A/7601).

Antonius, George. *The Arab Awakening.* New York: Capricorn, 1965.

The Arab Refugee Problem: How It Can Be Solved: Proposals Submitted to the General Assembly of the United Nations. n.p.: 1951.

Arberry, A. J. *Religion in the Middle East.* London: Cambridge University Press, 1969. 2 Volumes.

Avnery, Uri. *Israel Without Zionists: A Plea for Peace in the Middle East.* New York: Macmillan, 1968.

Badeau, John S. *The American Approach to the Arab World.* New York: Harper, 1968.

Barron, J. B. (ed.). *Palestine: Report and General Abstracts of the Census of 1922.* Jerusalem: Greek Convent Press, 1922.

Beatty, Ilene. *Arab and Jew in the Land of Canaan.* Chicago: Regnery, 1957.

Begin, Menachim. *The Revolt: The Story of the Irgun.* London: W. H. Allen, 1951.

Bein, Alex. *Theodore Herzl: A Biography.* London: East and West Library, 1957.

Bell, J. Bowyer. *The Long War: Israel and the Arabs Since 1946.* Englewood Cliffs, N.J.: Prentice-Hall, 1969.

Ben-Gurion, David. *Israel: Years of Challenge.* New York: Holt, Rinehart & Winston, 1963.

Bentwich, Norman. *Palestine.* London: Ernest Benn, 1934.

Berger, Morroe. *The Arab World Today.* New York: Doubleday, 1962.

Book of Documents, General Assembly of the United Nations Relating to the Establishment of the National Home for the Jewish People. New York: The Jewish Agency for Palestine, 1947.

Bright, John. *A History of Israel.* Philadelphia: Westminster, 1959.

Brockelmann, Carl. *History of the Islamic Peoples*. New York: Capricorn, 1960.
Brown, David. *The Restoration of the Jews: The History, Principles, and Bearings of the Question*. London: Hamilton-Adams, 1861.
Buber, Martin. *Israel and Palestine: The History of an Idea*. New York: Strauss and Young, 1952.
————. *To Hallow This Life*. New York: Harper, 1958.
Burns, E. L. M. *Between Arab and Israeli*. Toronto: Harrap, 1962.

Caplan, Samuel, and Harold U. Ribalow (eds.). *The Great Jewish Books*. New York: Horizon, 1963.
Childers, Erskine B. *The Road to Suez: A Study of Western-Arab Relations*. London: MacGibbon & Kee, 1962.
Corbon, Jean. *Western Public Opinion and the Palestine Conflict*. Lebanon: Fifth of June Society, 1967.
Coudenhove-Kalergi, Count Heinrich. *Anti-Semitism Through the Ages*. London: Hutchison, 1935.
Cremeans, Charles D. *The Arabs and the World*. New York: Praeger, 1963.

Davis, John H. *The Evasive Peace*. London: Murray, 1968.
Dawood, N. J. (tr.). *The Koran*. Baltimore: Penguin, 1956.
Dayan, Shmuel. *Pioneers in Israel*. New York: World, 1961.
Deutscher, Isaac. *The Non-Jewish Jew and Other Essays*. New York: Oxford, 1968.
Dimont, Max I. *Jews, God, and History*. New York: Simon & Schuster, 1962.
Draper, Theodore. *Israel and World Politics: Roots of the Third Arab-Israeli War*. New York: Viking, 1967.

Eban, Abba. *My People: The Story of the Jews*. New York: Behrman, 1968.
————. *Voice of Israel*. New York: Horizon, 1957.
Edelman, Maurice. *Ben-Gurion: A Political Biography*. London: Hodder & Stoughton, 1964.
El-Khatib, Rouhi. *Jerusalem: Israeli Annexation*. Jordan: 1968.
Elliot, Elizabeth. *Furnace of the Lord*. New York: Doubleday, 1969.
Encyclopedia Americana. 1961 (Can. Ed.). Toronto: American Corporation of Canada, Limited, 1961.
Esco Foundation for Palestine, Inc. *Palestine: A Study of Jewish, Arab, and British Policies*. New Haven: Yale University Press, 1947. 2 Volumes.

Faber, George S. *View of the Prophecies*. Boston: Andrews, 1809.
Fein, Leonard J. *Israel: Politics and People*. Boston: Little, Brown, 1967.
Feinberg, Abraham L. *Storm the Gates of Jericho*. Toronto: McClelland & Stewart, 1964.
Flannery, Edward H. *The Anguish of the Jews*. New York: Macmillan, 1965.
Frankfort, H. and H. A., John A. Wilson, Thorkild Jacobsen. *Before*

Philosophy: The Intellectual Adventure of Ancient Man. Baltimore: Penguin Books, 1954.

Frankfort, Henri. *The Birth of Civilization in the Near East.* Bloomington: Indiana University Press, 1959.

Gervasi, Frank. *The Case for Israel.* New York: Viking, 1967.

Goldman, Nahum. "The Future of Israel," *Foreign Affairs,* 48:3 (April 1970), pp. 441-459.

Grayzel, Solomon. *A History of the Jews.* New York: New American Library, 1947.

Great Britain and Palestine, 1915-1945. New York: Royal Institute of International Affairs, 1946.

Grey, John. *The Canaanites.* London: Thames and Hudson, 1964.

Hadawi, Sami. *Bitter Harvest: Palestine 1914-67.* New York: New World, 1967.

―――. *Land Ownership in Palestine.* New York: The Palestine Arab Refugee Office, 1957.

―――. *Palestine Before the United Nations.* Beirut: Institute for Palestine Studies, 1965.

―――. *Palestine in the United Nations.* New York: The Arab Information Center, 1964.

―――. *The Palestine Problem Before the United Nations, 1966.* Beirut: Institute for Palestine Studies, 1966.

―――. *United Nations Resolutions on Palestine, 1947-1966.* Beirut: Institute for Palestine Studies, 1967.

Harris, George L. *Jordan, Its People, Its Society, Its Culture.* New Haven: Human Relations Area File Press, 1958.

Hitti, Philip K. *A Short History of the Near East.* Toronto: Van Nostrand, 1966.

Hodgkin, E. C. *The Arabs.* London: Oxford, 1966.

The Holy Bible: Revised Standard Version. New York: Nelson, 1959.

Hoskings, Halford L. *The Middle East: Problem Area in World Politics.* New York: Macmillan, 1957.

Hughes, Philip. *A History of the Church.* Volume II, *The Church and the World.* London: Sheed & Ward, 1948.

Hurewitz, J. C. *Diplomacy in Near and Middle East: A Documentary Record, 1914-1956.* Toronto: Van Nostrand, 1956.

―――. *Middle East Dilemmas: The Background of United States Policy.* New York: Harper, 1953.

―――. *Middle East Politics: The Military Dimension.* New York: Praeger, 1969.

―――― (ed.). *Soviet-American Rivalry in the Middle East.* New York: Praeger, 1969.

The Interpreter's Dictionary of the Bible: An Illustrated Encyclopaedia in Four Volumes. New York: Abingdon, 1962.

Israel Yearbook, 1950-51. New York: Zionist Organization of America, 1951.

Israel Yearbook, 1952-53 (and annually thereafter). Tel Aviv: Israel Publications Limited, 1953.

The Jewish Case: Statements and Memoranda: Before the Anglo-American Committee of Inquiry on Palestine as Presented by the Jewish Agency for Palestine. Jerusalem: The Jewish Agency for Palestine, 1947.

Jiryis, Sabi. *The Arabs in Israel.* Lebanon: Fifth of June Society, 1969.

————. *The Arabs in Israel.* Beirut: The Institute for Palestine Studies, 1968.

Johnsen, Julia E. *Palestine: Jewish Homeland?* New York: Wilson, 1946.

Kadi, Leila S. *Arab Summit Conferences on the Palestine Problem. 1936-50; 1964-68.* Beirut: Palestine Liberation Organization, 1966.

Kahler, Eric. *The Jews Among the Nations.* New York: Ungar, 1967.

Kamil, Murad. *Coptic Egypt.* Cairo: Le Scribe Egyptien, 1968.

Keesing's Research Report. *The Arab-Israeli Conflict.* New York: Scribners, 1968.

Kellogg, Samuel H. *The Jews.* New York: Randolph, 1883.

Kertzer, Morris N. *What Is a Jew?* New York: Macmillan, 1960.

Khadduri, Majdia. *The Arab-Israeli Impasse.* Washington: Luce, 1968.

Khouri, Fred J. *The Arab-Israeli Dilemma.* Syracuse: Syracuse University Press, 1968.

Kirk, George E. *A Short History of the Middle East.* London: Methuen, 1948.

Koestler, Arthur. *Promise and Fulfilment: Palestine 1917-49.* London: Macmillan, 1949.

Lall, Arthur. *The UN and the Middle East Crisis, 1967.* New York: Columbia University Press, 1968.

Landau, Jacob M. *The Arabs in Israel: A Political Study.* New York: Oxford, 1969.

Landau, Rom. *Islam and the Arabs.* New York: Macmillan, 1959.

Laqueur, Walter. *The Israeli/Arab Reader.* New York: Citadel, 1968.

Latourette, Kenneth Scott. *The Nineteenth Century in Europe: The Protestant and Eastern Churches.* New York: Harper, 1959.

Lenczowski, George. *The United States Interests in the Middle East.* Washington: American Enterprise Institute for Public Policy Research, 1968.

Leumi, Vaad. *Three Historical Memoranda: Submitted to the United Nations Special Committee on Palestine.* Jerusalem: General Council of the Jewish Community of Palestine, 1947.

Lewis, Bernard. *The Arabs in History.* New York: Harper, 1966.

————. *The Middle East and the West.* Bloomington: Indiana University Press, 1964.

Lilienthal, Alfred M. *There Goes the Middle East.* New York: Bookmailer, 1958.

————. *What Price Israel?* Chicago: Regnery, 1953.

MacDonald, Robert W. *The League of Arab States.* Princeton: Princeton University Press, 1965.

Margolis, Max L. and Alexander Marx. *A History of the Jewish People.* New York: World, 1958.

Marlowe, John. *Arab Nationalism and British Imperialism: A Study in Power Politics.* London: Cresset, 1961.

Meinertzhagen, Richard. *Middle East Diary, 1917-56.* New York: Thomas Yoseloff, 1959.

Memoranda Prepared by the Government of Palestine for the Use of the Palestine Royal Commission. London: H. M. Stationery Office, 1937.

Memoranda Prepared by the Government of Palestine for the Use of the Palestine Royal Commission. Jerusalem: Government Printing Press, 1947.

Memorandum on the Administration of Palestine under the Mandate. Jerusalem: Government Printing Press, 1947.

Merlin, Samuel. *The Search for Peace in the Middle East.* New York: Thomas Yoseloff, 1968.

Mez, Adam. *The Renaissance of Islam.* London: Luzac, 1937.

Mezerik, A. G. (ed.). *Arab-Israel Conflict and the United Nations.* New York: International Review Service, 1962.

————— (ed.). *Arab Refugees in the Middle East.* New York: International Review Service, 1958.

————— (ed.). *The Crisis in the Middle East.* New York: International Review Service, 1958.

————— (ed.). *The Arab-Israel Conflict and the UN.* New York: International Review Service, 1969.

The Middle East in the Contemporary World. New York: American Professors for Peace in the Middle East, 1967.

Middle East Record, 1960. Tel Aviv: The 1960 Israel Oriental Society, 1960.

Miller, Irving. *Israel, the Eternal Ideal.* New York: Farrar-Strauss, 1955.

Miller, Madeleine S. and J. Lane (eds.). *Harper's Bible Dictionary.* New York: Harper, 1952.

Ministry of Foreign Affairs. *Facts About Israel, 1969.* Jerusalem: Keter Books, 1969.

Mohamad, Fadhil Zaky. *The Evolution of American Policy in Palestine.* Baghdad: Ministry of Education, 1963.

Moscati, Sabatino. *Ancient Semitic Civilizations.* New York: Putnams, 1957.

—————. *The Face of the Ancient Orient.* London: Routledge and Kegan Paul, 1960.

Nasir, Musa. *Towards a Solution of the Palestine Problem: A Selection of Speeches and Writings 1946-1966.* Bir Zait, 1966.

National Association of Democratic Lawyers. *The Middle East Conflict: Notes and Documents (1915-1967).* Brussels: National Association of Democratic Lawyers, 1967.

Nichols, James Hastings. *History of Christianity, 1650-1950: Secularization of the West.* New York: Ronald, 1956.

Noth, Martin. *The Old Testament World.* London: Adam & Charles Black, 1966.

Nutting, Anthony. *The Arabs.* New York: New American Library, 1965.

Oldenbourg, Zoe. *The Crusades.* New York: Ballantine, 1966.

Palestine and Trans-Jordan. Naval Intelligence Division, Government of Great Britain, 1943.

Palestine: Blue Book, 1937. Jerusalem: Government Printer, 1937.

Palestine Royal Commission Report. London: His Majesty's Stationery Office, 1937.

Palestine: The Promised Land. Amman, Jordan: 1968.

Papers on Palestine II: A Collection of Articles by Leading Authorities Dealing with the Palestine Problem. New York: Institute of Arab American Affairs, 1947.

Papers on Palestine III: A Collection of Articles by Distinguished Jews Who Oppose Political Zionism. New York: Institute of Arab American Affairs, 1947.

Parker, James. *A History of the Jewish People.* Baltimore: Penguin, 1964.

Peretz, Don. *Israel and the Palestine Arabs.* Washington: The Middle East Institute, 1958.

Pinner, Walter. *The Legend of the Arab Refugees.* Tel Aviv: Economic and Social Research Institute, 1967.

Plaut, W. Gunther. *The Case for the Chosen People.* Garden City: Doubleday, 1965.

Poliakov, Leon. *The History of Anti-Semitism.* New York: Vanguard, 1965.

The Political History of Palestine Under British Administration: Memorandum by His Britannic Majesty's Government presented in 1947 to the United Nations Special Committee on Palestine. Jerusalem: British Information Center, 1947.

Polk, William R. *The United States and the Arab World.* Cambridge: Harvard University Press, 1969. Rev. Ed.

Prittie, Terence. *Israel: Miracle in the Desert.* Baltimore: Penguin, 1967.

Qualben, Lars P. *A History of the Christian Church.* New York: Nelson, 1942.

Refugees in the Middle East: A Solution in Peace. New York: Israel Information Services, 1967.

Report of the Commissioner-General of the United Nations Relief and Works Agency for Palestine Refugees in the Near East. 1 July, 1966-30 June, 1967. New York: United Nations, 1967. Also, same title, 1968, and 1969.

Report of a Committee Set Up to Consider Certain Correspondence Between Sir Henry McMahon and the Sharif of Mecca in 1915 and 1916. London: His Majesty's Stationery Office, 1939.

Report on Palestine: Report to the General Assembly by the United Nations Special Committee on Palestine. New York: Somerset, 1947.

Rodinson, Maxime. *Israel and the Arabs.* Baltimore: Penguin, 1968.

Rosten, Leo. *The Joys of Yiddish.* New York: McGraw-Hill, 1968.

Royal Institute of International Affairs. *The Middle East: A Political and Economic Survey.* New York: Royal Institute of International Affairs, 1954.

Sachar, Abram Leon. *A History of the Jews.* New York: Knopf, 1965.
Safran, Nadan. *From War to War: The Arab Israeli Confrontation 1948-
    1967.* New York: Pegasus, 1969.
St. John, Robert. *Jews, Justice, and Judaism: A Narrative of the Role
    Played by the Jews in Shaping American History.* Garden City:
    Doubleday, 1969.
Samuel, Maurice. *Light on Israel.* New York: Knopf, 1968.
Sands, William (ed.). *The Arab Nation: Paths and Obstacles to Ful-
    fillment.* Washington: Middle East Institute, 1960.
Sarkissian, Karekin. *The Witness of the Oriental Orthodox Churches.*
    Beirut: Bishop Karekin Sarkissian, 1968.
Sayegh, Fayez A. *The Arab-Israeli Conflict.* New York: The Arab In-
    formation Center, 1964.
Schechtman, Joseph B. *The Arab Refugee Problem.* New York: Philo-
    sophical Library, 1952.
Schwarz-Bart, Andre. *The Last of the Just.* London: Secker & Warburg,
    1961.
Selzer, Michael. *Zionism Reconsidered: The Rejection of Jewish Nor-
    malcy.* Toronto: Collier-Macmillan Canada, 1970.
Smith, Wilbur. *Israel/Arab Conflict and the Bible.* Glendale, California:
    Regal Books, 1968.
Sokolow, Nahum. *History of Zionism, 1600-1918.* London: Longmans-
    Greene, 1919. 2 Volumes.
Stein, Leonard. *The Balfour Declaration.* London: Mitchell, 1961.
Stevens, Georgiana G. (ed.). *The United States and the Middle East.*
    Englewood Cliffs, N.J.: Prentice-Hall, 1964.
Stevens, R. P. *American Zionism and US Foreign Policy, 1942-47.* New
    York: Pageant, 1962.
*Supplementary Memorandum by the Government of Palestine, Including
    Notes on Evidence Given to the United Nations' Special Committee
    on Palestine up to the 12th of July, 1947.* Jerusalem: Government
    Printer, 1947.
*Survey of Palestine, Prepared in December 1945 and January 1946 for
    the Information of the Anglo-American Committee of Inquiry.*
    Jerusalem: Government Printer, 1946.

Tannouns, Izzat. *The Policy That Invited Soviet Russia to the Middle
    East.* New York: Palestine Arab Refugee Office, 1958.
Tartakower, Arieh, and Kurt R. Grossman. *The Jewish Refugee.* New
    York: Institute of Jewish Affairs of the American Jewish Congress
    and World Jewish Congress, 1944.
Tension and Peace in the Middle East. New York: The Palestine Arab
    Refugee Office, 1956.
Tibawi, A. L. *American Interests in Syria, 1800-1901: A Study of Edu-
    cational, Literary and Religious Work.* London: Oxford University
    Press, 1966.
———. *British Interests in Palestine (1800-1901): A Study of Religious
    and Educational Enterprise.* London: Oxford University Press, 1961.
To Make War or Make Peace: A Symposium on the Middle East. Tel
    Aviv: The New Outlook, 1969.
Twice in a Lifetime. Beirut: UNRWA, 1968.

Udin, Sophie A. (ed.). *The Palestine Year Book.* Washington: Zionist Organization of America, 1945 and 1949. Volumes I and IV.

United Nations Documents, including Records, Documents, and Reports of UN General Assembly, Security Council, Trusteeship Council, UN Conciliation Commission for Palestine, UN Emergency Force, UN Relief and Works Agency for Palestine, UN Secretary-General, UN Special Committee on Palestine, UN Truce Supervisory Organization. New York: United Nations, 1945-69.

United States Senate, Committee on Foreign Relations. *A Select Chronology and Background Documents Relating to the Middle East.* Washington: Government Printing Office, 1969. (Rev. Ed., May 1969.)

Velie, Lester. *Countdown in the Holy Land.* New York: Funk & Wagnalls, 1969.

Vilnay, Zev. *The New Israel Atlas: Bible to Present Day.* Toronto: McGraw-Hill, 1969.

Walz, Humphrey. *The Story of the American Palestine Committee.* New York: American Council for Judaism, n.d.

Warburg, James P. *Crosscurrents in the Middle East.* New York: Atheneum, 1968.

Wardi, Ch. (ed.). *Christian News From Israel.* Jerusalem: Government of Israel & Ministry of Religious Affairs, XIX, May, 1968.

Weisgal, M. W. *Chaim Weizmann: Statesman, Scientist, Builder of the Jewish Commonwealth.* New York: Dial, 1944.

Wight, Martin. *British Colonial Constitution 1947.* Oxford: Clarendon, 1952.

Williams, Ann. *Britain and France in the Middle East and North Africa.* London: Macmillan, 1968.

Wright, G. Ernest and Floyd V. Filson. *Historical Maps of Bible Lands.* Philadelphia: Westminster.

Wright, G. Ernest and Reginald H. Fuller. *The Book of the Acts of God: Contemporary Scholarship Interprets the Bible.* Garden City: Doubleday, 1960.

II. *Miscellaneous Publications of the Following Organizations*

1. American Council for Judaism,
   201 East 57th Street,
   New York, N.Y. 10022.

2. Americans for Justice in the Middle East,
   P.O. Box 4841,
   Beirut, Lebanon,
   including *The Middle East Newsletter.*

3. Arab Information Center,
   225 Metcalfe Street,
   Ottawa 4, Canada,
   including *The Arab Case: Documents and Testimonies,* and *The Arab World.*

4. Israel Information Service,
   11 East 70th Street,
   New York, N.Y. 10021.
5. Palestine Research Center,
   Beirut, Lebanon.
6. Zionist Organization of America,
   145 East 32nd Street,
   New York, N.Y. 10016,
   including *The American Zionist.*

Index

DATE DUE

F			
OC 22'80			
AP 15'81			
OC 28'81			
MR 17'82			
OC 26'83			
NOV 18 '83			
SEP 24 '86			
NOV 23 '87			
GAYLORD			PRINTED IN U.S.A.